D1600259

Shop Floor Citizens

Shop Floor Citizens

Engineering Democracy in 1940s Britain

James Hinton

University of Warwick
Coventry, England

Edward Elgar

Published by
Edward Elgar Publishing Limited
Gower House
Croft Road
Aldershot
Hants GU11 3HR
England

Edward Elgar Publishing Company
Old Post Road
Brookfield
Vermont 05036
USA

British Library Cataloguing in Publication Data
Hinton, James
    Shop Floor Citizens: Engineering
    Democracy in 1940s Britain
    I. Title
    331.01120941

Library of Congress Cataloguing in Publication Data
Hinton, James
        Shop floor citizens: engineering democracy in 1940s Britain /
    James Hinton.
        232p. 22cm.
        Includes bibliographical references and index.
        1. Engineers—Great Britain—Societies. 2. Engineering—Great
    Britain—Political aspects. 3. Trade unions—Great Britain—
    —History—20th century. 4. Industrial relations—Great Britain—
    History—20th century. I. Title.
    TA157.H519   1994   94–13035
    331.88'12'0094109044—dc20   CIP

ISBN 1 85898 081 X

Printed and Bound in Great Britain by
Hartnolls Limited, Bodmin, Cornwall.

Contents

List of Tables

Abbreviations

(Abbreviations used only in the footnotes are explained in the Bibliography.)

AESD	Association of Engineering and Shipbuilding Draughtsmen
AEU	Amalgamated Engineering Union
BEC	British Employers' Confederation
CP	Communist Party
EAC	Engineering Advisory Council
EEF	Engineering Employers' Federation
FBI	Federation of British Industries
ICI	Imperial Chemical Industries
JPC	Joint Production Committee
MAP	Ministry of Aircraft Production
NPAC	National Production Advisory Council
PEP	Political and Economic Planning
ROF	Royal Ordnance Factory
SSNC	Shop Stewards' National Council
TGWU	Transport and General Workers' Union
TUC	Trade Union Congress
TUDPC	Trade Union District Production Committee
WEA	Workers' Education Association
WVS	Women's Voluntary Service

Acknowledgements

Once again it is the generous sabbatical arrangements of the University of Warwick which have done most to make this book possible.

I am grateful for the help of a large number of archivists, notably those at Warwick's Modern Records Centre, the Working Class Movement Library in Manchester, the Communist Party and Labour Party archives, and the Public Records Office in Kew. I am grateful to the Transport and General Workers' Union and the Engineering Employers' Federation for permission to make use of their records.

I would like to thank particularly Richard Croucher (whose own researches, since their earliest stages, have done much to stimulate and inform my own interest in these issues), Nina Fishman, Tony Grainger, Yvonne Kapp, Yvette Rocheron, Nick Tiratsoo, Pauline Wilson, Chris Wrigley and Jonathan Zeitlin for the various kinds of help and support they have offered me in the preparation of this study. I also thank several current and ex-members of the Centre for Social History at Warwick with whom I have discussed these questions: I seldom agree with them, but their corrosive scepticism has forced me to clarify my ways of thinking.

Introduction

The British labour movement during the 1940s – when it reached the peak of its power – has attracted considerable historical attention. Two rather contradictory trends are apparent in the recent literature. On the one hand emphasis is being placed on the more libertarian aspects of socialist thinking in the 1940s, challenging the view that Labour approached the task of post-war reconstruction in a mood of triumphalist social engineering. Faith in the power of the state to refashion society was often hedged around and qualified by a liberal concern to protect civil liberties and to sustain the autonomy of non-state bodies in civil society.[1] At the same time, however, the actual record of popular self-activity – which, ever since the heroic days of 1940, has occupied a central place in accounts of wartime and post-war Britain – is being scrutinised in a critical spirit. A good deal of recent writing has emphasised the indifference of ordinary people to political and social change, or their cynical resistance to the ethos of heroic self-sacrifice with which official propaganda sought to clothe the disruptions of their everyday lives.[2] The present study contributes to the first of these trends by establishing the existence of a sustained campaign for industrial democracy among engineering trade unionists in the 1940s. These activists, and the many strands of progressive opinion which lent them their (more or less qualified) support, saw state planning of economic life as a means of creating opportunities for popular participation, not as an alternative to it. The new stress on popular apathy is treated here as more problematic. The movement for industrial democracy described in these pages was ultimately frustrated. But it was not without potential, nor popular appeal – particularly during the wartime production crisis of 1941–42.

It has often been argued that British trade unions have been indifferent to production and hostile to productionist intervention by the state.[3] In a recent study of the French aircraft industry, Herrick Chapman drew a sharp contrast between Communist productionism

1

in France during the 1930s and 1940s, and contemporary British trade unionists who, he argues, compounded indifference to production with a rooted determination to keep the state at arm's length from their bastions of power on the shop floor.[4] Chapman's account rests on an accurate reading of the existing literature on British industrial relations. But it is, nevertheless, quite wrong. During the 1940s, as this book will show, productionist attitudes gained a significant hold among militants in British engineering factories.

What most obviously distinguishes my approach from most of the existing literature is the weight it gives to Communist thinking and activity. Historians of the Labour Party, influenced no doubt by the sectarian and anti-Communist attitudes which suffuse their sources, frequently underestimate the importance of the Communist contribution to the dynamics of the British labour movement. This is particularly debilitating in writing about the 1940s, when Communist Party membership and influence were at their height. Thus a recent study of the Attlee Government's attempts to stimulate productivity in private sector industry presents a picture of trade union attitudes polarised between a supportive TUC hierarchy and an indifferent rank and file. This is simply to write out of history those thousands of trade union activists, many of them Communists, whose commitment to productionism between 1941 and 1947 must be an important factor (so it is argued here) in any reckoning of the potential for radical change in British economic life during these years.[5]

This book is concerned not only to fill a gap in socialist and trade union history, but also to contribute to the debate about whether the Attlee Government could have used post-war reconstruction to lay the foundations for a 'developmental state' in Britain – a practice of state intervention capable of tackling the deep-rooted inefficiencies in the industrial economy exposed by the 'audit of war'.[6] During the war the most intensively planned economy ever constructed in a capitalist society had been built in Britain. In 1945 few people believed that the planning apparatus could be dismantled instantly, and the return of a Labour Government ensured that planning would play an important part in post-war reconstruction. Whatever the hopes of some of its more left-wing members, however, the Labour Party had no intention of taking more than a minority of productive industry into public ownership. For the foreseeable future, therefore, planning and private ownership would be likely to coexist across large sections of British industry – including the complex of engineering industries discussed in this study. The relationship between planners and private enterprise was mediated by the tripartite consultative structures established during the war between employers, organised workers and the Whitehall apparatus.

The indispensability of the engineer to the war effort and to post-war reconstruction, together with the new role taken by the state in the administration of production, helped to create significant openings for trade union demands for participation. By allying themselves with state officials and enlightened management, trade unionists sought to break the stranglehold of employer autocracy and unleash worker creativity in industry. The unions found important allies for some of their demands, both in Whitehall and among employers. From 1942 Joint Production Committees (JPCs) were established throughout the industry, involving workers to a greater extent than ever before or since in joint consultation with management over production issues. For the engineering unions the JPCs were only the first base, from which they hoped to build a much more general participation of organised workers in production planning – linking shop floor workers, through the tripartite machinery at regional and sectoral levels, to national economic planning as a whole. They pursued this goal from 1942 until 1947–48, when the persistent indifference of the Labour Government combined with the new turn in Communist politics caused by the onset of the Cold War to undermine the basis for productionist politics among trade union activists.

In the debate over industrial reconstruction, questions both of efficiency and of democracy were involved, and they were intimately related to one another. Effective planning implied a transfer of authority from individual firms to state agencies. Any such transfer was likely to create opportunities for organised workers to seek the assistance of the state in their own attempts to encroach on employer autocracy in the factories. It was the opinion of many trade union activists that only by allying itself directly with organised labour in the factories would the state be able to acquire effective authority to persuade either employers or workers to put national needs before private and sectional interests. Through such an alliance, they argued, workers would be convinced that they were working for the nation, not for profit, and employers could be forced by simultaneous pressure from above and below to subordinate the pursuit of profit to the fulfilment of national economic needs. In this way effective reconstruction of Britain's capitalist economy could be pressed forward by co-operation between a Labour Government and the trade union movement.

The Government, while anxious to enhance its own power to steer and initiate in industrial life, had to balance such ambitions against the need to foster good relations with a business community whose continuing economic muscle commanded respect. In negotiating any such balance, the question of worker participation was a wild card whose deployment by Government would represent a high-risk strategy as likely to alienate employers as to intimidate them. The Attlee Government – unlike its post-war counterparts in a number of Western European countries – did little to entrench worker participation in private industry. Much of what Communists and other reformers demanded by way of planning and participation – tripartite planning committees at national and regional levels, statutory workers' councils – was not unlike measures that contributed positively to the institutionalisation of a productionist alliance in several of Britain's capitalist rivals.[7] In German industry, the statutory enforcement of co-determination helped to construct a collaborative 'productivity coalition' at the level of the enterprise which was widely seen as contributing to post-war economic success.[8] In France, as Herrick Chapman has argued, militants in aircraft factories, inspired by Communist productionism, were able to forge a positive alliance with technocratic state officials, which contributed much to the capacity of the French aircraft industry to perform competitively despite fierce ongoing conflicts on the shop floor.[9] The contrasting experience of Britain's capitalist neighbours suggests that, had the proponents of planning and participation met with a more favourable response from the state, then a significant transformation of shop floor attitudes to production might have occurred, even within a capitalist economic order. Certainly such participation would have enriched the quality of democratic life in Britain.

Reflecting on his experience as President of the Board of Trade in the Attlee Government, Harold Wilson argued that 'in this problem of the relation between Government and private industry we have what is almost a vacuum in Socialist thought.'[10] Although historians have generally endorsed this judgement,[11] what Wilson had actually identified was less a vacuum than a disjuncture: the debilitating rift between parliamentary socialism and the industrial left.[12] Trade union demands for the subordination of employer power within a regime of detailed planning and worker participation held little appeal to the new thinkers on Labour's right for whom macro-economic demand management, rather than dirigist industrial interventionism, held the key to the socialist future.[13] But the issues raised by the engineering unions were well supported on the Labour Left, some of whose more thoughtful members were just as prepared as the Communists to acknowledge that the most urgent economic problems demanded the development of strategies for state (and worker) control over the private sector rather than outright nationalisation.[14] Whatever appeal these ideas might have had in Government circles, however, was fatally weakened by the fact that the necessary dialogue between the Government and the shop floor would depend on the good offices of Communists. There were other important reasons why the Attlee Government was unresponsive to the demands of the engineering unions, including its desire to remain on good terms with employers and its respect for deep-seated codes of voluntarism built into the British political culture. Nevertheless, reluctance to embrace an alliance with Communist shop stewards was itself a major cause of governmental indifference to industrial democracy. That reluctance was understandable. By the time Wilson was writing, Communist support for productionism had disappeared: the Cold War left the British Communist Party with no choice but to abandon its exploration of productionism and participation in favour of a return to the narrowly economistic militancy which, beneath the revolutionary talk, had always provided Communists with their main *raison d'être* in shop floor politics.[15] On their own the Labour Left had little to offer. Only the Communists could mobilise effective support in the factories.[16]

It may seem strange to suggest that the Communist Party was a potential agency of capitalist modernisation in Britain. But, between 1941 and 1947 this was indeed the role that it sought: making capitalism work, first to win the war and then to consolidate the peace. Throughout these years, Communists had been ready to work with others to build structures of democratic participation within the existing order, abandoning revolutionary negativism for a constructive reformist agenda. The doctrinal considerations involved are explored in Chapter 1.

The particular combination of attitudes displayed by the people at the core of this book – a passion for increasing production, a belief in the capacity of the state to plan economic life, a commitment to maximising the participation of ordinary workers in the running of industry – would be difficult to find at any period outside the 1940s. Nevertheless, successive generations of socialist thinkers have wrestled with the dilemma of reconciling planning with popular participation. The agitations and arguments described here should be seen as part of a democratic tradition linking together the Guild Socialist movement of the period around the First World War with debates about worker participation in the 1960s and 1970s. Since the 1970s the tides of history have not created a great deal of space for the development of that tradition. But tides turn. In the face of persistent capitalist crisis, and probably insurmountable problems of combining the rule of market forces with the preservation of the ecological balance, planning and its democratic twin, participation, may not be irrelevant to our futures. As the planning debate re-emerges, this book will, I hope, help to inform it with some past experience – both of the activities of productionist industrial democrats, and of the deep roots of resistance to their ambitions in Britain's industrial and political culture. Whether read as a might-have-been in the history of Britain's failing capitalism, or as part of an ongoing socialist debate about participation in a planned economy, these experiences deserve to be analysed in detail.

NOTES

1. S. Brooke, *Labour's War. The Labour Party during the Second World War*, Oxford, 1992, pp. 20–21, 267–70, 289–92; G. Finlayson, 'A Moving Frontier: Voluntarism and the State in British Social Welfare, 1941–49', *Twentieth-century British History*, 1, 2, 1990, p. 193.
2. For the stress on popular 'apathy' and conservatism see A. Mason and P. Thompson, 'Reflections on a revolution? The political mood in wartime Britain', and S. Fielding, 'Don't Know Don't Care', both in N. Tiratsoo (ed.), *The Attlee Years*, 1991; S. Fielding, 'What did the people want. The meaning of the 1945 General Election', *Historical Journal*, 35, 1992, pp. 623–39. For the resistance to officially-fostered heroic myth see Tony Lane, *The Merchant Seamen's War*, Manchester, 1990.
3. C. Barnett, *The Audit of War*, 1987, pp. 187–92; P. Thompson, 'Playing at being skilled men; factory culture and pride in work skills among Coventry car workers', *Social History*, 13, 1, 1988, pp. 67–9. For a review and corrective see T. Nichols, *The British Worker Question: A New Look at Workers and Productivity in Manufacturing*, 1986.
4. H. Chapman, *State Capitalism and Working-class Radicalism in the French Aircraft Industry*, University of California Press, Oxford, 1991, *passim*.
5. N. Tiratsoo and J. Tomlinson, *Industrial efficiency and state intervention: Labour 1939–51*, 1993, pp. 164–5.
6. Barnett, *op.cit.*, Ch. 8. On the 'developmental state' see D. Marquand, *The Unprincipled Society. New Demands and Old Politics*, 1988, *passim*.
7. Although Soviet examples were most frequently cited by the advocates of workers' participation in Britain, they were not unaware of the relevance of French or German models. David Karzun, 'Joint Production Committes in France', *Communist Review*, July 1947, pp. 202–6; Communist Party, *The Way to Win*, May 1942, pp. 15–18.
8. W. Streek, 'Co-determination: the fourth decade', in B. Wilpert and A. Sorge (eds), *International Perspectives on Organisational Democracy*, 1984, p. 415 and *passim*; Report of the Committee of Inquiry on Industrial Democracy (Bullock Report), January 1977, Cmnd. 6706, p. 57.
9. H. Chapman, *op. cit.*, *passim*. For a systematic comparison between the French and British experiences see J. Hinton, review of Chapman, *Social History*, 17, 3, 1992, pp. 523–7.
10. H. Wilson, 'Personal Covering Note', 17 May 1950, CAB 124/1200.
11. J. Leruez, *Economic Planning and Politics in Britain*, Bath, 1975, pp. 61–2; K.O. Morgan, *Labour in Power, 1945-1951*, Oxford, 1984, p. 130; H. Mercer, 'Labour and Private Industry, 1945–51', in N. Tiratsoo (ed.), *The Attlee Years*, 1991, p. 71; J. Tomlinson, 'Productivity, Joint Consultation and Human Relations: The Attlee Government and the Workplace', paper for Conference on Management, Production and Politics, Glasgow University, 24–25 April 1992, p. 2.
12. For a fuller analysis of Wilson's position see below, pp. 202–30.
13. E. Durbin, *New Jerusalems: The Labour Party and the Economics of Democratic Socialism*, 1985, *passim*.
14. Ian Mikado was particularly imaginative. (J. Schneer, *Labour's Conscience: The Labour Left 1945-1951*, 1988, pp. 97–9.) Bevan, on the other hand, tended to make a fetish of nationalisation and could see only the dangers, not the opportunities implicit in tripartite corporatism. (S. Brooke, *op. cit.*, pp. 262–3, 266, 293–4.)
15. N. Fishman, 'The British Communist Party and the Trade Unions, 1933-1945: the dilemmas of revolutionary pragmatism', London PhD, 1991, *passim*.
16. Although Jonathan Schneer points out that the Labour Left had an independent presence in the AEU, he also accepts that it was the alliance with the Communists

which gave the Labour Left its 'power' in the immediate post-war years. (Schneer, *op. cit.*, pp. 134–5.)

1 Planning, Participation and the Communists

The demand for participation in the engineering factories calls into question the view that the planning movement of the 1930s and 1940s was predominantly technocratic and uninterested in ideas of popular participation.[1] Confronted by the coincidence of capitalist collapse following the Wall Street crash of 1929 and the planned industrialisation of the Soviet Union, a wide range of opinion came to see planning as an essential component of economic reconstruction, whether under capitalist or socialist relations of production. But, however much the mystique of planning tended to invest the state with near-magical powers of social regeneration, there was nevertheless a widespread acknowledgement that what the planning state needed from its subjects was not merely passive obedience but active participation. Even Barbara Wootton, whose concern to defend the planners against the irresponsible populism of elected politicians placed her on the technocratic wing of the British planning movement, nevertheless set ambitious targets for popular participation: 'I hope we shall see the time when every household has at least one member serving on some ... active public body.'[2]

G.D.H. Cole, reverting to the Guild Socialist themes of his youth after his 1930s' explorations of centralised planning, was not alone in insisting that British socialism would draw on 'a strong tradition of independent ... associations standing outside the State machine ... on the alert to defend our personal liberties against would-be autocrats and bureaucrats with a will to power.'[3] Even in the sphere of welfare, where top-down statism often appeared to be carrying all before it in the post-war years, ministers in the Attlee Government displayed considerable sensitivity to the arguments of those who sought a continuing role for voluntary organisations in partnership with, not subordination to, the expanded state.[4] The small change of progressive talk at the end of the war was not so much a hymn to the limitless power and benevolence of the state, as an anxious concern to match expanding state power with popular self-activity. Since the state was bound to play such a central place in the post-war world, popular initiative in partnership with the state was the only alternative to '1984'. To this end the citizens must educate, organise and activate themselves. 'Active citizenship,' wrote the editors of a series of left-of-centre books designed to promote 'The New Democracy' after the war, 'is the indispensable condition of freedom in a planned society.'[5]

This view was certainly shared by Michael Young, wartime director of Political and Economic Planning (PEP), the think-tank of 'middle opinion' established in 1931.[6] Young well understood that planning, by itself, 'would not revitalise democracy': indeed its tendency was to by-pass 'widely-dispersed initiative' in favour of 'authority from above'. If planning was to be reconciled with freedom, then ways must be found to replace the passive consent of the governed with an 'active democracy'.[7] To this end Young persuaded PEP to devote considerable efforts to investigating mechanisms through which citizens could be encouraged to participate in the administration of the new order: in the welfare services, local government and industry.[8] Behind closed doors, PEP members worried about whether planning could ever be democratised. Was Hayek right? Did the attempt to control market forces necessarily lead to authoritarian centralisation of power? While progressives could draw inspiration from the popular self-activity generated by the wartime emergency – the voluntary and neighbourly effort provoked by the Blitz was a constant point of reference – did this really give hope for the future? Or was the trend towards anomie and individual powerlessness bound to reassert itself once the stimulus of war had passed?[9]

Most socialists entertained no such doubts about the ultimate compatibility of democracy and planning. Nevertheless many of them were equally committed to the fostering of active citizenship. Admirers of Soviet planning imagined that its apparent successes rested not only on the directing power of the state, but equally on popular initiative and participation. Even the Webbs, when they eulogised Soviet Russia as a new civilisation, had in mind not only the empowerment of a public-spirited technocratic elite ('the vocation of leadership'), but equally the involvement of the mass of ordinary mortals in the day-to-day governance of their communities. It was this vision of active citizens working in partnership with a planning state that the admirers of Stalinism preached to their enormous audiences of pro-Soviet admirers in the years of Russian Glory that followed Hitler's invasion of the Soviet Union in June 1941.[10]   At the height of the war, the democratic credentials of Gosplan were accepted well beyond the Fabian or Communist Left. According to a PEP report written in the autumn of 1941, the prevalence of 'rigidity, bureaucratisation and the warping of individual initiative' in Soviet planning had been greatly exaggerated:

> The central plan itself is drawn up in close consultation with the ... Trade Unions. In its application to individual factories and plants it is then closely scrutinised by the trade unionists of the productive unit concerned, amendments are usually suggested and the draft travels back to Gosplan where the criticisms are considered and, as far as possible, embodied in the final version of the plan. Its execution is then helped and checked by the Trade Union Groups in the various factories.... The scope of the Unions' activities is such that the workers are given an opportunity to play a part in the administration of production as well as in its physical execution. This workshop democracy is apparently a powerful incentive to conscientious work.[11]

While such writing undoubtedly illustrates the capacity of British planning enthusiasts to delude themselves about what was going on in the Soviet Union, what is significant in the present context is that the utopia which commentators projected onto Stalinism was informed at least as much by values of democratic participation as it was by a technocratic faith in the capacity of the state to master economic life. Gosplan, as reconstructed in the imaginations of British reformers, confirmed that economic planning, far from being incompatible with popular participation, could only be successfully pursued in conditions of active democracy. Many socialists claimed that the balance between centralism and self-activity which they perceived in the Soviet model could be adapted to planning in a capitalist economy.

Twenty years ago Angus Calder emphasised the participatory character of the wartime mobilisation:

> a ferment of participatory democracy.... The people increasingly led itself. Its nameless leaders in the bombed streets, on the factory floor, in the Home Guard drill hall, asserted a new and radical popular spirit. The air raid warden and the shop steward were men of destiny ... the people surged forward to fight their own war.[12]

While this passage faithfully reflects the tone of much progressive writing during the crisis of 1940–42, Calder's overall conclusion was more sombre. As things turned out the populist rhetoric served the purposes of power, not of popular emancipation. Entrenched elites, who owed their survival in the face of Hitler to the efforts of the aroused masses, were able to cheat the people of the democratic fruits of their victory. The post-war welfare state underwrote a top people's peace, not the social revolution glimpsed in the popular energies unleashed by imminent national disaster after 1940.[13]

Calder's book was a child of the 1960s: it interrogated the social history of the war with an optimism about popular capacities and a bitterness about elite obstruction that owed much to the events of 1968. More recent historical writing has confirmed the power of elites to resist democratic change in the 1940s,[14] but the argument of popular upheaval frustrated by the manoeuvres of the powerful has given way to a scepticism about whether the 'ferment of participatory democracy' evoked by Calder was ever a reality. It is the biddability, rather than the initiative, of the people that has impressed historians. War did much to assuage the bitter divisions of class in British society, fostering remarkable levels of social discipline. National danger and the promise of fair shares sustained an ethos of national service and public responsibility. Looking back through eyes conditioned by the dismaying aftermath of the 1960s, historians since Calder have been more inclined to stress the discipline than the self-activity. The individualism and hedonism engendered by affluence, the degeneration of participation into a sectionalised warfare of each against all, the decay of the 'civic culture': these attributes of political modernity cast the civil obedience of the 1940s in a retrospectively positive light. After 1945, as Paul Addison so precisely put it, 'the home front ran on, even without a war to sustain it'. Social disciplines held. Even wages policy worked.[15]

Some recent historians have suggested that popular obedience owed more to subaltern passivity and limited horizons, than to any positive identification with the goals of the state.[16] While evidence of popular political 'apathy' is seldom far to seek, it is questionable how much weight should be given to it in a decade marked by uniquely high levels of electoral turnout and partisan affiliation.[17] Moreover, the balance between passive obedience (or resistance) and active participation was itself the issue at stake. 'Apathy' is a social construct, an outcome as much as an explanation. 'Don't know, don't care' – the disillusioned summary of popular political attitudes offered by Mass Observation in 1947 – expresses a defensive reaction to relative disempowerment, not the final rejection of civic responsibility on any terms. The record of the JPCs themselves, as we shall see, can be read as confirming the view that British workers by and large were indifferent to production. But it can equally well be read as a missed opportunity to develop a productionist culture among a workforce stimulated by the national danger of war, missed because of employer resistance and the indifference of the state. Those who worked for a more participatory democracy in the 1940s were not naive romantics unacquainted with the profound sources of popular 'apathy'. The project of active democracy did not assume the overnight creation of Athenian levels of participation. However much wartime mobilisation might, on occasion, inspire activists and intellectuals with a sense of awakening popular competence, most evidence about popular attitudes emphasised the downside. Mass Observation issued a stream of reports stressing 'to an extent unbelievable to those who have not investigated it, many people are passive-minded, letting things be done to them, hardly thinking of what they could get done, if they would co-operate with their neighbours or fellow citizens.'[18] While such judgements partly reflected the Mass Observers' own frustrated high hopes for a more participatory democracy,[19] there is no reason to doubt that most British citizens remained indifferent to the visions of participation that so excited activist minorities. The common people, as is well known, have plenty of defences against those earnest minorities who seek to rescue them from what one such improving organisation called 'desultory living'.[20]

No-one expected the alienated masses to awaken to their responsibilities overnight. Rather, reformers looked towards an alliance between a vigorously reforming Government and a bridgehead of especially active citizens as the means of prizing open the defensive shell of popular un-idealism and winning the masses towards an active sense of their own political competence.[21] PEP's Michael Young, who became the Labour Party's research director after the war, was well aware that a fully participatory democracy in which each individual felt personally responsible for the administration of community affairs was a project for the distant future, if ever. In the meantime, he was fond of suggesting, the practical goal of democrats should be to expand the minority already taking place in their own government: 'If we can raise the 3% elite to 8 or 10% than we shall have achieved a social revolution.'[22] Supporters of Joint Production Committees showed a similar belief in the need for activist minorities to leaven the stolid mass of ordinary workers.

In the summer of 1942 G.D.H. Cole's reaction to opinion poll evidence of mass political apathy and ignorance was to stress the vital role played by what he called the 'democratic elite' of active citizens in stimulating the masses to 'intelligent political action.' Looking back, more than a little nostalgically, to the work of such minorities in late Victorian non-conformist chapels and trade union branches, Cole seized on the JPC experiment as a means of creating a new 'democratic elite' of workers committed both to maximising productive efficiency for the common good and to facilitating the active participation of the mass of their fellow workers. Though worried about the implications of Communist leadership in the JPC movement, Cole was hopeful that the new ethic of productionism would provide the emergent 'democratic elite' with some protection against future policy somersaults.[23] The Communists themselves, of course, were fully committed to the view that a specially active vanguard of politically conscious workers had a vital part to play in awakening the masses to political participation.

Between June 1941 and the end of 1947 the Communist Party was very well placed to mobilise a bridgehead for productionism within the engineering industry. According to Jack Tanner – the (non-Communist) President of the Amalgamated Engineering Union (AEU) – Communists made up 'a very large proportion of the leading shop stewards in the engineering industry'.[24]   They had established this position during the later 1930s, when the Party took the initiative in organising sections of the engineering industry, especially aircraft, as rearmament brought it out of recession.[25] After Soviet entry into the war in June 1941, party membership grew very rapidly in the factories, and by the end of 1942 the number of functioning factory groups 'considerably exceeded' local area groups for the first time in the Party's history.[26]   In the Communist stronghold of Coventry membership increased tenfold in the twelve months following June 1941, and most of the new members were organised in factory branches.[27]

The AEU was certainly the Communist Party's most successful recruiting ground, providing up to a third of the delegates at CP Congresses during this period, and far more support for the Communist campaign for affiliation to the Labour Party in 1943 than any other trade union.[28]   In 1942 Ted Bramley, the London District secretary of the CP, told a Party meeting that 'the AEU was the main weapon of the Communist Party now.'[29]   Among elected officials in the Engineering union itself the Communists were much less well entrenched, having only two members on the National Executive – Joe Scott, an aggressive Londoner, and Gilbert Hitchings, a mild man from the South West with a technical bent whose soul, according to one of his colleagues, probably consisted of a finely wrought aircraft engine. Wal Hannington, who had led the unemployed workers' movement in the inter-war years, was elected as a National Organiser of the union in 1942.   Claude Berridge, who had cut his teeth with Scott and Hannington in the West London Shop Stewards' Movement at the end of the First World War,[30] presided over the Party's strongest base in the engineering factories of North and West London as the AEU's Divisional Organiser.   Elsewhere in the country, however, the AEU's full-time organisers remained predominantly hostile to

Communist influence. Even in Coventry, despite the CP's success in the factories, the Party failed to capture the District Committee, and the full-time organiser Billy Stokes was a relentless opponent: as an ex-Communist himself 'he knew all the moves.'[31]

Despite its weakness among the elected officials, the Communist Party was able to exercise a leading role in the industry through two main routes. Firstly, it controlled the Engineering and Allied Shop Stewards' National Council, an under-resourced and rather ramshackle unofficial body which nevertheless held a number of important national conferences. Its full-time secretary, Len Powell, did much to co-ordinate shop steward lobbying activity around Whitehall and Westminster during the war.[32] The Council also published a national shop steward paper for the aircraft industry – the *New Propeller* – with a circulation of at least 25,000,[33] which played a major co-ordinating role. Secondly, Communist delegates, though a minority, were usually able to command a majority for their resolutions at the National Committee of the union, which met for two weeks each year to debate and lay down union policy – a unique forum for detailed policy debate in the trade union movement.[34] An analysis of National Committee voting patterns between 1941 and 1947 shows them winning 9 of the 12 votes taken on issues directly concerned with the CP's own campaigns.[35] Throughout these years the Communists were helped by the fact that Jack Tanner, the union's charismatic leader, whose keynote speeches did much to orientate delegates at the National Committee, was, though not himself a Communist, extremely close to the Communist line. In fact many of his National Committee speeches were themselves drafted by the union's chief research officer, herself a member of the Party.[36]

There is no doubt that Communists took their responsibility for maximising production seriously. During the war, the exhortation to workers to put behind them the traditional view that production was the boss's concern not their own, rang out from hundreds of shop steward papers and leaflets, thousands of speeches.[37] The party poured pamphlets, leaflets and posters into the factories urging increased production; it organised 'socialist competition' between departments and between factories; it helped to set up 'Tank Weeks',

'Russia Weeks' and 'Africa Weeks' in an effort to boost output. One Communist shop steward urged his members not to let managerial inefficiency 'brown us off'. Instead of moaning about idle time caused by bad planning and bottlenecks, workers should 'use it in discussing new ways and means of speeding up, in replanning our jobs, in designing new tools and jigs and in forging new methods of production.'[38] Communists prided themselves on practising what they preached, taking the most unpleasant jobs and working to the limits of endurance in 'Party Shock Brigades'.[39] In a pamphlet significantly entitled *We Pledge the Lads* – a phrase redolent with Communist belief in their leading role – the comrades at one Liverpool factory manufacturing aircraft engines called on workers to make production their 'personal responsibility': 'Total war means also total war production, which can only be accomplished when we have the *conscious* participation of every worker in the factory in the drive to produce engines, *conscious* of all that this war means to us and our future, *conscious* of the problems that stand in our way.' The pamphlet left no doubt that the 'lads' were not, yet, sufficiently 'conscious', but that no effort would be spared in example and explanation to make them so.[40]

The Communist Party placed itself at the forefront of the movement for planning and participation in the engineering industry. Both the drive for JPCs and the more complex demands for the integration of the unions into the planning apparatus above the level of the firm owed much to Communist initiative. So long as the war continued, however, the Communists were extraordinarily reticent about the longer-term implications of the JPC campaign. In line with their enthusiastic support for the war effort from June 1941, the demands for nationalisation and workers' control which had figured so prominently in the politics of the factories during the First World War were now ruled out. While Communists had no doubt that a socialist society would be able to wage war more efficiently – was indeed doing so in the Soviet Union – the struggle to achieve socialism was bound to be both long and bitter; to unleash it now would destroy national unity and risk a fascist victory.[41] Demanding workers' control, as Len Powell explained to a shop steward at the Vickers works in Barrow 'is putting the cart before the horse. We will have no hope of controlling industry unless we defeat Fascism, and therefore surely we have got to organise the workers for the maximum production and ... for real production planning.... To the degree we do this will mean what sort of peace we will win after having defeated Hitler. To prepare for a new social order is meaningless without taking the above into account'.[42]

Even within capitalism much could be done to increase efficiency, and most of what urgently needed to be done, though it did not involve changes in ownership, did involve a very real transfer of control over private industry both to the state and to the organised workers. Against those on the left who proposed nationalisation and workers' control as the answer to the crisis of war production, Communists argued that the task of the moment was to fight to incorporate a high degree of workers' participation in the war economy.[43] But they were extremely reluctant to speculate about the ways in which JPCs might be laying a basis for future socialist advance. Jack Tanner was happy to talk, if only vaguely, about the JPCs as a stage on the road to socialism: 'By accepting a share of responsibility to-day in the difficult task of speeding production still tied to private ownership, with all that means in the way of organising output in the private interests of the owners, the workers will learn to shoulder the greater responsibility which will be theirs once they succeed to the control of industry.'[44] But such speculations remained firmly at the back of Communist minds.

So long as the main priority was the defeat of Hitler all talk about the implications of the wartime experience for any post-war strategy of transition to socialism was considered counter-productive. According to Douglas Hyde the comrades understood the long-term goals, but didn't talk about them openly for fear of destabilising wartime national unity. In 1942, Palme Dutt, the Pope of Party orthodoxy, warned the central committee that no judgement could yet be made about whether the political situation at the end of the war would require a continuation of the politics of national unity or the unleashing of immediate revolutionary struggles. Consequently, he insisted, the Party should keep its options open by saying as little as possible about post-war objectives; 'only in the concrete situation at the end of the war can the Party correctly judge the character of the immediate programme it should present'.[45] In the same spirit, Dutt repeatedly instructed members to 'check all attempts at diversion from the urgent tasks of the present struggle into speculation on the post-war settlement after victory'.[46] Yvonne Kapp, who attended regular briefing meetings provided by the Party centre to its militants in engineering, has no memory of any discussion of longer-term perspectives. The meetings were simply concerned with day-to-day tactics, and Dutt's rule against speculation about the strategic future seems to have been rigorously observed.[47] When Trevor Robinson, a leading Sheffield shop steward and chairman of the Shop Stewards' National Council, sought to raise the possible 'dual power' implications of the drive to establish JPCs, the Party leadership refused to engage in discussion of the issue.[48] It seems probable that most Communist shop stewards buckled down to winning the war, with a vague and unworked-out assumption that the increased status they won in the war factories would stand them in good stead when class struggle resumed after the war. The possibility that workers' organisation might be weakened by the processes of co-option unleashed by the JPCs, a possibility which worried some more thoughtful stewards, was not seriously confronted. Thus, Eddie Frow, a leading Communist engineer in Manchester, fended off criticisms of the JPC campaign in the *AEU Monthly Journal*, while refusing to discuss either the pros or cons of viewing production committees as 'a step in the direction of the socialisation of industry.'[49]

During the war CP shop stewards operated with an uneasy combination of productionist commitment – 'Tanks for Joe' – and an economistic determination to win the best possible wages and conditions for their members. Most of the time these two loyalties ran side by side rather than actively reinforcing one another – though arguments that increased production would flow from improvements in wages and conditions were easily mobilised. Communist activists did their best to avoid strikes and became adept at using the other means available to press their case in a full employment, state-controlled economy. But when, despite their best efforts, the logic of productionism and that of economism came into conflict with one another the shop stewards' democratic accountability to the shop floor normally ensured that economism would take priority.[50]

At the end of the war the Communist Party committed itself to the view that some objective basis existed for an alliance between 'progressive capital' and the labour movement to carry through a 'state capitalist' reconstruction programme. While the construction of socialism was not yet on the immediate agenda, such a reconstruction would entrench organised labour in a way that would pave the way for a relatively painless, perhaps even gradualist, assumption of power by the working class when conditions were ripe. The origin of this view was to be found in the speculations of Earl Browder, leader of the US Communist Party, about the shape of the post-war world. If long-term peaceful coexistence between capitalist America and the Soviet Union was possible, then there must be such an animal as a progressive capitalist. And, more importantly, the still-capitalist economy must be able to be freed from those fetters which would inevitably drive the world towards a new slump. In the United States, Browder argued, the balance of forces required the dissolution of the Communist Party and the abandonment of socialist aims in the medium term.[51]

In Europe conditions were more favourable for socialism, and 'liquidationism' gained little support within the British Party. Nevertheless the Party leadership rejected the idea that the war period was 'a sort of interim after which we get down to the "real" class conflict with "our own" capitalists'.[52] Against a background of ongoing co-operation between the Soviet Union and its capitalist allies the Party spelled out its post-war policy as being for: 'a Better Britain today and a Socialist Britain tomorrow.' 'Today' the CP worked for the establishment of a democratic 'state capitalism' with a government committed to international economic co-operation, piecemeal nationalisation, and progressive social reform. 'Tomorrow' it would be possible to go beyond this, embarking on a more or less rapid, and probably peaceful transition to socialism.[53] For the time being, it was to the establishment of the first, 'state capitalist', phase of reconstruction that the leadership devoted its attention, arguing that economic expansion, planning, full employment and significant redistribution of income could be achieved without any major transfer of industry from public to private ownership.[54]   Under state capitalism the productionist initiatives of the workers would replace market forces as the main driving force of economic progress.   To this end, the CP called on the Labour Government to take workers into partnership, as the state's main agents in achieving the production targets set by the planners.   It was assumed, moreover, that dominant sections of the capitalist class were now willing to collaborate in the construction of a democratic state capitalist order, despite the fact that such an order would involve fundamental popular encroachments on capitalist power and open the door to further advances towards socialism.[55]

The Communist belief that continuing private ownership of industry might not, at least in the medium term, be incompatible with the elaboration of a system of participatory planning, was reinforced by the fact that not all employers were entirely hostile to such ideas.   Forced by pressure both from their workers and from the state to accommodate the JPCs, the Engineering Employers' Federation (EEF) concentrated its resistance on the higher levels, where the pincer movement between Whitehall and shop floor organisation presented the most serious challenge to managerial prerogative.   A minority of employers, however, adopted a more positive attitude, seeing in the emerging tripartite structures a means both of sorting out the bottlenecks created by Whitehall's over-centralised and ill-coordinated system of contracting for military supplies, and of sustaining a measure of business autonomy despite the overwhelming power of the wartime state.[56]   While the contradictions involved were too great for any formal alliance to emerge, the existence of such sentiments in business circles played a role in sustaining the left-wing movement for participatory planning.

Riding out the confusion caused by a grossly misjudged decision to go into the 1945 election campaign calling for a continued Labour/ Conservative coalition, the Communist Party leaders re-worked these underlying perspectives as the basis of their policy of critical support for the Attlee Government under the slogan 'fight for the Britain you voted for'.[57]   This meant that a special responsibility for increasing production would continue to fall on 'the Marxist political leadership within the working class movement'.[58]   The constructive role played by Arthur Horner in tackling the acute problems of production in the coal industry was held up for general admiration by Party spokesmen.[59] At the same time, however, the Government was criticised for failing to plan the economy coherently, and much effort went into spelling out the kind of economic planning that would meet with the Party's approval. To lay the basis for successful reconstruction and national independence (from the Americans) Britain's resources of engineering manpower should be concentrated on exports and capital equipment.[60] The alleged failure of the Government to prevent firms from devoting resources to more immediately profitable domestic consumer goods provided the Party with a constant source of puritanical complaint that resources were being wasted on fripperies.[61] In contrast to their wartime refusal to discuss the implications of planning for the balance of class power, planning was now advocated explicitly 'as a means of changing the balance of class forces.' Its central aims should be to 'strengthen the working-class grip on Britain's economy, win new footholds of power. Planning means power to enforce plans, i.e. to coerce capitalists where necessary.'[62] Party educationalists tried to wean members from the catastrophic view that only economic disaster could open the way to socialism, holding out the prospect that implementation of their planning demands would 'take key economic positions out of the hands of capitalists ... and put power in the hands of workers'. Our aim should be – through confidence to power, rather than to power through disillusion.'[63] Or, as Harry Pollitt had put it in November 1945, pleading with old-style class warriors skulking in the ranks: 'Are we never going to learn? I have been in too many campaigns which had as their main motive *against*, and not sufficient with the main motive *for*...'.[64]

How convinced the militants were by this commitment to gradualism it is difficult to say. The new revisionism had been adopted by the leadership with little consultation with the Party rank and file, and it provoked a major outburst of criticism at the Party Congress in November 1945.[65] No doubt many expected a frankly revolutionary policy to re-emerge in the fullness of time. But for the time being the class struggle had become a war of position within the emerging structures of 'state capitalism' designed to open up practices of democratic participation though which working people could gain the awareness, confidence and ambition to make the transition to socialism, by whatever means, when the time came. By the time the Party got round to publishing its own plan for progress, in December 1947, the international earthquake of the Cold War had rendered the whole project redundant. Although Communist leaders were initially reluctant to adandon productionism altogether, the issue disappeared completely from the pages of the *Metalworker* (the re-named paper of the Shop Stewards' National Council).[66] Despite this, what matters in the present context is that for more than two years after the end of the war Communist attitudes to production had remained constructive. It was this that opened the way to the movement for industrial democracy analysed in later chapters.

NOTES

1. T. Smith, *The Politics of the Corporate Economy*, 1979, Ch. 4.
2. B. Wootton, 'Freedom Under Planning', in H. Morrison, *et al.*, *Can Planning be Democratic?*, 1944, p. 52.
3. G.D.H. Cole, *Guide to the Elements of Socialism*, Labour Party Research Department, June 1947, p. 26. On the evolution of Cole's ideas see A.W. Wright, *G.D.H. Cole and Socialist Democracy*, Oxford, 1979.
4. 'The ideology of voluntarism ... ran through statism.' G. Finlayson, 'A Moving Frontier: Voluntarism and the State in British Social Welfare, 1941–49', *Twentieth-century British History*, 1, 2, 1990, p. 193 and *passim*.
5. 'The New Democracy', Preface to G. Williams, *Women and Work*, 1945.
6. J. Pinder (ed.), *Fifty Years of Political and Economic Planning*, 1981, p. 13; D. Ritschel, 'A Corporatist Economy in Britain? Capitalist planning for industrial self-government in the 1930s', *English Historical Review*, 1, 1991.
7. 'The New Pattern', *Planning*, 178, 30 September 1941.
8. Michael Young, 'PEP After the War', February 1944, PEP A/13/4; PEP Executive, *Minutes*, 9 May 1946, PEP M/7; 'Review of the Programme', *Planning*, 289, 18 October 1948.
9. PEP Executive, *Minutes*, 18 July 1944, PEP A/13/4; 'Discussion of draft on "active democracy"', 13 May 1946, *idem*, A/12/1.
10. 'Soviet Planning in Wartime', *Planning*, 196, 17 November 1942. For a similar stress on the two-way dialogue involved in Soviet planning see A. Albu, *Management in Transition*, Fabian Society Research Series, 68, London, 1942, p. 22.
11. N. Barou, *British Trade Unions*, Gollancz, 1947, p. 235; M. Young, *Small Man: Big World. A Discussion of Socialist Democracy*, Labour Party, 1949, pp. 7–8.
12. Angus Calder, *The People's War, Britiain 1939–45*, 1971, p. 21
13. *Ibid.*, pp. 20–22.
14. Kevin Jefferys, *The Churchill Coalition and Wartime Politics, 1940–45*, Manchester, 1991; K. Middlemass, *Power Competition and the State Vol 1: Britain in Search of Balance 1940–61*, 1988; P. Hennessy, *Whitehall*, 1990.

15. P. Addison, *Now the War is Over*, 1985; J. Cronin, *Labour and Society in Britain 1918–1979*, 1984; S. Beer, *Britain Against Itself. The Political Contradictions of Collectivism*, London, 1982.
16. S. Fielding, 'Don't Know Don't Care', in N. Tiratsoo (ed.) *The Attlee Years*, 1991; S. Fielding, 'What did the people want. The meaning of the 1945 General Election', *Historical Journal*, 35, 1992, pp. 623–39.
17. K.O. Morgan, *op. cit.*, pp. 327–8.
18. Mass Observation, *An Enquiry into People's Homes*, 1943, p. 208.
19. C. Madge and T. Harrison, *Mass Observation*, 1937, pp. 29–30, 46–8. For discussions of the reliability of Mass Observation material see: T. Jeffery, *Mass Observation – A Short History*, 1978; P. Summerfield, 'Mass Observation: Social Research or Social Movement?', *Journal of Contemporary History*, 20, 3, 1985; A. Calder, 'Mass Observation', in M. Bulmer (ed.), *Essays on the History of British Sociological Research*, 1985.
20. 'Ethical Union', preface to Mass Observation, *Puzzled people. A study in popular attitudes to religion, ethics, progress and politics in a London borough*, 1947, p. 8.
21. W. Crofts, *Coercion or Persuasion? Propaganda in Britain after 1945*, 1989, pp. 53–4, 67–9.
22. 'Discussion of draft on "active democracy"', 13 May 1946, PEP A/12/1; Conference on the psychological and sociological problems of modern socialism, 15–16 September 1945, *Minutes*, p. 17, Fabian Society Papers, G49/10; 'Watling revisited', *Planning*, 270, 15 August 1947, pp. 78, 81.
23. G.D.H. Cole, 'Opinion in the Making', *New Statesman*, 15 August 1942; G.D.H. Cole, 'Production Committees', *ibid.*, 3 October 1942.
24. Labour Party Conference, *Report*, 1946, p. 224.
25. R. Croucher, *Engineers at War, 1939–1945*, 1982.
26. *World News and Views*, 28 November 1942.
27. *Ibid.*, 7 March 1942; Communist Party, *Party Organisation for Victory*, March 1943.
28. Croucher, *op. cit.*, p. 144; *New Propeller*, May 1943.
29. Special Branch Report, 3 April 1942, CAB 66/23.
30. N. Fishman, 'The British Communist Party and the Trade Unions, 1933–1945: the dilemmas of revolutionary pragmatism', London PhD, 1991, pp. 50ff.
31. Interview with Jack Cohen, March 1979. Both in Manchester and Glasgow right-wing officials could normally count on the District Committee majority.
32. Len Powell, 'The Shop Stewards' National Council', 23 October 1942, in Len Powell Papers.
33. This is the figure estimated by a TUC official who acquired the handwritten balance sheet for the SSNC covering the period May 1940 to February 1941. Hartwell to Citrine, 2 December 1942, TUC 292/225/1. The circulation is unlikely to have fallen subsequently, but its expansion may have been restricted by paper shortages.
34. L. Minkin, *The Labour Party Conference. A Study in the Politics of Intra-Party Democracy*, 1978, p. 182.
35. The same voting records show the CP's main strongholds as being London and the South East (where the Party almost always got its way); Scotland (but not Glasgow itself, where things were more evenly balanced); Lancashire (except North Lancs where the anti-Communists were in a majority); South Yorkshire; and Birmingham. The strongholds of anti-Communism were in Wales; the South West; the East Midlands; and East and West Yorkshire. Elsewhere – the South, Bristol, East Anglia, the South and North Midlands, the North East – the two sides were more or less evenly balanced.
36. Interview with Yvonne Kapp, June 1992. Kapp moved to the AEU job from working for the LRD. The LRD, which pumped out a stream of well-researched information

to shop stewards and trade union officials, was itself a major source of Communist influence in industry.

37. See the factory papers held in the Working-Class Movement Library, Manchester; surviving examples of productionist speeches by shop stewards include one by the convener at English Electric, Preston on 23 October 1941 (E. and R. Frow, *Engineering Struggles. Episodes in the story of the shop stewards' movement*, Manchester, 1982, pp. 173–4; full text in my possesssion (JH)), and one by E.W. Darling at Philco on 16 April 1942. (Darling Papers, Hoover Institution on War, Revolution and Peace, Stanford University.) The response to the AEU Production Enquiries in 1941–42 clearly revealed the breadth of productionist sentiment among shop stewards. AEU, *Third Report on Production*, 1942, *passim*.

38. E.W. Darling, *op. cit.* Darling worked for a particularly enlightened firm which was keen on promoting joint consultation: *Summary* of enquiry into JPCs in the Radio Industry (Philco), EEF 237/3/1/313 (W4/108/File 6); D.F. Hutchinson, 'Joint Consultation – an Experiment', *Industrial Welfare*, January 1946, pp. 8–10.

39. *World News and Views*, 12 September, 13 October 1942; Sam Blackwell, *Birmingham Against Hitler*, n.d. (1943?); *Shock Brigades – A Guide. How to start them. How they work.*, Y.C.L. n.d. (1942?).

40. *We Pledge the Lads*, Communist Party group at Napiers (Sabre Engines), Liverpool, n.d, (1944?).

41. R.P. Dutt, *Britain in the World Front*, 1942, pp. 132–4.

42. Powell to Montgomery, 30 March 1942, Len Powell Papers.

43. 'How to set up JPCs', n.d. (February 1942?), Len Powell Papers; L. Powell, 'For a Real Ministry of Production', *Labour Monthly*, April 1942; E. Burns, *Labour's Way Forward*, July 1942; M. Dobb, *Economics of Capitalism. An Introductory Outline*, n.d. (1942?), p. 5. Contrast M. Edleman, *Production for Victory, not Profit!*, 1941, pp. 124–5, 177.

44. AEU, National Committee, *Report*, 1942, p. 293; *idem*, 1943, p. 218. See also C. Riegelman, *British Joint Production Machinery*, Montreal, 1944, p. 190.

45. 'Draft for Central Committee', 7 December 1942, Dutt Papers, British Library, K4.

46. E.g. Political Letter, 12 February 1942, Dutt Papers, British Library, K3. In May 1942 he wrote: 'There are a host of controversial issues of the past and the future which at the appropriate time will repay careful review in order that the full political lessons of the period may be drawn. But the present is no time for recriminations over the past or philosophising over the future. The present hour requires unity in action of all who stand for victory over the fascist enemy' (R.P. Dutt, *Britain in the World Front*, 1942, p. i). Such present-mindedness in a radical political party, however understandable in the face of Hitler, was a serious obstacle to political creativity.

47. Interview with Y. Kapp, June 1992.

48. N. Fishman, *op. cit.*, p. 290.

49. Articles by Jennison and Frow in *AEU Monthly Journal*, December 1941, January, June 1942.

50. Croucher, *op. cit.*, *passim*.

51. Browder's speech of 10 January 1944 was reprinted in *World News and Views*, 22 January 1944.

52. Nan Brewer, *World News and Views*, 26 August 1944.

53. H. Pollitt, *How to Win the Peace*, 1945, pp. 90–91; Pat Sloan, *World News and Views*, 8 July 1944.

54. *Britain for the people*, May 1944; H. Pollitt, *op. cit.*, pp. 26–8; H. Pollitt, *Answers to Questions*, pp. 25ff.

55. H. Pollitt, *How to Win the Peace*, p. 12; H. Pollitt, *Answers to Questions*, *passim*; Nan Brewer, *World News and Views*, 26 August 1944.

56. See below, pp. 35–9

57. Communist Party, Report of Executive to 19th National Congress, 1946.
58. R.P. Dutt, *Labour Monthly*, September 1945.
59. 'We show the way', CP Executive statement, 15 March 1947 in Executive Report to 20th Congress, 1947.
60. J.R. Campbell, 'The Planless Planners', *Communist Review*, April 1947.
61. R. Birch, 'From an Engineering Shop', *Labour Monthly*, July 1947.
62. 'Discussion Guide on Looking Ahead', *World News and Views*, 23 August 1947.
63. 'Labour Government and Socialism', CP training manual, in Labour Party Archive, GS/1/4; H. Pollitt, Weekly Letter 46, 28 November 1946, Communist Party Archive.
64. *Communist Policy for Britain*, 1945, p. 32.
65. K. Morgan, *Harry Pollitt*, Manchester, 1993, pp. 143–4, 146–7.
66. For the evolution of Pollitt's views on the issue see: *World News and Views*, 20 December 1947, p. 385; *For Britain Free and Independent*, 1948, p. 47; *Daily Worker*, 13 September 1948. Already in October 1947 Party leaders responded to the formation of Cominform by instructing the *Daily Worker* to stop printing 'sunshine stories' about the success of workers' initiatives in sorting out production bottlenecks. D. Hyde, *I Believed. The Autobiography of a Former British Communist*, London, 1952, pp. 231–2.

2 The Production Debate, 1941–42

Dunkirk, and the two years of military reversals that followed, created a crisis of legitimacy for Britain's elites. As long as the threat of invasion remained acute discontent was muted, but the combination of a marginally increased sense of national security by the spring of 1941, and continuing defeat at the hands of Hitler's armies in North Africa, Greece and Crete, triggered an outburst of criticism of the Churchill Government which did not finally subside until Montgomery's armies ended the retreat at El Alamein in November 1942. Such criticism was greatly reinforced by the surprising resilience of the Soviet Union in the face of Hitler's onslaught. The apparent contrast between Soviet effectiveness and British muddle fostered dissatisfaction with the British war effort far beyond the ranks of those politically predisposed to admire the Communist state.

Discontent expressed itself in many forms. From the Hornsey by-election in late May 1941, through to the autumn of 1942 the Government suffered a series of defeats at the hands of independent candidates contesting Tory-held seats in defiance of the electoral truce between the parties. Most of the challengers supported Churchill, but attacked his ministers in the name of national efficiency. By the spring of 1942 the Labour Party was becoming seriously worried by the success of the independents, and its Annual Conference in May 1942 came close to precipitating a political crisis by withdrawing support from the electoral truce. Opinion polls told the same story: the number of people saying they were dissatisfied with the Government's conduct of the war rose from 30% in June 1941 to a wartime peak of 50% in March 1942.[1] In the early months of 1942, as Malaya fell to the Japanese, popular disenchantment with the Government's record fuelled the extraordinary rise of Stafford Cripps, briefly seen as national saviour when he returned from a term as ambassador to the Soviet Union, trailing clouds of Russian Glory. While this crisis passed, the defeat of Churchill's North African hopes at Tobruk in June 1942 brought him closer to resignation than at any other moment of the war, despite his continuing popularity.[2]

For the critics of the Government one key explanation of the continuing military reversal was the disorganised state of Britain's war industries. During the second half of 1941 a broadly-based agenda for the reform of war production emerged, combining calls for greater co-ordination at the top (a Ministry of Production), with decentralised administration at regional level (Regional Boards), and the direct participation of workers in the factories (Joint Production Committees). Significant alliances took shape around each of these demands, creating a degree of optimism among more radical critics that the crisis might be opening the way for fundamental change. Analysis of the response of the Government to the demands for a Ministry of Production and Regional Boards (Joint Production Committees are dealt with in later chapters) goes some way to explain why the radicals were ultimately to be disappointed. The very allies whose support made moves towards participatory planning appear practical politics – businessmen, Whitehall officials – ensured that those moves would be hedged around with protection for existing structures of authority. Moreover, while the Government showed enough flexibility to assuage many of its more powerful critics, it stood firm against changes which would have seriously jeopardised the perceived interests of important members of the governing coalition. In line with the arguments advanced by much recent literature on elite responses to the 'people's war', analysis of the state's response to the production crisis in 1941–42 reveals how little changed, not how much.

During the 12 months following the entry of the Soviet Union into the war Government, employers and trade unions conducted their negotiations against the background of a major public debate about the organisation of war production. According to opinion polls, the proportion of respondents giving top priority to production and man-power issues in the problems facing the Government rose from only 4% in March 1941 to 18% in August and 40% in December. In March 1942 57% believed that the complaints about war factories were justified, compared with a mere 16% who positively rejected this view.[3] Such attitudes were echoed and amplified by extensive parliamentary and press criticism both of war industry itself and of the Government's handling of the situation.

Mass Observation, which undertook a major study of war production over the winter of 1941–42, argued that the war factories were not nearly as inefficient as the general public had been led to believe, and placed much of the blame for popular misconceptions on sensational reporting in the national press, in particular the readiness of journalists with little respect for accuracy to give 'currency to "newsy" anecdotes of inefficiency and frustration' supplied by disaffected shop stewards.[4] Mass Observation's judgement, which echoed its long-standing hostility to the popular press, almost certainly underestimated both the probity of the industrial correspondents of the main newspapers and the degree to which they understood what was going on in war industry.[5] Nevertheless, the readiness of journalists to listen to, and amplify, shop stewards' accounts of industrial matters was part of a more general crisis in relations between the press and the established authorities in the early years of the war, a crisis which climaxed in Herbert Morrison's threat to suppress the *Daily Mirror* in March 1942. In their coverage of production issues, as on other matters, newspapers played an important part in expressing, and no doubt also in shaping, the upsurge of public dissatisfaction with established elites during 1941–42.[6]

Following the lead given by successive reports of the Select Committee on National Expenditure, and of back-bench critics in parliamentary debates, the press took a dim view of the effectiveness of war industry. Widespread publicity was given to a statement by Sir John Wardlaw Milne, Conservative chairman of the Select Committee in a Commons debate on production in July 1941, that industry was only producing at 75% of its capacity.[7] Outside the pages of the *Daily Express*, which often read more like a public relations hand-out for its proprietor than a newspaper,[8] negative headlines bemoaning the 'chaos in production'[9] outweighed positive ones by a factor of two to one. And many of the latter echoed workers' pledges to speed up arms production rather than ministerial attempts to reassure the public that the Government had production under control.

A systematic reading of the seven largest circulation national daily newspapers (*Express, Mirror, The Times, Herald, Mail, News Chronicle, Telegraph* and *Sketch*) during periods when the production debate was at its height during 1941–42 revealed 549 items dealing with production issues.[10] Where the source could be identified from the report, journalists were three times more likely to rely on information supplied by trade unions than by employers.[11] This bias in the sources, however, may not in itself have determined the tone of the reporting. The press study undertaken for the Royal Commission on the Press in the 1970s found a similar predominance of trade union sources.[12] The major difference between the two periods was not in where journalists gained their information, but in the conceptual framework within which that information was handled. In the 1970s the focus was on industrial disputes, where workers were normally seen as the initiators of disruption. In the war the issue was production failure, for which employers were much more likely to be held ultimately responsible.[13] Analysis of the 1941–42 sample shows an equal balance between articles blaming workers and those blaming employers for problems in war production. As one would expect the Conservative press concentrated on the former, the Labour and Liberal press on the latter, (see Table 2.1) Such balance across the national press as a whole was in itself probably a departure from the normal anti-union bias, and it is notable that among Conservative papers both the *Mail* and the *Telegraph* carried a significant number of stories criticising management. Only the *Sketch*, the lowest circulation paper in the sample, sustained a completely uncritical attitude to the employers.

Certainly employers themselves found the climate of public opinion uncomfortable. The main effect of employer allegations that absenteeism and bad time-keeping was a major cause of production delays was to stimulate trade unionists to counter-attack with charges of managerial incompetence which received very much wider press coverage.[14] Nothing in the right-wing press criticism of workers matched the ferocity with which the *Herald* and the *Mirror* laid into

Table 2.1 Production stories in the national press, 1941–42

Number of stories attaching blame to (a) workers (b) employers: in each case the percentage given is of the total number of production stories analysed in the paper or group of papers concerned.

	Blame Workers		Blame Employers	
	No	%	No	%
Herald	2	2	18	17
Mirror	7	8	11	13
News Chronicle	7	10	7	10
Lab./Lib.	16	6	36	14
Mail	15	27	5	9
Telegraph	12	22	6	11
Express	4	6	3	4
Sketch	6	11	0	0
Cons.	37	16	14	6
The Times	2	3	4	6
Total	55	10	54	10

the Blimps in the boardrooms: 'Managerial laziness. Proprietorial prejudice. Subjugation of public welfare to private profit. Red tape. Sheer selfishness. Sheer obstinacy', stormed the *Daily Herald*. Its solution lay in 'opening up and maintaining a direct route of co-operation between the workers and Whitehall ... craftsman and statesman must work as one.' The intervening layer of management and capitalist enterprise had, on this account, nothing at all to contribute to the solution: 'The Government wants 100% production. The workers want to give 100% production. But between the workers and the Government there are obstructions which confound the desires of both.'[15] A similar message was carried by a *Mirror* cartoon showing a worker and a tank trapped inside a bottle. Blocking the bottle neck with its bony finger is a skeletal hand – the 'dead hand of mis-management'.[16] While hostile stereotyping of management played a major role in the treatment of production issues there were no cartoons of selfish workers obstructing output. In October 1941 Gallup found only one individual among its sample of 2,045 people who believed that curbing shop steward power was the key to increasing war production – stereotypically enough she was a retired, upper-class, Conservative-voting spinster.

While dissident employers and managers played an important role in building up the production crisis,[17] the great body of employers remained, as Mass Observation put it, 'practically mute': presumably because they believed that, as the results of earlier attacks on absenteeism had shown, anything they said would be turned against them.[18] The Engineering Employers' Federation kept a low profile, briefing industrial correspondents, but deciding against a general press campaign to counter union allegations of inefficiency because of fears that this would only give such allegations even more prominence.[19] When the press got hold of a circular advising federated firms not to co-operate with a production questionnaire issued by the AEU, the Federation tightened its security, but made no public statement on the substantive issue.[20] At the height of the production crisis in January–February 1942 the TUC General Council issued a press statement which received wide coverage and helped to keep allegations of managerial incompetence flowing in. The employers took no similar initiative, concentrating instead on off-the-record briefings which gave little help to their friends in the newsrooms: 'These are the people who know the facts of industry,' complained the *Daily Mail*: 'It is up to them to tell the public, they cannot shift the whole of that duty onto the shoulders of politicians and the Press.'[21]

Both sides of industry could agree, however, on blaming Whitehall for the production crisis, and the main thrust of press criticism was aimed at the Government. In July 1941, for example, Maurice Webb's appeal in the *Daily Herald* for politicians not to allow the slanging match about absenteeism versus managerial incompetence to divert them from the need for greater Government co-ordination and planning, was echoed by a leader in the *Telegraph* despite the fact that the *Telegraph* had itself made a good deal of fuss about absenteeism.[22]   Similarly *The Times* endorsed management complaints that the competing demands of different supply ministries for labour, raw materials and production capacity sowed chaos and hold-ups in industry and it printed a major feature article on the production situation which alleged that it was lack of proper control by the state that was 'breaking the hearts of producers, both managements and workpeople.'[23]

Formal co-ordination of production administration lay with the Production Executive, which brought together the three supply ministries (Aircraft Production, Admiralty and the Ministry of Supply) under the chairmanship of the Minister of Labour, Ernest Bevin.   This, however, was a toothless body: 'a meeting of high contracting parties.   Sovereignty was not merged or waived.'[24] While the TUC initially argued that only the merger of the existing supply ministries into a World War One-style Ministry of Munitions would bring the necessary co-ordination,[25] the most commonly proposed solution was the appointment of an overlord Minister of Production with authority to direct the work of the supply ministries.[26]   By the end of 1941 the demand for a Ministry of Production was being pressed by *The Times* – following two anonymous articles by Beveridge[27] – as well as the *Herald* and the *Mirror*, though most of the Conservative papers remained sceptical and only came round to cautious support for the idea after Churchill moved to allay his critics by appointing Beaverbrook as Minister of Production early in February.

Most of those demanding a Ministry of Production did not think that this, by itself, would provide the answer.   Rather they sought to combine greater co-ordination at the centre with a devolution of authority and initiative to the production machinery in the regions.[28] The Regional Boards (known as Area Boards until May 1941) had originated in January 1940 as a means of co-ordination between regional officers of the Whitehall departments involved in war production.   In August 1940 so-called 'industrial' members were added to the Boards, representative of local employers and trade

unionists.[29]   Subsequently the Boards became a major focus of
attention for those on both sides of industry who wanted to combine
centralised planning of war production with autonomy and initiative
from below.[30]

Since the outbreak of war the TUC had campaigned actively for
the devolution of power to Regional Boards seeing this as a
significant means of extending trade union influence in the war
economy.[31]   Left-wingers were equally enthusiastic, seeing the
Boards as a key link in 'the drive from below' to overcome obstacles
to maximum output.   Communists linked demands for an all-
embracing Ministry of Production with agitation for 'open access
from the factories' to the Regional Boards which, they argued,
would give 'the life-giving free contact' necessary to counterbalance
'the dead hand of bureaucratic routine or dilatory Whitehall
centralisation'. In the Communist plan: 'The [transformed] Ministry
of Production, in place of directly seeking to control 50,000
enterprises, would act through the Regional Boards, allocating to the
regions (with consultation) their share in the national plan on the
basis of knowledge of their capacity. The main executive organs
would be the Regional Boards', on which the direct representation of
workers would have been considerably increased.[32] Argonaut, the
anonymous author of *Give Us the Tools*, a book which eloquently
expounds the productionist thinking in the autumn of 1941, paid
tribute to the achievement of some Regional Boards both in
overcoming the influence of Whitehall rivalries in their areas, and
building a real co-operation between employers and unions: 'This
regional harmony is a standing reproach to the absence of real co-
operation at the centre.'[33]

Talk of 'regional harmony' was a polemical exaggeration.
Nevertheless arguments for enhancing the powers of the Regional
Boards were at least as appealing among reform-minded
businessmen as on the Left.[34] For business opinion, the Boards had
a central role to play in adapting 1930s' doctrines of 'self-
government in industry' to wartime conditions.[35] As developed by
'middle opinion' before the war the object was to devolve statutory
powers onto trade associations so that they could meet the need for
greater co-ordination between firms on research, production and

marketing and other issues while keeping the state at arm's length.[36] In wartime, however, the penetration of Whitehall into the affairs of individual firms was far too extensive for 'self-government in industry', in this pure sense, to provide anything more than a gleam in the eyes of businessmen planning post-war escape routes from state control. In a situation where the state was the sole buyer for the products of whole sectors of industry, and where shortages of machinery, manpower and raw materials made allocation through the market impossible, a large measure of direct state control over industry was clearly unavoidable. Consequently, business opinion shifted towards a qualified version of 'self-government in industry' in which, within an overall framework of state control, businessmen claimed the right to administer their own affairs. The main institutional framework for self-government was provided, as in the 1930s, by the trade associations, organised on national lines and negotiating directly with their sponsoring ministries. A major advantage of the trade association as a line of communication between business and Government was that there was never any question of trade unions participating at this level.[37] By contrast, those businessmen who chose, instead, to concentrate their energies on the development of Regional Boards were ready to accept, if only for the duration, that trade unions had a legitimate role to play in the organisation of production. This is why the Left was so keen to build up the Boards. It was here that they could hope, in co-operation with the more progressive employers, to create the framework within which trade unionists could move from a merely external and advisory relation to production planning into a direct engagement with the every-day details of the administrative process.

Two businessmen in particular played a central role in the development of the Regional Boards. George Dickson, managing director of a medium-sized engineering firm in Kent, has not previously attracted a mention in a single history book; but his imagination, energy and inexhaustible letter writing make him a central presence in surviving Whitehall, employer and TUC files. A Christian socialist member of the management movement, with a background in the shipyards of Red Clydeside, Dickson enjoyed his reputation as an intelligent crank.[38] At key moments throughout the

1940s he exchanged views with Norman Kipping, the other businessman central to the story of the Regional Boards. Kipping's subsequent career as post-war Director General of the FBI was to make him a leading figure in the evolution of state–industry relations until the mid-1960s.[39]

In 1940 Dickson used his position as an employer representative on the London and South East Regional Board to pioneer the establishment of Capacity Clearing Centres, which enabled companies to avoid bottlenecks by *ad hoc* borrowing of temporarily unused tools and machines from other local firms. In the aftermath of Dunkirk, Dickson believed that the normal obstacles of trade secrecy and competitive rivalry could be overcome by a vigorous call to patriotic sentiment.[40] Working with a group of local employers and trade union officials, Dickson improvised the first Clearing Centre in the offices of his Rochester factory.[41] The subsequent success of the Capacity Clearing Centres, he argued, provided 'astounding proof of the value of group integration around a common interest with some measure of autonomy to get a job done quickly but wisely'. The Centre worked informally:

> At our meetings, after the three trade unionists, the three employers and the two [officials] had really got to know each other, our agendas, which were wide, were covered comprehensively and quickly by intelligent knowledgeable discussion interspersed every here and there by suggestions of 'Don't let that worry you. When you go to such and such a firm, ask for so-and-so and tell him that I sent you. He has been a friend of mine for years. He will help you'.[42]

Beyond simple patriotism, there was a rich vein of frustrated managerial professionalism waiting to be tapped – a point which Dickson later impressed on the author of an admiring PEP report on the Clearing Centres:

> Once managers are introduced to one another they start to lend or exchange tools, gauges, fixtures, drawings, progress methods, and often specially skilled personnel.... Those men and women who have developed their production technique within the factory walls, nine times out of ten jump at the chance to meet others who speak their own production language. They just like doing their jobs and are delighted to do them better.[43]

Not all businessmen were so co-operative. The response to similar proposals for breaking down trade secrecy presented to a conference of the Institute of Mechanical Engineers in 1943 shows what Dickson was up against: industry was 'not a Garden of Eden where everybody told everybody else about everything' and such practices would not take root until 'the manufacturers sprout wings!'[44] Nevertheless the Federation of British Industries lent its support to Dickson's initiative, and helped to extend the Capacity Clearing Centres from Rochester to the country as a whole. The Centres dealt not only with the exchange of resources between firms, but also with more general problems affecting local industry – labour supply, housing, transport, and so on.[45] In May 1941, when the functions of the Boards were extended, the Centres were formally required to advise supply ministries where their uncoordinated contracting policies were in danger of overloading local firms responsible for contracts (or sub-contracted orders) originating in different parts of the Whitehall machine.[46]

These moves did not satisfy the decentralisers, among them Norman Kipping. In 1941 Kipping was works manager of the Standard Telephone and Cable factory in East London, and chairman of his local Capacity Clearing Centre. He proposed that neighbouring factories should set up local manufacturers' associations, so that Clearing Centres could 'do the majority of their business by getting into direct touch with only six or ten key firms acting as the leaders for their groups instead of dealing with hundreds of firms.' Within each group labour, machine tools and raw materials would become completely interchangeable, 'thus eliminating the idle men and unused machine tool capacity within a mile or so of an overloaded firm'. Presenting his ideas to a meeting of leading London industrialists in May 1941, Kipping concluded:

> They must surely press to a conclusion the question of decentralisation or delegation of authority, until people knowing local conditions, were empowered to settle local problems, to place local contracts, and deal with matters which would never properly be solved by civil servants sitting aloof in headquarters.[47]

By early 1942, Kipping was proposing that Capacity Centres should be given a power of veto over contracts issued from Whitehall, in

order to ensure that they were placed with due regard for the
capacity of firms to complete them, an idea already current in trade
union circles where the complex sub-contracting arrangements of the
major firms were often viewed with hostility.[48] Although in later
years Kipping looked back on these proposals as 'naively
impractical', similar ideas were being promoted by West Midlands
businessmen.[49] Moreover Kipping's arguments brought him to the
notice of Oliver Lyttelton, Minister of Production from March 1942,
and contributed to Kipping's own appointment as Head of the
Regional Division of the new Ministry.[50]

Some of the employers who backed a greater role for the Boards
showed little interest in fostering collaboration with the trade
unions,[51] but it was clear to most – including Dickson and Kipping –
that labour could not be excluded. This convergence between some
of the more imaginative business leaders seeking a measure of 'self-
government in industry' via the empowerment of Regional Boards
and trade unions' demands for participation was to be a persistent
feature of the debate on planning into the post-war years. It was
never an easy collaboration and neither side lost sight of the interests
of its own constituency. During the winter of 1941–42, the support
coming from both sides of industry for regional devolution did
something to counterbalance the language of class conflict deployed
in the Left's offensive against managerial incompetence.
Nevertheless for left-wing advocates of participatory planning the
basic problem remained – how to sustain the combination of shop
floor self-assertion and co-operation in production in a creative
tension, and prevent the divergent interests of workers and
employers from destroying the project of empowering workers
through their constructive engagement in the war economy.

One key to achieving this would be the extent to which the
reformers' demands found an answering response within the power
structures of the state. The state's response, however, was far from
straightforward. The reform package of tighter control at the top (a
Ministry of Production) and greater devolution (strengthened
Regional Boards) intersected with the concerns of Whitehall and
Westminster in contradictory ways. In the face of mounting
pressures, Churchill resisted the establishment of a Ministry of

Production until February 1942, and even when the new Ministry was set up it lacked the powers of overall direction which reformers had been calling for.

At one level the problem was political. The creation of an overlord Minister of Production would have had serious implications for the balance of power between Conservatives and Labour within the Coalition Government, for Churchill's own power, and for the political futures of the two major antagonists in the argument, Beaverbrook and Bevin. At another level the problem was administrative. The three ministries responsible for weapons procurement – Aircraft Production, Supply and the Admiralty – possessed formidable powers of bureaucratic resistance to any attempt to subordinate them to control by a super-ministry: and the Ministry of Labour was no more willing to see its concerns subordinated to such a ministry. Most fundamentally the reform agenda was entirely incompatible with some of the deepest structures of the British state, the unwritten rules and assumptions governing the way in which the state apparatus conducted its relationships with civil society. It is as a challenge to the 'governing code' of the British polity that the reformist currents of 1941–42 take on their most general significance.[52]

For many reformers, particularly in Fleet Street, the obvious solution was to make Beaverbrook production supremo.[53] In the summer of 1940, when defeat and invasion had seemed closest, the outcry against the Men of Munich who had left Britain defenceless was matched only by the readiness of war workers to respond to appeals for unrelenting effort. Beaverbrook's controversial achievement as Minister of Aircraft Production cashed in on this public mood, which enabled him to ride roughshod over due process and long-term planning to turn out Spitfires as fast as the limits of human endurance would permit.[54] Following Hitler's invasion of Russia, Churchill put Beaverbrook in charge of the Ministry of Supply, charged with doing for tanks for the Russian front what he had earlier done for planes for the Battle of Britain.

It was Beaverbrook's war on Whitehall red tape that appealed to his supporters – 'he whistles round the civil service like a vacuum cleaner in a family tomb', wrote Casandra in the *Daily Mirror*.[55] To legitimate his appeals for ever greater effort from the workforce as well as his disregard of established Whitehall procedures, Beaverbrook's style required public agitation about production failures. 'We thrive on unrest', he told Churchill in July 1941.[56] As A.J.P.Taylor has shown, Beaverbrook used his position at Supply to construct a new public persona for himself as leader of the pro-Russian sentiment that swept Britain in the aftermath of Hitler's invasion of the Soviet Union. Declaring his support for the early opening of a Second Front in Western Europe, and insisting on his right to consult directly with shop floor representatives over the heads of the trade union leadership, Beaverbrook gained considerable popularity among shop stewards and the tactical support – for what it was worth – of the Communist Party. But his grasp of the real dynamics of Coalition politics was in danger of being overwhelmed by the excited products of his own populist imagination. At those moments when his asthma wasn't getting the better of his euphoria, he would fantasise that the public clamour would lift him into the role of home-front dictator, with overall control of war production.[57]

Many of those who pressed for a Ministry of Production, however, doubted whether Beaverbrook's talents – however appropriate they may have been during the Battle of Britain – were what was now needed for the long-haul build up of weapons for the Eastern front and, eventually, the attack in the West.[58] Production, Bevin insisted to a chorus of approval from the anti-Beaverbrook press, was 'a question of rhythm not of stunts. If you lose the rhythm it takes a good time to get it going again.'[59] Even Beaverbrook's fans in Fleet Street struggled to reconcile their conviction that only he had the charisma and dynamism to pull the whole production effort together, with the evidence that their hero's methods of work were not at all what was required to develop a smooth and balanced programme of arms production.[60] Beaverbrook was notoriously resistant to the efforts of Bevin, chairing the Production Executive, to bring some order into the production effort as a whole. On one occasion, after Bevin had moved the meetings into Beaverbrook's own office in an effort to force him to attend, Beaverbrook was said to have slipped out of the room during a discussion of shortages of aluminium in order to buy up the whole Canadian output for his own Ministry. The Beaver's methods of rush and grab, it was argued, produced tanks or planes only by spreading shortages and disorganisation around the rest of the production programme.[61]

Whether or not Beaverbrook, given sufficient authority, could have brought order to the production effort, his centralist and dictatorial style made him an unlikely agent for the reformist programme as a whole. While the reformers linked their demand for a Ministry of Production with devolution to the regions, Beaverbrook thoroughly disliked the participatory aspect of the Regional Boards. The reformers, he argued, entirely misunderstood the logic of their own proposals: 'Decentralisation implies rejection of the idea of the production Ministry, not its acceptance: the destruction of our present ministerial authority and not its reinforcement.'[62] Within weeks of taking office he was encouraging his own officials to boycott the Capacity Clearing Centres whose activities, he and his officials believed, threatened to undermine the authority of the Minister. They had become 'an independent force. Already they seek and obtain access to plants and give directions. They require information and demand returns.' In September he launched an all-out war to replace the Centres with machinery under the joint control of the three supply ministries, rather than the Regional Boards.[63] This provoked furious resistance from the Boards and their Whitehall supporters and by mid-December Beaverbrook had been forced to acknowledge defeat, writing to Churchill:

It is my advice that you should let the Regional Boards and the Capacity Clearing Centres run. The cause is lost. It would now be too difficult to dispose of these institutions. They are firmly established. They have their paid officials, chairmen and local members. All of these would struggle to hold on. They have, too, a state of public opinion which would give them support, in the belief that struggles over priorities go on between ministries and that the Production Executive [and its Regional Boards – JH] is the way to the Production Ministry.[64]

Beaverbrook's capitulation followed a thinly veiled threat from Bevin that any attempt to scrap the Regional Board machinery would produce 'a very nasty reaction'.[65]

Bevin had been a consistent supporter of devolution to the Boards and the Clearing Centres from the beginning,[66] and in the opinion of some reformers he was the main alternative to Beaverbrook for the job of production overlord. Any attempt by Bevin to attain such a position would, however, have flown in the face of the strategy he consistently pursued throughout the war years to maximise Labour's influence without jeopardising either the survival of the Coalition Government, or the independence of the labour movement. On the first count it was clear that giving Bevin more power than he already possessed as Minister of Labour and chairman of the (albeit toothless) Production Executive would hardly be compatible with the survival of the Coalition. (Beaverbrook, mischievously perhaps, proposed to Churchill on various occasions that Bevin should be given the supreme position – but only when he had 'improved his position with the middle classes upwards' – that is, the Tory backbenchers – a vain hope.)[67]

More fundamentally, the prospect of a production overlord putting together the empires of the supply ministries and the Ministry of Labour – as in Lloyd George's Ministry of Munitions in the First World War – raised issues about the relationship between labour, business and the state which Bevin had no wish to open up. Even if it had been politically possible for Bevin to become Minister of Production, taking his labour responsibilities with him, he would have been unlikely to approve of such a direct fusion of industrial relations and production policy. The institutional separation of the Ministry of Labour from the ministries responsible for production matters was a key feature of the social settlement achieved in Britain after the upheavals of the First World War.[68] Bevin was no more anxious to revive the all-powerful state control implicit in Lloyd George's Ministry of Munitions than were his officials. In particular he was concerned to protect the independence of the unions. Too close an incorporation of the unions into the war economy would, he believed, undermine the credibility of union leaders with their members and precipitate the kind of industrial unrest that had, apparently, brought Britain to the verge of revolutionary chaos at the end of the First World War. An administrative structure driven simply by the need to maximise production would be unlikely to foster the degree of autonomy and the recognition of legitimate divergences of interest and conflict within industry necessary to maintain social order and cohesion. To simple-minded proponents of national efficiency, who wished to organise society on the model of the army, Bevin replied that only through the careful balancing of divergent interests could a viable national unity be sustained. The day-to-day work of Ministry of Labour conciliation officers, whose brief was as much to cultivate good industrial relations as it was to press for maximum output, was as essential to the war effort – and to the social stability without which war could not be successfully prosecuted – as was the more directly productionist work of the supply departments.[69] As Minister of Labour Bevin worked to protect the institutions of free collective bargaining against the ambitions of planners to take wage determination out of the market place and subordinate it comprehensively to the needs of planning. It was the operation of the system of industrial relations, facilitated but not controlled by the state, which constituted, for Bevin, the core achievement of British 'democracy':

> Voluntary in its nature, democratic in its functioning, united by law and yet stronger than law because it rests on men's words, it stands stronger than anything else man has yet conceived.... I believe, however much the political battle may rage, however much parties may divide, this great machinery of industrial relations which has stood us in such good stead during the years of war, will see us back to an orderly industrial society, at the end when victory is won.[70]

The autonomy of the Ministry of Labour from the production ministries provided a critical line of defence for this voluntary system of collective bargaining against the careless interventionism of the war-driven state. It was Bevin's commitment to voluntarism that underpinned his support for the Regional Boards and what they represented. By the same token, however, it made him hardly less antagonistic to the full agenda of the participatory planners than was Beaverbrook. Consequently the reform consensus lacked coherent backing in Government. Bevin supported the Regional Boards but was lukewarm about a Ministry of Production. Beaverbrook supported a Ministry of Production but was hostile to the Boards. Meanwhile Churchill had his own reasons for resisting the clamour to appoint a Production overlord.

Probably Churchill feared that such a Minister would seriously encroach on his own overall control of the war effort, and might even – if things continued to go so badly – become a potential rival for the premiership itself. Certainly that was the lesson suggested by Lloyd George's career at the Ministry of Munitions in the First World War. Moreover, the appointment of Bevin to the job would have been unacceptable to his own backbenchers, and any attempt to give Beaverbrook the kind of authority over Bevin's empire at the Ministry of Labour that a Ministry of Munitions solution would have involved would probably have led to Labour's withdrawal from the Coalition Government. It was Bevin's role as manpower supremo which symbolised the new role of organised labour within the British state.[71] In any case Churchill was far from convinced that a Ministry of Production would improve the co-ordination of production. In practice the really important decisions were taken, not by Bevin's Production Executive, but by a publicly unknown Cabinet committee working under Churchill's personal control.[72] What finally persuaded Churchill that a Minister of Production was needed was not so much the public clamour – though he was in considerable political difficulties as the military disasters mounted in the early months of 1942 – but the entry of the United States into the war in December 1941. It was now essential to have a single Minister capable of defending British interests in allied negotiations over the co-ordination of arms production, and Beaverbrook, who accompanied Churchill on his visit to the US over Christmas and formed good relations with the men in charge of the US production programme, was the obvious man for this job.[73]

The days preceding Beaverbrook's appointment saw an intense battle over the powers of the new Ministry. The main substance of this battle concerned its relation with the supply departments,[74] but the political excitement and the attention of the press, was focused on the old antagonism between Beaverbrook and Bevin. If Beaverbrook got the post, would Bevin be prepared to yield up any of his power over labour supply? Although much of the press blamed Bevin for sabotaging a coherent Production Ministry in order to protect his empire at the Ministry of Labour,[75] and Bevin himself was clearly extremely worried, there is no evidence that his power was, in fact, seriously threatened.[76] Most of the press reacted to the new Ministry as a shoddy compromise which established none of the clear lines of authority they had been demanding, and would depend for its working on the unlikely flowering of friendly co-operation between Beaverbrook and Bevin.[77] In the event Beaverbrook, who was in any case at loggerheads with Churchill over policy towards Russia, had no stomach for the challenge. Exasperated by his failure to win significant authority over the supply ministries, bruised, betrayed, and finally blackmailed by Churchill into accepting the job, Beaverbrook gave up within two weeks, resigned from the Government and went off to America to brood on the next stage of his political career.[78]

The Ministry, however, survived under Oliver Lyttelton, a Conservative businessman who was prepared to take on the co-ordinating job despite the absence of effective authority over the rival departments. Lyttelton, like Bevin, understood that effective co-ordination of anything as complex as British war production would depend at least as much on the devolution of authority to the Regions as it would on the exercise of dictatorial powers from Whitehall. If the Ministry of Production, from the stand-point of the reformers, was something of a damp squib, its very lack of power at least had the advantage of ensuring that the new Minister would give serious attention to enhancing the power of the Regional Boards.

During Beaverbrook's brief term of office he had been persuaded, under pressure from the TUC and the Regional Boards, to set up a committee chaired by the TUC General Secretary, Walter Citrine, to make recommendations on the future of the Boards. When Lyttelton took over he lost no time in encouraging the Citrine Committee to think radically, well understanding that the Boards provided one of the few means at his disposal for overcoming the sectionalism of the supply ministries. In particular he asked the Committee to give serious consideration to Norman Kipping's scheme for grouping firms under the Clearing Centres.[79] The Committee recommended that the Boards be given advance notice of significant contracts to be awarded in the region, and the opportunity to delay the implementation of the contract while any difficulties they anticipated were investigated. It was also proposed that the Clearing Centres, renamed District Offices (with District Advisory Committees representing employers and unions attached), should be asked to identify sub-contracting firms suffering from overloading or managerial incompetence. Such 'danger lists' had been proposed by the FBI as an alternative to Kipping's much more radical idea of giving the Clearing Centres the power to veto further contracts.[80] Overruling vigorous protests from the supply ministries, the Government accepted these recommendations.[81]

Despite support from Bevin, who was impressed by Kipping's approach, the full Kipping scheme of grouping the smaller firms for contract allocation purposes was not supported by the committee. Employer members pointed out that this would entirely disrupt the normal commercial procedures of contracting between firm and firm.[82] The desire of the enthusiastic pioneers of the Capacity Clearing Centres to rationalise the system of sub-contracting on a local basis under the control of an office accountable to a partnership of employers, trade unions and officials, conflicted with the complex practices of placing sub-contracts in many parts of the country, particularly characteristic of the major aircraft companies.[83]

Forced to accept an enhanced role for the Regional Boards, the supply ministries tried to turn back the advancing tide of unofficial participation by excluding employer and trade union members from the Executive Committees which, under the Citrine recommendations, would conduct the real work of the Boards. While accepting that 'politically we must do something to strengthen the Regional organisation', the Minister of Aircraft Production protested that the Citrine scheme 'would load the administrative machine ... with many hundreds' of non-official representatives independent of Whitehall control whose interference would turn production into 'an obstacle course', strewn with 'quasi-political' issues.[84] The supply ministries insisted that the Regional Board Executives 'would function with greater freedom and there would be more chance of building up a real team spirit if their work did not have to be conducted in the presence of outsiders'.[85] Contesting such attitudes, officials of the new Ministry of Production retorted: 'The Minister of Aircraft Production seems to forget that the workers and employers are as keen on getting more production as he is. They do not want to raise obstacles but remove them, and they feel that they have been treated as outsiders who are expected to obey orders rather than as partners in the general production drive.'[86] Such rhetoric made no impact on the supply ministries, whose belief in the need to maintain 'an untrammelled authority in the exercise of their responsibilities' was no less passionately held than the conviction of the 'unofficials' – and their friends in the Ministry of Production – that Whitehall should be made to 'pay attention to their specialised or local knowledge'.[87]

Faced down by the supply ministries, Lyttelton capitulated, and accepted that 'at least at the beginning' the Executives should consist only of officials.[88] When this decision was announced it caused outrage in TUC headquarters. Within two weeks a joint deputation of the TUC, and the two employers' organisations – itself a 'historic' first – met Lyttelton to protest. Reminding him that 'his office was created as a result of public resentment and anger at the production muddles which were taking place as a result of over-centralisation', the deputation told him that both sides of industry considered this a matter of principle on which they would not give way.[89] This gave the Minister of Production the backing he needed to bring the supply ministries into line, and the earlier decision to exclude the unofficial members was swiftly reversed.[90] The Ministry of Production itself might not have a lot of power, but the outcome of this lobby fully vindicated Beaverbrook's view that the Regional Boards had acquired too much independent support outside Whitehall for it to be feasible to close them down.[91]

By the summer of 1941 public confidence in the competence of Britain's elites had reached a low point and, for another nine months, it carried on down. In the debate over war production both employers and Whitehall found themselves on the defensive, while their critics had a field day. The crisis enabled radical voices to gain a hearing, and helped to create an alliance between reformers on both sides of industry around demands for a Ministry of Production and a devolution of authority to tripartite Regional Boards. The reformers' overlord ministry was ruled out both by considerations of political balance within the Coalition, and, at a deeper level, by the voluntarism which lay at the heart of Britain's political system. But the Regional Boards cut with the grain of that voluntarism and were able to see off attempts by centralist supply ministries to emasculate their powers. A niche was thus created within the system of wartime production administration around which advocates of worker participation could hope to construct a flexible and authoritative link between Whitehall and the workshop. Before examining the fate of trade union attempts to use their access to the Regional Boards in this manner (Chapter 5), we must turn to the more fundamental struggle, conducted during these same crisis months, to establish worker participation within the factories themselves.

NOTES

1. BIPO: 'Are you satisfied or dissatisfied with the Government's conduct of the war?'

	Sat.	Dissat.	DK
	%	%	%
June 41	57	30	13
Oct. 41	44	38	18
Mar. 42	35	50	15
May 42	62	24	14
Jul. 42	42	41	17

2. Angus Calder, *The People's War. Britain 1939–45*, 1971; Paul Addison, *The Road to 1945. British Politics and the Second World War*, London, 1982, Ch. 4; Paul Addison, 'By-Elections of the Second World War', in C. Cook and J. Ramsden (eds), *By-Elections in British Politics*, 1973; Kevin Jefferys, *The Churchill Coalition and Wartime Politics, 1940–45*, Manchester, 1991, p. 67; S. Fielding, 'The "movement away from party": wartime popular politics reconsidered', unpublished paper, 1992; Richard Sibley, 'The swing to Labour during the Second World War: when and why', *Labour History Review*, 55, 1, 1990, pp. 23–34; S. Brooke, *Labour's War. The Labour Party during the Second World War*, Oxford, 1992, Ch. 3.

3. G.H. Gallup (ed.), *The Gallup International Public Opinion Polls, Great Britain, 1937–1975*, Vol.1 (1937–1964), New York, 1977. For March 1941 figure see *News Chronicle*, 7 May 1942.

4. Mass Observation, *People in Production. An Enquiry into British War Production*, Penguin Special, 1942, pp. 13–14, 40, 49–52.

5. T. Harrison, 'What is Public Opinion?', *Political Quarterly*, August 1940, pp. 375–6.

6. J. Curran and J. Seaton, *Power Without Responsibility. The Press and Broadcasting in Britain*, 1988, pp. 66–73; S. Koss, *The Rise and Fall of the Political Press in Britain*, Vol. 2, 1984, pp. 605–8.

7. HC Deb., Vol. 373, Col. 336, 10 July 1941. Bevin confirmed this figure with a call for a 40% increase in production: *The Times*, 20 October 1941. See also Twenty-First Report from the Select Committee on National Expenditure, August 1941, P.P. 1940–41.

8. 'The Man Who Can Produce Results!' 'Huge Gun Output. Beaverbrook gives news to hearten you', *Daily Express*, 1 July 1941, 29 January 1942.

9. *Daily Herald*, 10 July 1941.

10. The following dates were selected for systematic reading: 1–12 July 1941, 13–26 October 1941, 12 January to 21 February 1942, 27 April to 9 May 1942.

11. Only the *Telegraph* and *Sketch* relied on employer sources equally with trade union ones.

12. D. Mcquail, *Analysis of Newspaper Content*, Royal Commission on the Press, Research Series 4, Cmnd. 6810, 1977, p. 139.

13. J. Turnstall, *The Problem of Industrial Relations News in the Press*, Royal Commission on the Press, Working Paper 3, pp. 348–9.

14. Absenteeism was given prominence in the Fifteenth Report of the Select Committee on National Expenditure, May 1941, P.P. 1940–41. For the counterproductive effects of employer allegations see the remarks of the Glasgow Industrial Relations Officer on 28 February 1942 (LAB 10/363), and of his colleague in the North West on 21 June 1941 (LAB 10/379). Ten of the 16 stories in the press sample which blame workers for absenteeism were in the *Mail* or *Telegraph*. The 43 stories blaming managerial incompetence were distributed as follows:

Herald	11
Mirror	8
News Chronicle	7
Telegraph	5
Mail	5
The Times	4
Express	3
Sketch	0

15. *Herald*, 29 January 1942.

16. *Mirror*, 21 October 1941.

17. Gordon England, managing director of General Aircraft and Chairman of the Engineering Industries' Association, was frequently quoted in the press: *The Times*, 25 September 1941; *Mirror*, 22 January 1942; *Sketch*, 23 October 1941. See also the major role played by an anonymous works manager in building up the production crisis in Coventry: *Coventry Evening Telegraph*, 17 January 1942.

18. Mass Observation, *People in Production*, p. 52.

19. E. Wigham, *The Power to Manage, a History of the Engineering Employers' Federation*, 1973, pp. 150–51.

20. EEF Management Board, *Minutes*, 25 September 1941, EEF 237/1/1/39.

21. *Daily Mail*, 16 January 1942. Employers may, however, have been more effective in influencing the local press. In the autumn of 1941 the TUC alleged that editors of Midlands local papers had been 'instructed' by a group of employers to 'soft pedal' on the Regional Board's campaign for Joint Production Committees, to which initially they had given favourable coverage. Walter Citrine, briefing for NJAC, 4 December 1941, TUC 292/106.45.

22. *Herald*, 5 July 1941; *Telegraph*, 8 July 1941.

23. *The Times*, 1, 8, 11 July 1941; Oscar Hobson in *News Chronicle*, 21 October 1941.

24. J.D. Scott and R. Hughes, *The Administration of British War Production*, London, 1955, p. 423.

25. TUC, *Report*, 1942, p. 169; in May 1941 Citrine still held this view but admitted that there was no prospect of it being achieved. 'Notes of a meeting ... to discuss National Production', 28 May 1941, BT 168/6.

26. Scott and Hughes, *op. cit.*, p. 430; HC Deb., Vol. 373, cols 224–26, 9 July 1941; *The Times* 7 July 1941; Argonaut, *Give Us the Tools*, 1942, pp. 120–21.

27. Alan Bullock, *The Life and Times of Ernest Bevin, Vol. 2, Minister of Labour*, 1967, pp. 72–3, 148.

28. Ellis Smith, letter to *Manchester Guardian*, 30 October 1941. Smith, who was Labour MP for Stoke on Trent, was later to resign as PPS to Cripps at the Board of Trade in 1946 over the failure of the Attlee Government to plan the economy on socialist principles: Jonathan Schneer, *Labour's Conscience. The Labour Left 1945–1951*, Boston, 1988, pp. 82, 212.

29. Scott and Hughes, *op. cit.*, pp. 419–21; Committee on Regional Boards (Citrine Committee), *Report*, Cmd. 6360, 1942, paragraphs 8–11.

30. Some critics, however, argued for devolution of power to the Regional Boards, not as a complement to the formation of a Ministry of Production, but as an alternative route to containing interdepartmental rivalry: e.g. Sir John Wardlaw Milne, HC Deb., Vol. 373, cols 1334–35, 29 July 1941.

31. TUC 292/106.1/2; TUC *Report*, 1942, pp. 80, 169; 'Notes of meeting between Chairman of Production Executive and Chairmen and Secretaries of Regional Boards', 14 May 1941, TUC 292/106.44/1.

32. R.P. Dutt, *Britain in the World Front*, 1942, p. 136; Len Powell in *Labour Monthly*, April 1942; *Labour Research*, August 1941, p. 116, November 1941, pp. 166–7, January 1942, pp. 7–8.

33. Argonaut, *Give Us the Tools*, 1942, pp. 122–5.

34. A 'five point plan' put forward by the *Financial News*, presented regional devolution as the first step towards 'that ultimate decentralisation: the restoration of incentive'. The leading aim of this plan was to reduce Excess Profits Tax. (*Financial News*, 22 September 1941, 20 October 1941.)

35. Political responsibility for the development of the Regional Boards in 1940–41 lay with one of the major 1930s' advocates of 'self-government in industry', Harold Macmillan, who was chairman of the Industrial Capacity Committee. For Macmillan's advocacy of the 'democratisation' of production administration see Production Executive, *Papers*, 2 May 1941, CAB 92/55.

36. Nigel Harris, *Competition and the Corporate Society*, 1972; T. Smith, *The Politics of the Corporate Economy*, 1979.

37. S. Blank, *Industry and Government in Britain. The FBI in Politics, 1945–65*, 1973, pp. 31ff; meeting of employer representatives on NPAC, *Minutes*, 2 October 1941, FBI 200/F/1/1/145.

38. M.P.F., 'interview with Mr. G. Dickson, 11 December 1944', Cole Papers, B3/4/f/6; G. Dickson, *Already Our Children Sneer*, 1941. This later text, a passionate mixture of autobiography and polemic, survives because Dickson sent the typescript to Harold Laski. Laski gave this unsolicited gift to the LSE Library where the present writer found it, by a happy chance, in the cellar.

39. N. Kipping, *Summing Up*, 1972.

40. Dickson to Lithgow, 20 October 1940, BT 168/120.

41. Memo on Clearing Centres, n.d. (1941?), BT 168/6; Dickson to Churchill, 20 November 1940, BT 168/120; G. Dickson, *Already Our Children Sneer*, 1941, p. 13; Argonaut, *Give Us the Tools*, 1942, p. 123; 'Production Clearing Centres', *Planning*, 191, 28 July 1942; Interview with Mr. G. Dickson, 11 December 1944, Cole Papers, B3/4/F/6, p. 6.

42. G. Dickson *Already Our Children Sneer*, pp. 71–2.

43. 'Production Clearing Centres', *Planning*, 191, 28 July 1942.

44. BT 171/210.

45. London and South East Clearing Centres – Sources and Functions, BT 168/7; Clearing Centres for all Regions, BT 168/6; FBI War Production Committee, *Minutes*, 11 July 1941; employer representatives to the NPAC, *Minutes*, 18 July, 7

August 1941, FBI 200/F/1/1/145; 'Production Clearing Centres', *Planning*, 191, 28 July 1942.

46. Committee on Regional Boards (Citrine Committee), *Report*, Cmd. 6360, 1942, paragraph 9.

47. Coop to Young, 14 February 1941, BT 168/6; 'Notes of a meeting ... to discuss National Production', 28 May 1941, BT 168/6.

48. Memo by E.P. Harries, 24 March 1942; Harries to Chegwidden, 20 April 1942, TUC 292/106.4/2/4; Stokes to AEU Research Department, 3 December 1941, Stokes Papers, 289/8/3/10; *Labour Research*, October 1941, p. 151; meeting between GC members of NAC to Ministry of Supply and representatives of the engineering unions, *Minutes*, 18 July 1940; E.P. Harries, memo on interview with Ministry of Supply officials, September 1940, TUC 292/106.1/1. See also Committee on Regional Boards (Citrine Committee), *Report*, Cmd. 6360, 1942, paragraph 31.

49. N. Kipping, *Summing Up*, 1972, p. 5; memo for Midlands Regional Board, 25 February 1942, Stokes Papers, 289/8/3/10; Chance to Beaverbrook, 21 January 1942, Beaverbrook Papers, d/504; Chance at Conference of Production Machinery, 18 February 1942, Citrine Papers, 7/2.

50. Kipping's assistant, Robert Burns, who acted as 'guide, philosopher and friend' in introducing him to the mores of Whitehall (Kipping, *Summing Up*, p. 6), was also a convinced advocate of 'local self-government in industry.' (Burns to Kipping, 6 July 1942, BT 168/151).

51. E.g. Patrick Hannon, letter to *The Times*, 3 February 1942; see also article by group of industrialists in *The Times*, 25 July 1941.

52. For an elaboration of the idea of a 'governing code' see J. Bulpitt, *Territory and Power in the United Kingdom: An Interpretation*, Manchester, 1983, *passim*.

53. Beaverbrook's Fleet Street supporters were by no means limited to his own employees, and included both A.J. Cummings of the *News Chronicle* (e.g. 1 July 1941) and 'Casandra' of the *Daily Mirror* (e.g. 11 July 1941, 20, 31 January 1942). See also the file of Cummings' correspondence with Beaverbrook in Beaverbrook Papers, c/104.

54. A.J. Roberston, 'Lord Beaverbrook and the Supply of Aircraft, 1940-41', in A. Slaven and D.H. Aldcroft (eds), *Business, Banking and Urban History*, 1982; A. Chisholm and M. Davie, *Beaverbrook. A Life*, 1992, p. 396.

55. *Daily Mirror*, 31 January 1942, quoted in 'Casandra on Beaverbrook' in file of Beaverbrook's correspondence with William Connor, Beaverbrook Papers, C/98.

56. Beaverbrook to Churchill, 17 July 1941, quoted in A.J.P. Taylor, *Beaverbrook*, 1972, p. 51.

57. Taylor, *op. cit.*, pp. 482ff; Chisholm and Davie, *op. cit.*, pp. 420-23.

58. *Daily Herald*, 11 July 1941, 3 February 1942; Mass Observation, *People in Production*, pp. 57-9.

59. *Daily Mail*, 5, 7 July 1941; *Daily Telegraph*, 8 July 1941.

60. A.J. Cummings in *News Chronicle*, 1 July 1941.

61. Robertson, *op.cit.*, pp. 92-3; Macmillan to Beaverbrook, 12 November 1941, Beaverbrook Papers, D/82.

62. Beaverbrook to Churchill, 19 November 1941, Beaverbrook Papers, D/82.

63. Beaverbrook to Churchill, 19 December 1941; Beaverbrook, dictaphone notes for Macmillan, 10 November 1941, Beaverbrook Papers, D/82; Memo on Clearing Centres, n.d. (1941?); Midlands Regional Board to Young, 25 July 1941; Young to Myrddin Evans, 12 September 1941, BT 168/6.

64. Beaverbrook to Churchill, 19 December 1941, Beaverbrook Papers, D/82.

65. Bevin to Beaverbrook, 1 December 1941, Beaverbrook Papers, D/82.

66. Kipping, *Summing Up*, p. 6; Bullock, *op. cit.*, p. 13.

67. Beaverbrook to W.P. Crozier, 25 July 1941, quoted in A.J.P. Taylor, *op. cit.*, p. 479.

68. Rodney Lowe, *Adjusting to Democracy. The Role of the Ministry of Labour in British Politics, 1916–39*, 1986, pp. 11–13.

69. Alan Bullock, *The Life and Times of Ernest Bevin*, Vol. 2, Minister of Labour, 1967; S. Tolliday, 'Government, employers and shop floor organisation in the British motor industry, 1939–69', pp. 115–17 in S. Tolliday and J. Zeitlin (eds), *Shop Floor Bargaining and the State. Historical and Comparative Perspectives*, Cambridge, 1985.

70. K. Middlemass, *Politics in Industrial Society*, 1979, p. 335

71. J.M. Lee, *The Churchill Coalition, 1940–1945*, 1980, p.87; Chisholm and Davie, *op. cit.*, p. 429.

72. Scott and Hughes, *op. cit.*, pp. 425–9; Bullock, *op.cit.*, pp. 110–11; J.M. Lee, *op.cit.*, pp. 88–9.

73. A.J.P. Taylor, *op. cit.*, p. 519.

74. *Ibid*, pp. 508–9.

75. *Daily Sketch*, 11 February 1942; *Daily Mirror*, 11 February 1942; *Financial News*, 11 February 1942: 'It is quite fantastic that the MOP should be denied control of one of the main functions of production, just because the Minister of Labour is too able a man to be replaced.' But *The Times* (20 February 1942) grudgingly conceded that Bevin's special position in the country rendered untouchable the anomalous status of the Ministry of Labour.

76. Citrine, diary notes on establishment of Ministry of Production, pp. 18–19; diary, 4 February 1942, in Citrine Papers, 7/2 and 1/12.

77. E.g. *The Times*, 13 February 1942.

78. A.J.P. Taylor, *op. cit.*, pp. 511–18; Chisholm and Davie, *op. cit.*, pp. 438–41.

79. Citrine Committee, *Minutes*, 23 March 1942, FBI, 200 b/3/2/c938.

80. Locock to Citrine, 7 April 1942, TUC 292/106.4/2/4.

81. Committee on Regional Boards (Citrine Committee), *Report*, Cmd. 6360, 1942, *passim*; Minister of Production's Council, *Minutes*, 13 May 1942, BT 28/1131/MISC/75.

82. *Idem*; Chance to Citrine April 1942, TUC 292/106.4/2/4.

83. 'Production Clearing Centres', *Planning*, 191, 28 July 1942; Minister of Production's Council, *Minutes*, 7 May 1942, BT 28/1131/MISC/75.

84. 'Minister of Aircraft Production's comments', 12 May 1942, BT 168/131. In evidence to the Citrine Committee, MAP had proposed for the complete exclusion of non-officials from the Regional Boards: Citrine Committee, *Minutes*, 27 March 1942, FBI 200 b/3/2/c938/pt.1.

85. Lyttelton to Cripps, 19 May 1942, BT 168/131.

86. BT 168/131.

87. Scott and Hughes, *op. cit.*, p. 470.

88. Lyttelton to Cripps, 19 May 1942, BT 168/131.

89. Tewson to Lyttelton, 21 May 1942, E.P. Harries, *memorandum*, 19 May 1942; E.P. Harries, *briefing* for TUC deputation, 28 May 1942; *Report* of TUC deputation, 28 May 1942: all in TUC 292/106.4/2/4.

90. Regional Organisation Committee, *Minutes*, 2 June 1942, BT 168/239.

91. A BIPO poll conducted a few weeks later showed an overwhelming 82% rejecting the view that the 'Boards ... to be set up for encouraging better production ... should include only government officials [rather than] employers and workmen as well.'

3 Pressure from Below

In June 1941, Jack Tanner tried to place the issue of production firmly on his union's agenda. Opening the annual meeting of the National Committee, he insisted that continuing military defeat was a product of mismanagement on the home front. 'As engineers, we have a right to expect that if we make our utmost efforts to produce munitions, those efforts shall not be turned to nought by a group of incompetents.' Despite Labour's membership of the Government, Whitehall muddle and the power of vested interests were producing chaos in the factories. 'Labour must be bolder in its conceptions and more audacious in its strategy,' demanding, not only more coherent planning at the top, but also joint consultation in the factories to enable workers 'to express their ideas, develop their initiative and to give the benefits of their inventive genius and constructiveness in the interests of the nation equally with the employers.'[1] The National Committee, however, was not interested in such talk. Dismissing an earlier proposal by Bevin for factory councils to be elected regardless of trade union membership as an attack on shop steward organisation, the delegates were in no mood to follow Tanner's lead.[2] Consequently the union was left at something of a loss when Hitler's invasion of the Soviet Union, the day before the National Committee dispersed, transformed the political situation. In July, the AEU Executive, responding to press complaints that Tanner had attacked managerial incompetence without supplying convincing evidence, circulated shop stewards asking for details of production problems in the factories. Three thousand replies came in, many of them detailed and angry – convincing testimony to the frustration among trade union activists at their inability to influence production.[3] But while the AEU Production Enquiry did much to arouse interest in production issues among shop stewards, the union could do little to channel the shop stewards' anger in constructive directions. At this crucial moment the union's cumbersome decision-making procedures left it unable to take the initiative, despite Tanner's clear understanding of what needed to be done.[4] Others, however, were able to move faster.

The day after the Nazi invasion, shop stewards at the Napiers aero-engine factory in Acton – the CP's leading London stronghold – responded with a delegation to the Soviet Ambassador pledging themselves to fight for a new Government friendly to the Soviet Union and able to 'inspire the confidence of the working classes of the world' and to achieve 'a people's peace'. This, of course, was the pre-invasion policy, which the Communists had just succeeded in pushing through at the AEU National Committee, and leaders of the Shop Stewards' National Council felt that it should have been coupled with demands for 'more vigorous action to ... deal with the cases of inefficiency and mismanagement which are so rife in the factories. Incompetent [sic] managements must not be allowed to stand in the way of the utmost support being given to the Soviet Union.'[5] A briefing paper prepared by (or for) Len Powell, full-time secretary of the shop steward movement, pointed out that the wartime suspension of competition had removed a 'natural' check on waste and extravagance. The contracting systems used by Whitehall for weapons procurement did little to tackle inefficiency: indeed the cost-plus system was widely believed to act as a positive encouragement to firms to 'delay and hold up the work'. The solution lay partly in more effective contract policing by the state, but mainly in the replacement of (suspended) market pressures for efficiency by what was described as 'workers' control and checking', which was how Bevin's proposals for workers' councils, earlier denounced by Communists as class collaboration, were now understood.[6] Fully embracing the implications of this analysis the shop stewards' movement now argued that 'if the employers cannot end the existing muddle in industry, then the workers can – and will.'[7] Workers should mobilise 'to use their organisational strength to wipe out the inefficiencies, the redundancies, the horrible bloomers and blunders of capitalism.'[8]

Underpinning this strategy was a new recognition by the Communists of how greatly the war had enhanced the power of shop floor organisation. This was not simply a product of high levels of demand increasing the economic muscle of the workers, but also of the legal and administrative interventions of the state in the day-to-day affairs of the workshop. When Bevin introduced the Essential Works Order in March 1941 the CP had attacked it as an enslaving measure, paving the way for British fascism.[9] Now they discovered that the Order, which provided for appeals against dismissal and other disciplinary action, could be used 'in the interests of the working class to put compulsion on employers'.[10] Ministry of Labour officials had long been worried by the capacity of shop stewards to draw them in as allies in domestic battles over trade union recognition, bargaining rights, facilities for meeting in the works, use of the canteen for meetings and similar issues.[11] Expanding the agenda of this burgeoning workshop organisation from wages and conditions of work to production issues was a natural progression for the shop stewards, and one that was, indeed, already underway before the change in the politics of the war encouraged Communists to place this issue at the forefront of workshop politics.

The shift in CP policy produced an upsurge of proposals for shop steward involvement in solving production problems. At Armstrong Whitworth Aircraft, one of the Communists' main strongholds in Coventry, shop stewards demanded the institution of a regular weekly meeting with management to discuss production problems.[12] In Bristol, the Communist convener at the Bristol Aircraft Company asked Whitehall to intervene to persuade the management to accept proposals for the establishment of a Production Investigation Committee with members elected from each department to report on obstacles to greater production.[13] In London, at the East End works of Harris Lebus, a furniture factory working on aircraft, the shop stewards, rebuffed by management, set up their own production committee with regular factory and departmental meetings: 'Because we work with steel and wood and so on it is part of our lives and because of this when we come up against the snags we can solve them.'[14] A few managements accepted proposals for Production Committees at this early stage, though many more attempted to pre-empt the movement by establishing works committees which, because they included non-unionists, were unacceptable to the AEU and its more militant shop stewards.[15]

Pleased with the way things were developing, the shop stewards' movement called a major national conference to publicise the new politics of production. On 19 October – in what was probably the largest mobilisation of shop stewards undertaken by the Communist Party at any time in its history – over a thousand delegates assembled from factories in all parts of Britain at the Stoll Theatre in London. Speaker after speaker denounced managerial incompetence and production hold-ups, demanded the establishment of production committees in the factories and (not least) pledged every ounce of worker effort to war production.[16] The rhetoric left no doubt that the shop stewards were flexing their muscles. As Pollitt had explained in August, the new politics of co-operation could be expected to lead to 'an increased authority for the shop stewards' and workers' committees and enable them to become absolutely indispensable in everything that has to do with production questions.'[17] There was, moreover, no necessary conflict between productionism and the immediate material interests of the workers. The language of sacrifice was carefully balanced by the demand, in heavy type in the official report: 'Piece-rates and bonus earnings not to be cut, as fear of this is the greatest single obstacle to increased production.'[18] A shop steward from the Gloster aircraft factory, where a JPC had already been successfully established, claimed that the management had agreed to a guarantee of no price-cutting with the words: 'The sky's the limit'.[19] Nevertheless, Mass Observation was quite wrong to assert of the demands made by the conference that 'there is no suggestion that anything more of any sort is ... demanded of the *worker*'.[20] In fact the Communists were quite explicit about the need for more individual effort: 'If there is need for a Second Front in the West, there is also need for a Fighting Front in the Workshops. The workers should not be content only to make proposals that demand something should be done from the employers and government sides. We too have contributions to make.'[21] Early in September 1941 a Ministry of Labour conciliation officer had been surprised by a speech reported from an unofficial shop stewards' meeting in Liverpool urging that 'before demanding that the management put their house in order they should make sure that their own was shipshape'.[22] Similar sentiments were expressed at the Stoll Theatre, including a ferocious denunciation of slacking and absenteeism by an ex-sergeant major, also from Liverpool, who proposed that: 'If a man does not pull his weight ... he should be put in the army'. Rather astonishingly he was applauded by the assembled militants for this sentiment.[23]

This statement, quoted in several national newspapers the next morning, along with a resolution condemning inter-union demarcation disputes for holding up production, no doubt played a part in winning favourable press coverage for the Stoll Conference, including an enthusiastic leader in the *Daily Express* which remarked: 'In the last war shop stewards met to ask for improved conditions for the workers. They were more inclined to slow down production than to ginger it up. There was none of that mood yesterday.'[24] The assembled journalists can have been under no misapprehension about who was behind the conference but the tone of their reporting displayed a readiness to take the Communist conversion to productionism at face value. This was in sharp contrast to the attitude of the trade union leaders whose ineffectual attempts to proscribe the conference were condemned by the *News Chronicle*'s correspondent as revealing an obsession with 'the Communist bogey' as irrational as that embraced by 'the late Lord Rothmere ... in his most jittery moments.'[25] In fact it was not only the trade union leaders who were jittery.

Alarmed by the press coverage of the conference, the War Cabinet instructed the Ministry of Information 'to take suitable steps to ensure that undue publicity was not given' to the follow-up meetings planned for the regions by the shop stewards' movement.[26] Whatever the effects of such pressures, cultivation of journalists continued to play a key role in the Communist strategy. The Ministry of Labour's conciliation officer in Scotland was much impressed by the shop stewards' 'flair for publicity', and reported grumblings from the trade union officials that they could not get similar coverage for their own, less sensational, efforts to boost production.[27] One reason for the ready access enjoyed by the shop stewards to the press was, paradoxically, the Government's suppression of the *Daily Worker* in January 1941. Intended to crush the influence of the Communist Party, the ban not only gained them widespread support on grounds of press freedom, it also forced the Party to make use of the considerable journalistic expertise at its disposal in new ways. Making use of the *Daily Worker's* network of worker-correspondents in the factories, the Party put out a daily bulletin, 'Industrial and General Information'. Not only did this serve to give a lead to militants in the factories, it was also used to feed to the press a constant stream of stories about production hold-ups in the factories. With the aid of this bulletin, Communist journalists built up close relations with the industrial correspondents of several national newspapers.[28] No amount of subsequent pressure from the Ministry of Information was likely to undo the boost that the decision to ban the *Daily Worker* had given to the Party's search for lines of communication with the established press. Analysis of the press sample shows that the number of production stories based on information provided by shop stewards or local trade unions was roughly equal to the number based on statements by national trade union officials. While the *The Times*, *Telegraph* and *Daily Herald* favoured the national officials as a source, the rest of the national press gave greater prominence to local activists.

As delegates reported back from the Stoll Conference there was a major escalation of demands for the setting up of Joint Production Committees. Where managements resisted, the shop stewards' movement encouraged militants to produce detailed written accounts of production difficulties in the factory, and to use these to lobby support from union officials, workers in neighbouring factories, the press and the local MP. Beyond this, 'well-prepared and organised Shop Stewards' delegations to the House of Commons and the appropriate Ministry can also be useful.'[29] The full-time secretary of the shop stewards' movement, Len Powell, spent much of his time during these months guiding shop steward deputations around the institutions of Westminster, Whitehall and Fleet Street. The net result of all this activity, hopefully, would be to persuade Ministry of Labour or supply ministry officials to investigate the workers' allegations and to persuade the management to establish a Joint Production Committee.[30]

In March 1942 the *New Propeller* declared:

Deputations from the factories are getting things moving. Enquiries have been ordered into most of the cases brought to the attention of ministers and

MPs. Shop stewards have been helped by our national council in setting forth their case. The documents produced have been powerful statements well-supported by facts and figures.[31]

While attacking inefficient managers, the militants knew that it was only through alliances with efficient ones that they could hope to force the authorities to take their complaints seriously: by themselves workers lacked both the prestige and the technical know-how needed to persuade Whitehall that management had a case to answer.[32] In Coventry the impact of the shop steward agitation was greatly enhanced by the wide circulation of a detailed account of waste and inefficiency in the Coventry factories written by a senior local manager.[33] In what was seen as a model campaign, shop stewards at one West London factory produced a detailed record of mismanagement supported by a long and detailed statement from the Chief Progress Manager. Their agitation was quickly rewarded by a formal enquiry, at which the shop stewards were able to produce additional management witnesses. This enquiry, the shop stewards believed, 'put the Directors in such a positive scare that even if they are allowed to remain they will never dare risk creating conditions which would again put them right on the spot.... It was the workers, all of them, determination and solidarity that done it.'[34] This was exactly the kind of empowerment that Communist Party strategists hoped that workers would draw from the production campaign. This degree of success in calling in the state to sort out the bosses was, however, unusual.[35]

Many employers and officials were inclined to view the JPC campaign as mere mischief making by militants intent on 'placing the employers in a hot spot'.[36] In fact Communist leaders were both genuinely committed to increasing output, and genuinely convinced that only by mass mobilisation of the workers could the main obstacle to production–capitalist vested interests – be removed. They were also aware of the danger, identified clearly by the Scottish Conciliation Officer in November 1941, that the agitation they encouraged could itself become counterproductive: 'it is to be feared that a movement initiated for the improvement of output may have exactly the opposite effect.'[37] So, at the same time as they stoked up the agitation, they found themselves trying to hold its

potential for disruption in check. As a Party training syllabus put it
in late 1941: 'the question is not viewed simply as a struggle against
the management, but of winning its co-operation in a way that
strengthens both production and the initiative and organisation of the
workers themselves.'[38]

Where management was sympathetic, conflict could be avoided
altogether. Thus Sir Valentine Crittall called together shop stewards
at his Essex factory to deliver a detailed account of the way in which
inadequate Whitehall planning was causing delays and hold-ups in
the works. While fully endorsing the view that major changes were
needed at the centre, he also invited shop stewards to go back to
their departments and see what could be done to 'improve the use of
the ... plant in the common cause.' Such an attitude left the militants
with little to do but hope that workers would 'drop their inferiority
complex' and 'respond to the invitation of the Management [to]
bombard it with constructive suggestions.'[39] But Crittall, later
instrumental in establishing the pro-Labour 1944 Association among
progressive businessmen, was hardly a typical employer. Where
management was obstructive, the workers well organised and
Government closely involved – as in the Rootes aero-engine shadow
factory at Ryton (near Coventry) – a militant campaign could have
dramatic results without seriously disrupting production. Here two
senior managers had been removed, and the whole supervision
overhauled, following a trade union approach to the Regional Board
and intervention by the supply ministries. The *New Propeller* saw
this as a model campaign, reporting:

> that this has been achieved without strike action, the only stoppage being on
> the occasion of the mass demonstration of October 21st. Although feelings
> were running high, and an important element advocated strike action, we feel
> that our successes to date have been a vindication of the wiser council to
> abstain from any stoppage of work in the present situation.[40]

While shop stewards seldom found it possible to persuade
Whitehall to use its powers to remove inefficient managers, officials
could be induced to pressure reluctant managements into establishing
production committees. The JPC at the Gloster aircraft factory,
which had been reported to the Stoll Theatre Conference as starting
so happily with a pledge against price-cutting, fell apart after a few

meetings. After major ructions involving the AEU Executive and a Whitehall investigation, MAP officials persuaded the management to re-establish the committee on a sounder basis.[41] Elsewhere a little well-timed militancy may have proved sufficient even without official intervention to persuade the management to come to terms, as in the following example related to the Stoll Theatre Conference:

> This week we found that the management were very nasty to the Shop Stewards, so we called a stoppage for an hour; that stoppage was 100% including the inspection, timekeepers and progress, showing quite plainly that if the Shop Stewards get cracking on the job and are really able to organise and discipline the employees as well as the management, we will get somewhere with the war effort. I want to say that our Management have learned their lesson, and are kind to us now.[42]

As in the case of the Gloster factory, however, there was no guarantee that an early success in opening a dialogue with management on production issues would stick. In the adversarial world of industrial relations nice could turn to nasty with unexpected alacrity. Thus the February issue of *New Propeller* reported the successful establishment of a Joint Production Committee at Vickers' Openshaw factory in Manchester, including an elaborate structure of departmental committees, and the election of charge-hands in the toolroom. The new spirit in the works, said to stem from recent changes in the management, was embodied in the permission given to the Communist convener – Blackwell – to use the works loud-speaker to announce that the firm had agreed that in future the Production Committee would deal with absenteeism internally, instead of referring delinquents to the National Service Officer.[43] According to a detailed response to this article sent by Vickers' management to the EEF most of these claims were fantasy, and though Blackwell had made one broadcast about absenteeism he was certainly not allowed to repeat the experiment.[44] By the time the *New Propeller* article was published a new management team had been installed at Openshaw – men 'from the London Works of the Firm [who] were evidently not acquainted with Trade Union practices in the North.' Facilities previously granted to the shop stewards were withdrawn and the works committee disbanded on the grounds that, in accordance with AEU policy, it had no provision for the representation of non-unionists.[45]   Eventually agreement on establishing a JPC was reached at Openshaw, but only after the national agreement of March 1942 made this more or less obligatory for the firm.[46]

While it was clearly impossible to mount a campaign for production committees without provoking employer resistance, Communist leaders were worried by the attitude of some militants who seemed more interested in attacking the bosses than in solving production problems. Of one Worcester firm, Len Powell wrote in February 1941: 'a *demand* was made by stewards to be shown the firm's order books and details of production without any practical propositions or pledges from the workers. Result: whole thing wrecked.'[47]   It is unlikely that Powell would have approved the demands made by shop stewards in one electrical factory in South London, not only to 'open the books' but to establish a production committee with 'full power to carry out decisions' and to 'direct any members of the staff with regard to timekeeping, absenteeism, quality of work, etc.')[48] This had a similarly negative result. Even where militants were ready and able to secure 'practical ... pledges from the workers', their motives were not always as constructive as the pledges in themselves might imply. Thus early in 1942 shop stewards at the Duples factory in West London, where the Communist Party was well represented, responded to a management complaint about absenteeism by persuading the workers to give the stewards 'the mandate of the shop to deal with ... instances of irresponsibility or dodging'. Far from representing the dawn of a new era of co-operation, however, this decision was justified to the rank and file on the tactical grounds that 'we could not criticise management ... until we ourselves showed up regularly and continuously to perform our task. If we keep irreproachable hours and the work was still disorganised or delayed, THEN we could throw stones and boulders; THEN we could go forward and ruthlessly remove all bottle-necks in management'.[49] Worried by the excessive zeal of some of their own members, the Communist Party sent Walter Swanson and other shop stewards from the Napiers factory in Acton to persuade their counterparts at Napiers' Liverpool factory from going over the top in their criticisms of managerial inefficiency.[50]   By January 1942 the Communist leadership was becoming seriously worried that the lack of movement in the high politics of production, together with the resistance being put up by many employers to joint consultation on production issues in the factories, was producing a mood of cynicism in the factories: 'the growth of absenteeism ..., the increasing tendency to strike and stop production, the widespread complacency that everywhere abounds'. Even inside the Party, they implied, the idea that the war could be left to the Russians was gaining ground, and they warned the comrades not to accommodate themselves to 'the sense of frustration that exists in the factories', but to fight against it: 'Complacency is treachery.   Complacency is defeatism....   We call on every Communist to set the example, wherever they may be, in good timekeeping, skill and responsibility on the job, willingness to teach each other, discipline and leadership.'[51] Perhaps this was just the usual hyperbole, characteristic of official Party-speak, but Len Powell in the unrhetorical notes he made on the production situation a few weeks later was clearly worried by events in Coventry: 'workers expressing anti-T.U. attitude and cynicism regarding production'.[52]

Powell's anxiety about Coventry was well-founded.   When the shop stewards at Armstrong Whitworth had pressed for the establishment of a JPC in August 1941, the firm dismissed the demand, explaining to the EEF: 'production matters are entirely a Managerial function, and we feel it would be creating a dangerous precedent to accede to this request'.[53] When, later that year, the Armstrong management announced large-scale redundancies of skilled men, and their replacement with women dilutees, militants accused the employers of 'conscious or unconscious sabotage' and of using dilution, not to increase production, but to create artificial redundancies and facilitate the victimisation of 'shop stewards and the leaders of the drive to increase production'.[54] Such attitudes were characteristic of Coventry industry as a whole.   While in other parts of the country some firms were conceding, or indeed pre-empting, demands for JPCs, in Coventry the Engineering Employers Association remained adamant in its resistance.   Unconvinced by the new productionist rhetoric of the shop stewards, the employers' belief that shop stewards were out for control of industry was reinforced by demands like those made by militants at one large factory for the removal of the Works Manager and direct shop steward representation on the Management Committee.[55]   Mass Observation, conducting an enquiry into production in several armaments centres over the winter of 1941–42, found more dissatisfaction in Coventry than anywhere else.[56]   Commenting on stories of idle machinery at the works of one of Coventry's more reactionary firms, a local Labour Party leader told Mass Observation's investigator: 'There's fifth columnists about it somewhere.... I tell you it's fifth column, all that.'[57]   Matters were brought to a head in January 1942 by the sacking of a group of 108 sheet-metal workers, the aristocrats of Coventry industry, after a dispute over time off for Christmas shopping.   Despite winning their appeal against dismissal, the men's work was transferred by the firm to Manchester (where wages were lower) and they were declared redundant.   With banners protesting 'We Want Work' the men took to the streets, bitterly denouncing the management for being interested in nothing but increasing their profits: 'We wonder if the gentlemen who control Cornercrofts have heard of CRETE, MALAYA, SINGAPORE and the danger to BRITAIN itself from airborne invasion.   Are they concerned with winning the war or merely getting rid of organised workers?' Local indignation was heightened by the fact that the chairman of the offending firm was also the Conservative MP for Coventry.[58]

In this context of military reversals and allegations of managerial sabotage, the arrival of a delegation of Russian trade unionists in Coventry only served to intensify unrest, especially since the Russians pulled no punches in condemning the organisation of production in the Coventry factories: 'There are no idle machines in Moscow and I feel that if the Huns were as near to Coventry ... as they are to Leningrad and Moscow there would be no idle machines here.'[59]   This remark was given added authority by a long letter to the local press from the general manager of an (unnamed) Coventry factory which made detailed allegations about managerial waste and inefficiency in the city.[60]

A few days after the Russians left, an unofficial meeting of fifty shop stewards from the main Coventry factories met to discuss the production crisis and the sacking of the sheet-metal workers. Several speakers urged all-out strike action, an overtime ban or sit-down strikes. Two older men spoke of the lessons of the First World War: 'though they realised that the issues in this war were quite different from the last because it was no longer a capitalist war, they had found then that the workers had to use the only weapon they have got which is the power to strike and they were sure it was the same in this war.' Eventually, however, the Communist leaders were able to persuade the meeting to reject strike action, 'as they do not want to hinder production for Russia'. Instead they elected a delegation 'to go to Parliament and make a shindy'. Demanding a Government inquiry into the disorganisation of production in Coventry, the meeting declared: 'Repeated efforts have been made by the workers to get an improved flow of arms from this important munitions centre. All offers by the shop stewards to their respective managements for co-operation and the setting up of Joint Production Committees have been turned down by the employers.... The workers are told, in effect, "This is our factory and it is not your business how it is run."'[61] Though strike action had been ruled out for the time being, and the deputation received widespread publicity in the national press, Len Powell's anxiety about 'anti-T.U.' attitudes in Coventry must have been fed by a statement made by the (Communist) leader of the deputation that the official unions, incapable of responding to the situation, had become 'almost obsolete'.[62] By the time this remark was made, however, the official unions were finally getting their act together, and the Engineering Employers' Federation was moving towards a negotiated agreement on production committees. Nevertheless the Coventry movement, though more confrontational than the Communists were comfortable with, made a significant contribution to the eventual resolution of the production crisis. Alarmed by the favourable coverage their local trouble-makers were getting in the press as well as by news of national developments, the Coventry employers reluctantly accepted early in February 1942 that 'in spite of all efforts by local firms to resist the setting up of Production Committees, this district would be compelled to agree'.[63]

While Communist anxiety about the movement getting out of hand testifies to the sincerity of their commitment to increasing production, in fact there was little danger of their strategy misfiring in this way. If they could stay on top of the situation even in Coventry, where the employers were most adamant in their resistance, they were unlikely to lose control elsewhere. There was, certainly, an undercurrent of leftist opposition to the Communist position. At the Stoll Theatre a woman shop steward from West London argued that collaboration with the existing management would 'paralyse any independent action on the part of the working class' and moved a resolution demanding nationalisation and workers' control.[64] Although the delegates accepted Len Powell's position that 'this was not a question to raise now', similar ideas were endorsed by the Birmingham Trades Council after a series of debates in the winter of 1941–42. Initially the Trades Council called for democratisation of private companies, with 50% of the Boards of Management being elected by the workers – a policy much more radical than that supported by the CP. In January, however, they voted 48 to 37 against all forms of 'collaboration with employers', and in favour of full public ownership with control by technicians and workers.[65] But abstract debates at the Trades Council were much less significant than the enthusiastic support for JPCs shown by the Birmingham AEU.[66] Despite widespread public support for the nationalisation of the armaments industries during the winter of 1941–42, leftist arguments that co-operation in production should be withheld until such demands were granted had little purchase on the realities of factory politics.[67] Unlike the Communist Party, the Manchester District Committee of the AEU debated the issue of 'collaborationism' seriously, concluding:

> On the one hand we are working under a capitalist system, more highly organised for exploitation, even than in peace time. Every advantage that the employers can secure from collaboration ... will be, and is being, ruthlessly acquired throughout the industry. No sacrifices are being made by the employers. No fraction of managerial power is being surrendered.... On the other hand we are committed to intensified production.

To handle these 'complications' the District Committee adopted a permissive policy of approving Production Committees so long as they steered clear of the existing negotiating procedures, while relying on 'the discretion and experience of our shop stewards to secure the maximum advantage' from the new committees. They summed up this approach as 'a war on two fronts' against both Hitler and the employers – a phrase which echoed Communist responses to the outbreak of war in 1939, rather than the much less critical policy advocated since the Nazi invasion of the Soviet Union.[68] Whatever doubts were felt by the District Committee, however, this did not stop it from supporting a call for the Government to use compulsion to break employer resistance to the establishment of JPCs.[69]

Manchester's caution had less to do with the appeal of leftist ideas about workers' control, than with the strength of traditional labourist attitudes among the vigorously anti-Communist majority who dominated the District Committee. Swept along by the CP-led euphoria at their quarterly meeting in October, the shop stewards were in danger of being led into a trap: 'We should be foolish' warned the District President, 'to place our future in the hands of those who have [pre-June 1941] eminently demonstrated how tactless and misguided they are.' Shop stewards, he argued, could not simultaneously collaborate with management and defend the interests of their members. The way to improve the production position was through parliamentary intervention from above, not by a bottom-up politics of production which threatened to submerge the independence of the unions in ill-considered attempts at workers' control.[70] Very similar attitudes were noted a few months later by the Ministry of Labour's man in Glasgow. Opposition to JPCs was, he wrote, 'confined in the main to the older groups of leaders and their criticism is that in the absence of guarantees as to a new status for workers after the war it will be wrong to place the knowledge of the workers at the disposal of the employers because this will enable the latter to intensify exploitation when peace comes.'[71] This defensive hostility to a productionist stance was, as in Manchester, reinforced by suspicion of Communist activists who had been, until so recently, the leading opponents of any such collaboration in the workshops.[72] Richard Croucher provides an enlightening summary of these attitudes:

> Their view was that it might well be true ... that production was chaotic, and that the fault lay with management: as skilled men they were often quick to point it out.... The legitimate task of the AEU ... was not to do the management's job for them, but to improve wages and conditions by ensuring that management was deterred from telling them how to do their jobs. It seemed as if the area of control which they had always fought to retain, the legendary circle around the turner's lathe over which the foreman was advised not to step, was now threatened not only by the traditional enemy but by a disturbing tendency within their own unions to advocate joining with management in committees set up for the express purpose of invading that area of control.[73]

This kind of defence of traditional craft regulation on the shop floor against the new productionism preached by the young men of the Communist Party, was more prevalent in the Northern strongholds of craft regulation than in the Midlands or London. Such attitudes, and the employer traditionalism which they mirrored, probably go far to explain why the JPC campaign was much more successful in the South than in the North. According to the information collected by the AEU's Production Inquiry covering the first three months of 1942, a far higher proportion of firms had formed JPCs in the South (31%) than in Scotland (11%) or the North (14%). The Midlands, at 20%, fell in between[74] (see Table 3.1). In Manchester and Glasgow the evidence of significant resistance among some trade unionists, is born out by low levels of JPC formation reported in the AEU figures.

At the height of the agitation in January 1942, when well-publicised demands for Government inquiries into alleged managerial incompetence were being made by shop stewards in several Clydeside factories, the Scottish Conciliation Officer reported that 'the rank and file of the workers do not seem to be very much stirred about this production question. They grouse and complain, murmur and mutter, but the impulse behind this attitude seems to be the ordinary one which makes the Clyde employee inclined to grouse about his employer as a matter of habit'.[75] Clydeside, however, may have been a special case, and the more reliable judgement is probably that offered by Mass Observation in

December 1941 that 'workers are in a somewhat suggestible condition', ready to respond to productionist initiatives where shop stewards and management were able to work intelligently together (especially if these could be linked to the Russian cause), but equally likely to stand pat on traditional practices where no such alliance could be constructed.[76]

Table 3.1 JPCs established, January–March 1941[77]

District	% JPC	JPC	No JPC
Glasgow	15	6	34
Scotland W.	5	1	18
Scotland E.	11	3	24
Scotland N.E.	9	1	10
SCOTLAND	11.3	11	86
Tyne	11	3	24
Tees	14	3	19
Yorks W.	13	7	47
Yorks E.	19	5	21
Yorks S.	25	4	12
Lancs. N.	25	4	12
Lancs. Cent.	11	5	42
Manchester	18	7	33
Liverpool	22	2	7
NORTH	14.3	40	239
Midlands N.	6	2	29
Midlands E.	25	2	6
Birmingham	30	25	58
Midlands S.	14	5	31
East Anglia	10	3	26
South Wales	33	1	2
MIDLANDS	20	38	152
Bristol	38	6	10
South West	40	2	3
London N.	37	17	29
London S.	32	12	26
Kent	0	0	8
South	21	5	19
SOUTH	30.7	42	95

Whatever the exact balance between cynicism and productionism – and this clearly differed from region to region and factory to factory – what is clear is that rank-and-file indifference or hostility, where it existed, was insufficient to prevent the Communist-led campaign from achieving its primary gaols. By March 1942 Joint Production Committees had been established, according to the AEU Enquiry, in 8 of the 15 biggest factories employing more than 10,000 workers each, and nearly a third of the 73 factories in the next group (2,500–10,000). Altogether, of the 740 factories surveyed, 21% had JPCs. Some of these were long-standing works committees, but most of them had been formed since the beginning of the year.[78] This was no mean achievement for the campaign launched at the Stoll Theatre in October 1941.

The major impact of the Communist-led agitation was to push both employers and trade union leaders into accepting that something had to be done, if only to contain the growth of Communist influence. It was Bevin who forced them to face up to this fact.

NOTES

1. AEU, National Committee, *Report*, 1941, pp. 227–8.
2. *Ibid.*, p. 237.
3. W. Hannington, *The Rights of Engineers*, London, 1944, p. 86; AEU, *Enquiry into Production Committees: Third Report on Production*, December 1942, p. 1; interview with Yvonne Kapp, 11 June 1992.
4. Calls to re-convene the National Committee in order to look again at the production issue came to nothing: AEU Southall District Committee, *Minutes*, 11 September 1941.
5. 'Nazi German attacks Socialist Russia', n.d., Len Powell Papers; AEU, Proceedings of Twenty-third National Committee, *Report*, 16–23 June 1941, p. 252.
6. 'Notes on Production Hold-up', n.d., Len Powell Papers; W. Hannington, 'The A.E.U. and the Shop Stewards' Movement', *Labour Monthly*, February 1941, pp. 68–9.
7. D. Hyde, *I Believed. The Autobiography of a Former British Communist*, London, 1952, p. 117.
8. Engineering and Allied Trades Shop Stewards' National Council, *Arms and the Men*, 1941, p. 19.
9. K. Morgan, *Against Fascism and War*, Manchester University Press, 1989, pp. 189–96; *Labour Monthly*, March 1941; Deputy Chief Industrial Commissioner for Scotland, *Reports*, 22 March 1941, 31 May 1941, LAB 10/362.
10. *Labour Research*, September 1941, p.143.
11. S. Tolliday, 'Government, employers and shop floor organisation in the British motor industry, 1939-69', in S. Tolliday and J. Zeitlin, (eds), *Shop Floor Bargaining and the State. Historical and Comparative Perspectives*, Cambridge, 1985, pp. 111–14; R. Price, *Labour in British Society*, London, 1986, pp. 191–2;

Deputy Chief Industrial Commissioner for Scotland, *Reports*, 10 August 1940, 28 September 1940, LAB 10/361; North West Regional Industrial Relations Officer, *Reports*, 5, 12 July 1941, 6, 13 December 1941, LAB 10/379; London Chief Conciliation Officer, *Reports*, 4 October 1941, LAB 10/357.

12. P.G. Crabbe (AWA Works Manager) to H.R. Chapham (MAP), 4 July 1941, AVIA 15/2539.

13. On 17 September 1941, Imison (BAC personnel manager) wrote to Low (EEF Secretary) enclosing details of the shop stewards' demands. EEF 237/3/1/264; see also *Arms and the Men*, pp. 16–17,

14. *Labour Research*, October 1941, p. 151.

15. *Idem*, September 1941, pp. 141–2; Low to Imison, 22 September 1941, EEF 237/3/1/264; Minutes of Central Conference, 10 April 1942, EEF 237/1/13/63. About a quarter of the committees established before March 1942 were the result of managerial, not trade union, initiative: AEU, *Enquiry into Production Committees: Third Report on Production*, December 1942, p. 7.

16. Engineering and Allied Trades Shop Stewards' National Council, *Arms and the Men*, 19 October 1941.

17. *World News and Views*, 16 August 1941.

18. *Loc. cit.*, p. 24.

19. *Ibid.*, p. 12. Even so, such guarantees, which often paved the way for the establishment of JPCs, were not always demanded by the men because, as Len Powell explained, many workers preferred to protect their working conditions for the long term, rather than going all out for extra money: 'workers are looking at *their* post-war interests and therefore desire to maintain easy times on jobs'. 'Some Points on the Production Situation', n.d. (early 1942?), Len Powell Papers.

20. Mass Observation, *People in Production. An Enquiry into British War Production*, Penguin Special, 1942, p. 51.

21. H. Pollitt, in *World News and Views*, 16 August 1941, p. 514.

22. North West Regional Industrial Relations Officer, *Report*, 6 September 1941, LAB 10/379.

23. Douglas Hyde, in *World News and Views*, 25 October 1941; less suprisingly, this particular remark was toned down in the official report, *loc. cit.*, p.14.

24. *Daily Express*, 20 October 1941. Other approving reports and leaders appeared in *The Times, News Chronicle, Mirror* and *Mail*. The Chairman of the Conservative Party's 1922 Committee contacted Walter Swanson asking for details of the shop steward allegations of mis-management. W. Citrine, briefing to Joint Consultative Committee of Ministry of Labour, 4 December 1941, TUC 292/106.45.

25. *News Chronicle*, 18 October 1941. The AEU Executive complained to the *Daily Mirror* about its sympathetic reporting of the unofficial movement, AEU Executive *Minutes*, 7, 8, 10, 16 October 1941.

26. Cabinet Conclusions, 20 October 1941, CAB 35/19.

27. Deputy Chief Industrial Commissioner for Scotland, *Reports*, 27 December 1941, LAB 10/362; *idem*, 10 January 1942, 4 April 1942, LAB 10/363. See also Mass Observation, *op. cit.*, p. 49.

28. D. Hyde, *op. cit.*, pp. 102, 128–9; interview with Douglas Hyde, 31 October 1989; D. Hyde, 'Preparations for Illegality: Communist Party of Great Britain, 1941', *Our History Journal*, 14, 1989. On 27 January 1942 A.J. Cummings, the *News Chronicle* columnist, paid tribute to the ex-*Daily Worker* staff for their work in stimulating production in the factories.

29. Untitled typescript, n.d. (February 1942?), in Len Powell Papers.

30. The Len Powell Papers contain numerous examples of such campaigns. The undated typescript of ? February 1942 lays out step-by-step advice to shop stewards about how to launch a campaign.

31. *New Propeller*, March 1942. It may be further testimony to the effectiveness of the CP's press work that the *Financial News* carried an almost identically worded report on 2 March 1942 (quoted in *Labour Research*, April 1942).

32. 'Technically ... inefficient managements are subject to removal by the authorities, and proven cases of managerial inefficiency have been known. It is however, highly doubtful whether, unless accompanied by unrest so widespread that the authorities themselves are forced to institute an enquiry, cases of this kind, involving as they do questions of costing and other technicalities, are ever provable by the workpeople'. AEU, *Enquiry into Production Committees: Third Report on Production*, December 1942, p. 25.

33. *Coventry Evening Telegraph*, 17 January 1942.

34. S. Thompson to Len Powell, 21 March 1942, in Len Powell Papers.

35. Sir Charles Doughty, who conducted the 1942 enquiry, had already intervened for the Ministry of Labour a year earlier, and public criticisms of the management had been made by an Old Bailey judge in July 1941 when, following a celebrated trial, seven trade unionists from Swift's were bound over for their part in a strike against the victimisation of shop stewards. E. and R. Frow, *Engineering Struggles*, Manchester, 1982, pp. 159–60; correspondence between London Engineering Employers' Association and the EEF, EEF 3/1/264/77; Seven Trade Unionists' Defence Council, *Report*, 21 May 1941, in Len Powell Papers.

36. Local Conference between AEU and Glasgow EEA, *Minutes*, 26 January 1942, EEF 237/1/1/312.

37. Deputy Chief Industrial Commissioner for Scotland, *Reports*, 1 November 1941, LAB 10/362.

38. Communist Party, *The Communist Party and the National Front*, n.d. (late 1941?), a syllabus intended for use at cadre training schools.

39. Untitled typescript, notes on particular firms, n.d. (early 1942?), Len Powell Papers.

40. *New Propeller*, January 1942; W. Stokes to AEU Research Department, 3 December 1941, Stokes Papers, 289/83/8. No JPC was established, however, because of the obstructive attitude of the local Employers' Association, and complaints about front-line supervision continued to be made by the stewards: AEU, *Enquiry into Production Committees: Third Report on Production*, December 1942, p. 73 (establishment 686).

41. *Ibid.*, p. 86.

42. Engineering and Allied Trades Shop Stewards' National Council, *Arms and the Men*, 1941, p. 14.

43. *New Propeller*, February 1942. The Communists had won control of the shop stewards' committee the previous summer after a bitter fight with the right-wing, AEU Manchester District Committee, *Minutes*, 26 June 1941.

44. L. Levenan (Openshaw) to Bissett (Manchester Engineering Employers' Association), 27 June 1942, EEF 237/1/1/312.

45. AEU Manchester District Committee, *Minutes*, 5 March 1942.

46. *New Propeller*, May 1942, Levenan to Bissett, *op. cit.*

47. 'Some Points on the Production Situation', n.d. (early 1942?), Len Powell Papers.

48. Hugh Latter to Low, 19 March 1942, EEF 237/1/1/312. The attitude of shop stewards at the Rotax factory in London may have been similarly counter-productive as the following extract from their report to the AEU Production Enquiry suggests: 'The management refuse a mass meeting to be held in the canteen to explain to workpeople the necessity for a good production committee to be formed. So the shop stewards decided they might just as well not have one at all. The management did not mind whether they did or not.' AEU, *Enquiry into Production Committees: Third Report on Production*, December 1942, p. 78 (establishment 689).

49. Untitled typescript, notes on particular firms (Duples), n.d. (early 1942?), Len Powell Papers. A very similar argument appeared in the shop stewards' paper at Vickers, Openshaw, *Factory News*, November 1942.

50. R. Croucher, *Engineers at War, 1939-1945*, London, 1982, p. 157. In November 1941 the other factories in the group had refused to support a strike called by the Liverpool men: North West Regional Industrial Relations Officer, *Report*, 29 November 1941, LAB 10/379.

51. Communist Party Executive Committee, statement, 16 January 1942, PREM 4/64/5.

52. 'Some Points on the Production Situation', n.d. (early 1942?), Len Powell Papers.

53. P.G. Crabbe (AWA Works Manager) to H.R. Chapham (MAP), 4 July 1941, AVIA 15/2539.

54. Baginton Works Committee, *Bulletin*, 4, n.d. (Autumn 1941?); J. Steele to *Coventry Evening Telegraph*, 1 August 1941; 'Coventry Shop Stewards' Delegation', 22 January 1942, all in J. Steele Papers; Coventry Engineering Employers' Association Executive, *Minutes*, 21 July 1941, CEEA, 66.

55. Midland Conciliation Officer, *Reports*, 25 October, 8 November 1941, LAB 10/351.

56. Mass Observation, *op. cit.*, pp. 46-7.

57. V. Tester, *Report*, 26 January 1942, MO, Town Boxes. The Chairman of Alvis, T.G. John, was an outspoken reactionary who dismissed the idea that workers might have anything to contribute to management as 'just political nonsense': letter in *The Times*, 9 May 1942.

58. V. Tester, *Report*, 22 January 1942, MO, Town Boxes; Midland Conciliation Officer, *Report*, 3 January 1942, LAB 10/352; *Coventry Evening Telegraph*, 2, 5, 7, 12, 16 January 1942; National Union of Sheet Metal Workers' Coventry Branch, *Minutes*, 7, 10 January 1942, 4, 16 February 1942; Coventry Shop Stewards' Deputation, 22 January 1942, in J. Steele Papers.

59. *Coventry Evening Telegraph*, 13 January 1942.

60. *Ibid.*, 17 January 1942.

61. 'Points for a Policy for the Shop Stewards' Movement', memorandum attached to Z. Baker, *Report*, MO, Industry Boxes. Croucher, *op. cit.*, pp. 167-8 reproduces Baker's report. See also AEU Coventry District Committee, *Minutes*, 24 January 1942.

62. *The Times*, 23 January 1942.

63. Coventry Engineering Employers' Association Executive, *Minutes*, 2, 9, 18 February 1942, CEEA, 66; Midland Regional Board, *Minutes*, 17 February 1942, MRB 180 MRB/3/2.

64. Engineering and Allied Trades Shop Stewards' National Council, *Arms and the Men*, 1941, p. 14.

65. Midlands Conciliation Officer, *Report*, 8 November 1941, LAB 10/351; *idem*, 17 January 1942, LAB 10/352.

66. Report in *Financial News*, quoted in People's Convention, *Notes No. 3*, December 1941, People's Convention Papers, Marx Memorial Library.

67. According to Mass Observation, far more people looked towards nationalisation than to joint consultation as the key to solving the production problem. Joint consultation, an unfamiliar idea promoted by shop stewards, was unlikely to be spontaneously raised from the shop floor: 'there is no factory precedent for such a thought, and it does not seem immediately practicable' (Mass Observation, *op. cit.*, pp. 44-5, 254-5). In December 1941 Left Labour MPs moved an amendment to the King's Speech calling for nationalisation (S. Brooke, *Labour's War. The Labour Party during the Second World War*, Oxford, 1992, pp.85-9). For an exposition of the leftist view that co-operation in production should be withheld until the factories were taken into public ownership see M. Edleman, *Production for Victory, not*

Profit!, Left Book Club, London, 1941, *passim*. Paradoxically the most determined resistance to JPCs by workers occurred in a number of factories which were nationalised already – the Royal Ordnance Factories: Croucher, *op. cit.*, pp. 173–4.

68. AEU Manchester District Committee, *Minutes*, 23 December 1941; Croucher, *op. cit.*, p. 170.

69. AEU Manchester District Committee, *Minutes*, 5 February 1942. Early attempts to insist on worker-only production committees had been overwhelmingly defeated: *idem*, 30 October 1941.

70. E. Jennison, 'Production Committees', *AEU Monthly Journal*, December 1941; *idem*, June 1942. See also J.W. Sutton, 'Production Committees', *ibid.*, February 1942.

71. Deputy Chief Industrial Commissioner for Scotland, *Reports*, 28 March 1942, LAB 10/363.

72. *Ibid.*, 2 May 1942.

73. Croucher, *op. cit.*, pp. 168–9.

74. This figure is borne out by the fact that a third of the 222 firms responding to a circular sent out by the Southern Regional Board in February 1942, claimed to have production committees, though most of these would probably not have met with AEU approval since they were open to non-unionists: TUC 293/106.44/2. In Birmingham shop stewards reported that 18 JPCs had been formed by mid-March, while twice as many firms continued to resist union demands, figures roughly confirmed by the AEU Report: *Daily Herald*, 16 March, 1942.

75. Deputy Chief Industrial Commissioner for Scotland, *Reports*, 31 January 1942, LAB 10/363. Compare Mass Observation's report from a Northern factory: 'the real war which is being fought here today is still pre-war, private and economic': Mass Observation, *op. cit.*, pp. 24–5.

76. Mass Observation, 'Effects of Russian Campaign on Feelings About Industrial Output', *File Report*, 1050, 12 December 1941. For a similar assessment see Maurice Webb's report of a conference of Ministry of Supply officials in the *Daily Herald*, 27 January 1942.

77. These figures are based on a reworking of the data collected by the AEU Production Enquiries. I am grateful to Yvonne Kapp, who conducted the Enquiries in 1941–42, for lending me this material.

78. *Trade Union Report*, MO 'Industry' Topic Collection, (n.d. 1946?), p.107; W. Hannington, *op. cit.*, p. 93.

4 Defusing the Crisis

Since becoming Minister of Labour in May 1940, Ernest Bevin had been keen to promote joint consultation on the shop floor. But he had made little headway against the combined hostility of engineering employers and trade union activists, both of whom objected to any such interference with the traditional rules of the class struggle.[1] In the summer of 1941 reinforcement came from the chairman of ICI, Sir Harry McGowan, who wrote to Churchill pleading with him to give a lead in the matter. As a professional career manager, McGowan was contemptuous of the unimaginative defensiveness displayed by the engineering employers.[2] Bevin had a long-standing involvement with the development of ICI's labour policy, and had already invited Richard Lloyd Roberts, ex-labour director of ICI and a leading advocate of the 'human relations in industry' school of management thought, to join him at the Ministry of Labour.[3] Following up McGowan's letter, Bevin explained to Churchill:

> we cannot shut our eyes to the fact that intelligent workers do become cognizant of management blunders – blunders which inevitably have increased in number as the result of the expansion of industry and the dearth of people who really understand the art of management. This fact makes it all the more essential to convince managements of the wisdom of relying less on conventional 'authority' and more on the willingness of the workers.... If managements would explain promptly to the workers why they have to stand idle at a particular moment; why at another moment there is a special rush; why a certain change of method is going to be introduced, and so on, the reaction of the men would be immediate.

What was needed was 'a campaign for the establishment of what might be called a "round table" in every factory.... Well publicised, this "round table" phrase might acquire a great psychological value', helping to break down the adversarial language of the 'two sides' of industry.[4] Bevin fully embraced the new school of management thinking represented by 'human relations in industry' enthusiasts like

Lloyd Roberts, steering the Ministry of Labour into a campaign to persuade firms to institute changes in managerial techniques that some would see as almost revolutionary: 'It implies a willingness on the part of management to associate the ordinary worker much more closely with matters which have hitherto been regarded as outside his province.'[5]

At first Bevin's initiative showed every sign of running into the sands. While the Nazi invasion of the Soviet Union in June shifted the Communists from opposition to enthusiastic support for the idea, among trade union leaders the sudden Communist conversion served only to reinforce their suspicion about the whole project, and the opposition of the Engineering Employers' Federation was unrelenting. In this situation the supply ministries were reluctant to put pressure on their industrial partners.[6] In the West Midlands the employer Chairman of the Regional Board, General Baylay – himself a leading figure in the EEF – was persuaded by the enthusiasm of the AEU representative on the Board, Billy Stokes, to support the idea of production committees.[7] In October the Board launched an ambitious campaign to promote 'Production Enquiry Committees' in the factories, intending to bring pressure to bear on any employers who resisted the scheme. Despite initial enthusiastic welcome in the local press, the Board's initiative quickly ran into opposition from employers, and both Whitehall and the TUC were half-hearted about giving the green light to such local experimentation.[8] The national trade union executives, Bevin complained bitterly, remained apathetic, disorganised and unwilling to undertake new responsibilities.[9]

It was the Communists' Stoll Theatre Conference in October 1941 which enabled Bevin to cut through the inertia. Nine days later he met privately with TUC leaders, and told them that unless they did something positive to contain the unrest in the factories, he would be unable to prevent some of his fellow ministers, notably Beaverbrook, from dealing over their heads with the shop stewards.[10] Bevin's warning induced near-panic at the TUC General Council, with Deakin – Bevin's stand-in at the TGWU – insisting that any meeting between Beaverbrook and shop stewards 'in any shape or form' would represent an unacceptable attack on established trade union authority.[11] The apparent convergence between Beaverbrook and the Communists seriously alarmed the TUC. Despite a Cabinet ruling against him on the day after the Stoll Theatre Conference, Beaverbrook continued to insist on his right to talk directly with shop stewards about production issues.[12] Churchill, writing to his son, found it hard to decide which was more aggravating – the fact that the Communists were 'posing as the only patriots in the country', or the effect of the asthma season on Beaverbrook's relations with Bevin: 'Max fights every day and resigns every day'.[13] The issue rumbled on into the winter with the announcement that Beaverbrook would address meetings of shop stewards in Newcastle and Glasgow. A week before Beaverbrook's visit to Glasgow, the Communist MP William Gallacher was sent North to persuade the shop stewards 'to give the old lad a hearing'. The resulting newsreel footage of the Tory press lord hitting it off with the hard men of the Clydeside factories no doubt helped to feed Beaverbrook's populist fantasies, as well as providing the Communists with further confirmation that they had become a force to be reckoned with.[14] Communist leaders did not hesitate to lend themselves to the Beaverbrook mystique. Not only did the Party's arch-enemy, Bevin, hate him, but Beaverbrook could be boosted as the scourge of capitalist restrictive practices, trade union bureaucrats and civil service red tape: the man who got things done, and was pro-Soviet into the bargain.[15] Had Beaverbrook won the power-struggle of 1941–42, his penchant for dictatorial centralism would have offered little scope for the Communists to develop their schemes of worker participation; certainly less than they were able to find within the voluntaristic and decentralised regime within which Bevin was seeking to contain their energies. Fortunately he did not, and the main consequence of the emerging alliance between the Minister of Supply and the Communist Party was to help to persuade the TUC that something positive needed to be done if the agitators – high and low – were to be prevented from upsetting the apple cart.

It was Walter Citrine, TUC General Secretary, who broke the deadlock. For some time Citrine had been concerned about the lack of co-ordination among unions in the engineering and shipbuilding industries. Faced with the upsurge of unofficial shop steward activity, and the emergence of Joint Production Committees uncontrolled by official trade union machinery, he became convinced that the time had come for the main unions concerned to establish joint district machinery capable of supervising the activities of joint shop stewards' committees which, in the prevailing conditions of uncoordinated multi-unionism, were beyond the control of any official trade union body.[16] Early in January 1942 – such was the pace of the fragmented trade union bureaucracy's response to an emergency – the engineering unions were ready to agree that 'something had to be done, and done quickly', if the rapidly extending influence of the Communist Party was to be checked. At first the unions, worried about the potential enfranchisement of non-unionists, appeared to rule out direct election of production committees from the shop floor.[17] But this was hardly a sustainable position – as Sir Frederick Leggett, a senior Ministry of Labour adviser pointed out to Bevin: 'It seems difficult to expect representatives to have the confidence of workers in the shops unless the latter have a voice at some stage in their selection.'[18] Following an informal meeting with Bevin the unions worked out a compromise formula by which workers would elect representatives from people nominated by the unions: but nothing they produced, at this stage, made it clear whether the electorate was to include all workers or only trade union members.[19] To vet the nominations, and to oversee the work of the JPCs once they were established, Trade Union District Production Committees (TUDPCs) were to be set up bringing together all the unions organising in the engineering industry. It was emphasised that the new machinery was intended to deal solely with production problems, and not with questions of wages and conditions already covered by existing negotiating procedures.[20] Production questions were far less likely to divide unions than the bread-and-butter issues with which they normally dealt – a point made forcefully by the Engineers' President, Jack Tanner, two years later when Citrine, still anxious about the influence of the unofficial shop stewards' movement, tried unsuccessfully to use the precedent of the TUDPCs to persuade the engineering unions to merge their district organisation for normal collective bargaining purposes.[21]

The TUC rounded off its intervention by asking Bevin to amend the Essential Works Order to make JPCs compulsory.[22] Though the TUC was reluctant to risk rebuff by pressing for an immediate answer, the request was widely reported in the press and, during the weeks that followed, rumours of impending compulsion did much to hold the EEF to the path of negotiations.[23] At the end of January Sir Alexander Ramsay, the EEF Director, had told the AEU that, while he was in favour of more explanation of production problems being given to workers, he would resist 'panic ideas' about setting up new committees: 'I am not going to be a party to handing over the production of the factory and the problems concerning production to shop stewards or anyone else.'[24] These bold words belied the real weakness of the EEF's position. Two days later, the Federation privately accepted that it would have to come to terms.[25] It is clear that this decision owed more to shop floor pressures and fear of what Bevin might do than to any direct demands from the AEU. Although the union had finally got around to opening informal talks with the employers in December, they remained unsure and confused about what exactly they were demanding.[26] At first the employers' bottom line was that non-unionists must be fully integrated into any new machinery. While this stance certainly represented 'a large body of opinion' within the Federation,[27] it was not in reality compatible with the decision to negotiate: it was clear that the AEU would never agree to sit with non-unionists on the new committees.[28] Moreover there was a perplexing ambiguity in the EEF's stance. They were as worried as the unions by the rise of the unofficial movement, and they appear to have believed that they had a common interest with the unions in devising machinery to keep the militants under control: any new machinery, they minuted at the end of January, must be 'under the aegis of and in strict conformity with the official trade union movement'.[29] When the Glasgow Association discussed the issue with the unions in January, their chairman was clearly unsure how to respond to the AEU argument that the unions could only be expected to take responsibility for the good behaviour of the JPCs if membership was limited to organised workers.[30] Given this ambiguity on non-unionists the EEF would probably have had to abandon its stance in any case. In fact, on the

very day that its Management Board approved the detailed
negotiating position, it was rendered obsolete by an agreement
between the unions and the Ministry of Supply to establish JPCs in
the state-owned Royal Ordnance Factories.

At the end of January, while negotiations in the private sector
were stalled, the Ministry of Supply invited the AEU to discuss
production committees in the Royal Ordnance Factories. Informal
discussions followed around a detailed constitution drawn up by the
Ministry in consultation with the Ministry of Labour and the TUC.[31]
Agreement was easily reached, since the draft constitution embodied
a compromise on the non-union question devised (according to the
official historian) by Bevin: while membership of the JPC would be
limited to organised workers, all workers employed in the factory
would be eligible to vote.[32] When the formal negotiation took place
on 26 February the unions put up token resistance to this
enfranchisement of non-unionists, but finally accepted 'in view of
the special functions of the Production Committees'.[33]

When, three weeks later, the unions met the EEF they insisted on
taking the ROF agreement as the basis of negotiations. Although the
employers put up a fight over the exclusion of non-unionists from
membership of the committees, they had already privately accepted
that after the ROF agreement Bevin's compromise on this would be
impossible to resist.[34] They did, however, get Tanner's agreement
that the JPC's powers of co-option could be used to bring in non-
unionists with technical expertise to contribute. Moreover they
succeeded in limiting JPCs to firms with over 150 workers, and
prevented anything being said about the post-war continuation of the
committees. While resisting any formal agreement that JPCs should
be made mandatory in federated firms, the EEF volunteered to
'strongly recommend' their establishment.[35] However, where
existing Works Committees were dealing satisfactorily with
production questions it was accepted by the unions that the new
machinery need not be implemented.[36]

Following the March 1942 agreement, the number of firms
recognising JPCs spread rapidly (see Table 4.1 on page 83). A
survey by the AEU placed the peak of JPC formation between April
and June 1942. Of the establishments responding to this survey

54% had established JPCs by the autumn of 1942.[37] There seems to have been a second wave of JPC formations, especially in the smaller firms, in the first half of 1943. Thereafter reports of new JPCs slowed to a trickle.[38] While the EEF's promise to put pressure on its members to observe the agreement was by no means universally effective, figures covering a majority of the local associations, showed that, of 1,022 firms employing over 150 workers, 79.6% had JPCs or equivalent bodies by April 1943.[39] Many smaller, and non-federated, firms also established committees. The EEF figures are broadly consistent with a Whitehall estimate, made in June 1944, that JPCs existed in about 75% of the larger firms – 2,959 altogether. They reported a further 1,606 in firms employing under 150 workers. The regional bias towards the South apparent in the early stages of JPC formation appears to have persisted throughout the war.[40] Two weeks after the March 1942 agreement was signed TUC leaders agreed to withdraw their request that JPCs be made compulsory under the Essential Works Order.[41] The request had nevertheless served its purpose. Although Bevin was, as always, reluctant to use statutory powers, he had made it clear that he would do so if it was the only way 'to achieve the desired object'.[42] Merely hinting at the possibility had been sufficient to bring the EEF to heel. The employers knew that nothing they did could prevent Bevin from legislating, as he had done, in the face of united employer opposition, with the Essential Works Order a year before.[43] The only way to avoid the still greater disaster of compulsory JPCs was to negotiate their voluntary establishment with the unions. The danger of compulsion, as General Baylay, who had been trying to get production committees established in the Midlands since the previous autumn pointed out, was that, by demonstrating that the state was prepared to coerce the employers, it would encourage the militants to up their demands still further.[44] Such fears were confirmed in subsequent years, when those looking to develop the JPCs as a basis for post-war industrial democracy pressed for the committees to be given statutory form.[45] Once the employers had accepted joint consultation on a voluntary basis, however, Bevin was deaf to renewed TUC calls for compulsion.[46] In any case these calls lacked conviction since, whatever resolutions the AEU might persuade the Congress to adopt, the General Council held back from pressing the issue, fearing that in industries less well organised than engineering it would be difficult to resist employer arguments to permit non-unionists to sit on the Committees, opening the way to company unionism.[47]

In her contemporary study of the JPCs, Carol Riegelman suggested that 'when the movement for establishing the Joint Production Committees was in an early stage of development any intervention in open or active form by the Government would doubtless have so prejudiced the movement that it could not have achieved success'.[48] This gets the balance wrong. Bevin's forceful, if informal, interventions from an early stage played a vital part in preventing the movement for JPCs from precipitating a serious breakdown in industrial relations. The reflections of a Ministry of Labour official on what the Government should do about the future of JPCs at the end of the war, are suggestive about the considerations governing Bevin's policy in 1941–42. While 'the development of workshop collaboration ... must be a voluntary process based upon goodwill and the recognition of a common interest between management and employees', Government had a responsibility to help both sides of industry to recognise these common interests:

> There is a danger that the majority of employers may make no move in the matter on their own initiative and that if the initiative is left too much to the unions, workshop collaboration will not be developed as it should on a basis of common interest, but rather on a basis of worker control.[49]

Bevin's problem had, in fact, been more complex that this, since the unions, fearing for their own authority, had been initially as obdurate as the employers in resisting the demand for JPCs. By pushing first the unions (with the Beaverbrook/Communist card) and then the employers (with the threat of compulsion), Bevin forced the two sides of industry to reach an accommodation designed to defuse the crisis of authority in the war factories. Whatever fantasies the Communists may have entertained about the possibilities of an alliance with Beaverbrook, it was in reality Bevin, their most determined enemy, whose intervention forced the employers to give way to their demands for joint consultation in the factories.

Table 4.1   JPCs established by December 1942[50]

Engineering firms employing over 150 people known to have established JPCs.

Region	December 1942 Firms	Workers
SCOTLAND	131	114,000
North	73	99,000
N.West	190	186,000
Yorkshire	219	181,000
NORTH	482	466,000
Midlands	298	344,000
Wales	59	107,000
East	118	102,000
N. Midland	106	118,000
MIDLANDS	581	671,000
London & S.E.	564	414,000
S.West	131	126,000
South	148	123,000
SOUTH	843	663,000

In pursuing his policy of 'guided voluntarism' Bevin liked to stress his even-handedness. As he explained to the TUC leaders in November 1941: 'I have had to be very careful not to let it be thought that I am merely strengthening the hands of the unions'.[51] The engineering employers, however, perceived no such balance. The state, they believed, had forced them to accept what the militants wanted and they were filled with foreboding for the future. 'Nothing could be more harmful to production', wrote Low, Secretary of the EEF, in March 1942, 'than that managements should become imbued with an idea that their prerogatives are infringed, their status invaded, and their authority dissipated by a successful challenge from the workers, whether instigated by unofficial shop stewards or supported by a Governmental attitude' – or, he might well have added, by both at once.[52] The Ministry of Labour was anxious to reassure them, pointing out that while 'the new idea ... [will involve for] some firms a revolutionary change in their attitude and the expenditure of much time and energy', it would not in any way detract from 'the responsibilities now exercised by management'.[53] Bevin's objective was to re-legitimise managerial authority, not to undermine it. If he had intervened he had done so in order not to impose an intrusive regime of state supervision on industrial relations within the firm, but to foster a new atmosphere of co-operation – the psychology of the round table – in which state intervention could be minimised. Bevin's voluntarist intentions, however, were not sufficient to reassure the engineering employers. Was there, they wondered, a sinister agenda behind the contraction of the nomenclature used in official documents from 'Joint Production Consultative and Advisory Committees' – as they were described in the March 1942 agreement – to the less cumbersome (but also less qualified) 'Joint Production Committee'?[54] Could it be that, rather than defusing the crisis of managerial authority, Bevin's interventions had merely shifted the terrain on which a continuing battle for authority and legitimacy would have to be fought? Above all, would the dangerous alliance between insurgent shop stewards and an interfering state, which had forced the employers to accept the Joint Production Committees, now curl up and go to sleep? Or would the employers find their authority increasingly squeezed between an ongoing pincer movement of shop floor power and Whitehall intervention? At first, as the wider implications of the new production regime were worked out during the summer months of 1942, the answers to these questions were far from clear.

NOTES

1. 'Production Advisory Committees', n.d. (March 1942?), EEF internal briefing document, EEF 237/3/1/313; AEU, Proceedings of Twenty-third National Committee, *Report*, 16–23 June 1941, pp. 97–107, 237; W. Citrine, memorandum for NJAC, 4 December 1941, TUC 292/106.45; W. Hannington, 'The AEU and the Shop Stewards' Movement', *Labour Monthly*, February 1941. The Glasgow-based Deputy Chief Industrial Commissioner for Scotland was an early advocate of proproduction committees, *Reports*, 2, 23 November 1940, 15 February 1941, LAB 10/361–2.
2. McGowan to Churchill, 26 June 1941, Proproduction Executive, *Papers*, 22 July 1941, CAB 92/55. The immediate occasion for this letter were hints thrown out by Jack Tanner and Charles Dukes (leader of the National Union of General and Municipal Workers) at their union conferences a few days earlier. On McGowan see H. Perkin, *The Rise of Professional Society. England since 1880*, 1989, p. 295.
3. Roberts had been President of the Institute of Personnel Management. McGowan to Bevin, 26 June 1941, BT 168/166; W.J. Reader, *ICI, A History*, Vol. II, 1975, pp. 57–70, 298. Bevin conveniently forgot that, back in 1929, he had seen ICI's labour policy as distinctly anti-union. W.J. Reader, *op. cit.*, pp. 64–6.
4. Bevin to Churchill, 9 July 1941, Proproduction Executive, *Papers*, 22 July 1941, CAB 92/55.
5. 'Development of Joint Consultation in Factories', briefing prepared by Lloyd Roberts for Regional Industrial Relations Officers, n.d. (late 1941?), LAB 10/213.
6. EEF Management Board, *Minutes*, 25 September 1941, EEF 237/1/1/39; Robinson to Chapman, 27 September 1941, AVIA 15/2539.
7. Stokes was keen to promote production committees not only to foster good industrial relations but also in order to outflank the CP whose progress in the Midlands he viewed with alarm. (Stokes to Tanner, 27 November 1941, Stokes Papers 289/7/1/58; Stokes, 'Joint Production Enquiry Committees', *AEU Monthly Journal*, November 1941; AEU Executive, *Minutes*, 7 October 1941.)
8. W. Citrine, memorandum for NJAC, 4 December 1941, TUC 292/106.45; *Minutes* of MRB sub-committee, 19 September 1941; Collier to Chapman, 1 October 1941; Chapman to Stephenson, 4 October 1941; all in AVIA 15/2539, which also provides full documentation of the Whitehall response to the MRB initiative.
9. Bevin to Citrine, 1 October 1941, Citrine Papers, 7/3.
10. *Minutes* of GC side of NJAC, 28 October 1941, TUC 292/106.45.
11. *Minutes* of TUC GC, 29 October, 26 November 1941; *Minutes* of GC side of NJAC, 5 November, 4 December 1941, TUC 292/108.1/2. That Deakin was not alone is shown by the reaction of the trade union members of one Regional Board: 'Very strong opposition to the suggestion that Special Joint Production Enquiry Committees should be set up in the works came from the Trade Union representatives on the Board.... There was a real fear that representatives of the workpeople on these additional Committees might be elected, who had not the backing of the Trades Unions, and that in consequence there was a grave danger of undesirable people becoming members of these Committees and undermining the authority of both the Government and the Trade Unions.' *Minutes* of the East and West Riding Regional Board, 4 December 1941, BT 168/166.
12. Extract from Cabinet Conclusions, 20 October 1941, Beaverbrook Papers, D/504; Beaverbrook to Churchill, 22 October, 6 November 1941, Beaverbrook Papers, D/447.
13. Quoted in M. Gilbert, *Finest Hour*, 1983, p. 1227.
14. William Gallacher, letter published in *Daily Worker*, 13 June 1964; *New Propeller*, January 1942. According to the local Conciliation Officer the Glasgow meeting was

thinly attended and something of a disappointment for its promoters: Deputy Chief Industrial Commissioner for Scotland, *Report*, 6 December 1941, LAB 10/362.

15. Special Branch report on meeting of CP Industrial Bureau, 10 April 1942, WP (42) 168, CAB 66/23.

16. Citrine, memorandum on need for a National Advisory Committee for the Engineering and Shipbuilding Industries, 28 August 1941, TUC 292/86/1; Citrine, 'Joint Production Enquiry Committees', briefing for JCC MOL, 4 December 1941, 292/106.45; TUC, 'Munitions Production – Unofficial Machinery', 22 December 1941, TUC 292/106.45.

17. Conference of Engineering Unions, 7 January 1942, *Minutes*, TUC 292/106.45; Note on meeting of 7 January 1942 (n.d.), LAB 10/213; E.P. Harries, 'Memorandum for Group B meeting', 10 February 1942, TUC 292/86/1. On the bureaucratic reasons for the delay see Harries to Citrine, 8 December 1941, TUC 292/106.44/2.

18. Leggett to Bevin, 12 January 1942, LAB 10/213.

19. TUC Sub-Committee on production machinery, *Minutes*, 23 January 1942, TUC 292/106.45; Harries to Bevin, 8, 14, 19 January 1942, TUC 292/106.412/5. Bevin had already explained his ideas about the form that production committees should take to the TUC representatives on the JCC to the MOL on 5 November 1941, TUC 292/106.45.

20. TUC Sub-Committee on production machinery, *Minutes*, 23 January 1942, *loc. cit.*

21. NACSS&E, *Minutes*, 3 December 1943, 20 January 1944. TUC 292/225/1. Citrine had probably always intended to use the production committees as a stalking horse for the structural incorporation of shop stewards: cf. C. Riegelman, *British Joint Production Machinery*, Montreal, 1944, pp. 7–8.

22. Conference of Engineering Unions, *Minutes*, 5 February 1942, TUC 106.44/1. They also tried, without success, to draw the British Employers' Confederation into talks on the issue. Harries to Citrine, 27 February 1942, TUC 292/106.45; Forbes Watson to Low, 23 March 1942, EEF 237/3/1/313.

23. *Daily Express*, 23 January 1942, *Daily Telegraph*, 23, 29 January, 6 February 1942; Harries to Citrine, 29 January 1942, TUC 106.45 'Production Advisory Committees', n.d. (March 1942?), EEF 237/3/1/313.

24. Central Conference, *Minutes*, 27 January 1942, EEF 237/1/13/62.

25. EEF Management Board, *Minutes*, 29 January 1942, EEF 237/1/1/39.

26. 'Production Advisory Committees', n.d. (March 1942?), EEF internal briefing document, EEF 237/3/1/313; EEF Management Board, *Minutes*, 30 December 1941, EEF 237/1/1/39. It was not until 17 November that the AEU Executive agreed to approach the EEF over the issue.

27. 'Production Advisory Committees', n.d. (March 1942?), EEF 237/3/1/313.

28. R.Lloyd Roberts, 'Development of Joint Consultation in Factories', n.d. (December 1941?), LAB 10/213.

29. EEF Management Board, *Minutes*, 29 January 1942, EEF 237/1/1/39.

30. Glasgow local conference with AEU, *Minutes*, 26 January 1942, EEF 237/1/1/312 (North West).

31. C. Reigelman, *op. cit.*, pp.15–16; Harries to Citrine, 4 February 1942, TUC 292/106.45.

32. P. Inman, *Labour in the Munitions Industries*, 1957, p. 381. The full text of the agreement is reproduced in Reigelman, *op. cit.* pp. 223ff.

33. MOS Industrial Council, *Minutes*, 26 February 1942, WO 185/161.

34. 'Production Advisory Committees', n.d. (March 1942?), EEF 237/3/1/313.

35. Although the EEF assured Whitehall that 'practically every federated firm will do it' (Low to Chapman, 8 April 1942, EEF 237/3/1/313), it is clear that a substantial number of federated firms continued to resist, as well as many non-federated ones.

Bevin considered pressuring firms to conform by refusing to prosecute persistent absentees at firms without JPCs, but this was scrapped in favour of informal pressure brought by the supply ministries (Lindsay Scott, *Memorandum*, 24 March 1942, AVIA 15/2539).

36. 'Production Advisory Committees', n.d. (March 1942?), EEF 237/3/1/313; Central Conference, *Minutes*, 18 March 1942, EEF 237/1/13/62. Subsequently, in cases where employers had deliberately pre-empted the agreement by setting up production Committees including non-unionists shortly before it was signed, the unions insisted on reconstructing them to exclude the non-unionists. (NACE&SI, *Minutes*, 6 November 1942, TUC 292/106.451/2.) This led to major confrontations in a number of factories, including Dunlop in Coventry and Standard Telephone and Cables in East London. On the former see Coventry Engineering Employers' Association, Works Conference *Minutes*, 28 May 1942, CEEA 66/1/2/1/113; Coventry District Committee of the Confederation of Engineering and Shipbuilding Unions, *Minutes*, 7 July 1942, TGWU 126/JJ/CS/1; Jack Jones, *Union Man*, 1986, pp. 109–10. On the latter see Central Conference, *Minutes*, 10 April 1942, EEF 237/1/13/63.

37. AEU, *Third Report on Production*, December 1942, p. 7, in Michaelson Papers 233/3/3/5.

38. BT 168/168.

39. Summary of replies from Local Associations, April 1943, 237/1/1/312.

40. *Briefing*, n.d. (June 1944?), BT 171/210.

41. NJAC, *Minutes*, 30 March 1942, TUC 292/108.1/2.

42. Bevin, *Memorandum*, n.d. (January 1942?), LAB 10/213.

43. EEF General Council, *Minutes*, 27 February 1941, EEF 237/1/1/39.

44. Baylay to Forbes Watson, 27 March 1942, FBI 200/13/3/2/C961.

45. TUC *Report*, 1943, p. 206; NACE&SI, *Minutes*, 11 May 1943, TUC 292/106.451/2; Memorandum on AEU Resolution (War production) to TUC Southport, 1943, 11 April 1944, in TUC 292/106/2.

46. EEF Management Board, *Minutes*, 31 August 1944, EEF 237/1/1/41.

47. National Council of Labour, 21 April 1942, *Minutes*, TUC 292/106.44/2; Harries to Gunnell, 11 February 1944, TUC 292/106.45. In 1943, however, Harries seems to have been momentarily in favour of asking Bevin to make JPCs compulsory in the engineering industry: Harries, *Memorandum* for NJAC, 14 April 1943, TUC 292/106.45.

48. Riegelman, *op. cit.*, p. 91.

49. M.A. Bevan, 'Workshop Collaboration', 19 February 1945, BT 168/169. Similar fears had been articulated within the Ministry of Labour during the winter of 1941–42: Deputy Chief Industrial Commissioner for Scotland, *Report*, 1 November 1941, LAB 10/362; Lloyd Roberts, 'Development of Joint Consultation in Factories', briefing prepared for Regional Industrial Relations Officers, n.d. (late 1941?) LAB 10/213.

50. Paper for National Production Advisory Council, 31 December 1942, TUC 292/106.1/8.

51. NJAC, *Minutes*, 5 November 1941, TUC 292/106.45.

52. 'Production Advisory Committees', n.d. (March 1942?), EEF 237/3/1/313.

53. Lloyd Roberts, *op. cit.*

54. Leech to Latter, 8 October 1942, EEF 237/1/1/312.

5 Making Links

Summarising the changing nature of the reports sent in by shop stewards to the three production enquiries it conducted during 1941–42, the AEU claimed to detect a shift away from merely negative criticism of managerial inefficiency towards a constructive engagement with production problems: 'The workpeople have awakened to their responsibility for production.'[1] At their wartime height as many as 20,000 trade unionists may have served on JPCs: 'an unpaid and almost unheralded army of men and women who devoted their energies both during and after working hours to settling difficulties, answering questions, building morale and increasing production'.[2] This picture is echoed in the writings of union officials and shop floor activists, and well summed up by the worker JPC chairman portrayed in Mark Benney's 1943 novel *Over to Bombers*, based on his own experience in war industry, who urges his members to trade in the English working-man's privilege of grumbling in exchange for 'the new and better privilege of having some say in the ordering of our work.'[3]

In reality, however, the evidence of the day-to-day working of the JPCs, reviewed in the next chapter, lends scant support to the optimistic view that members of JPCs, let alone ordinary workers, effectively broke out of traditional defensive postures and reached for participation and a measure of control within the workplace. The mere establishment of production committees did little to solve the dilemma of how workers could develop a constructive productionism within the authority structures of the capitalist firm.

The key to shifting those structures, it was widely believed, was the integration of the firm into the wartime planning apparatus. Much of the confidence displayed by militants during the 1941–42 struggle for JPCs was rooted in their sense that the interventionist wartime state constituted a powerful new ally in their battles with the employers. Carol Reigelman's account of the JPCs, written for the International Labour Office when they were at the height of their influence in the autumn of 1943, argued that the full potential of the committees would only be achieved if they were developed not simply as a means of joint consultation between employers and their workers but as part of a triangular relationship between the state, the shop floor and management. The effectiveness of individual JPCs, she suggested, 'depended very largely on their connection with the special machinery developed ... for bringing employers and workers into constant consultation with the Government on war production problems.'[4] This argument reflected the trade union view that the fostering of a productionist culture in industry required not only the enlightened managerial techniques promoted by Bevin's Ministry of Labour, but also the closest possible integration between shop floor initiative and the state's planning apparatus.[5] From the outset JPC enthusiasts called for a close link between the JPCs and the Regional Boards.[6] Commenting on the demands of some Left Labour MPs for the nationalisation of war industry, *Labour Research* argued that the democratisation of the planning machinery would do more to secure immediate increases in production: 'Without effective state control, the activities of the JPCs will be seriously hampered; without workers' active participation, State control may mean little more than new machinery as cumbersome as the old.' In February 1942 Len Powell was urging shop stewards to take their problems to the Regional Boards both to get immediate redress, and to 'add impetus to the demand for full power to the Regional Boards, and give practical illustration to the need for same.' The Communists linked continuing demands for an all-embracing Ministry of Production with agitation for 'open access from the factories' to the Regional Boards which, they argued, would give 'the life-giving free contact' necessary to counterbalance 'the dead hand of bureaucratic routine or dilatory Whitehall centralisation'. In the Communist plan: 'The [transformed] Ministry of Production, in place of directly seeking to control 50,000 enterprises, would act through the Regional Boards, allocating to the regions (with consultation) their share in the national plan on the basis of knowledge of their capacity. The main executive organs would be the Regional Boards,' on which the direct representation of workers would have been considerably increased.[7] These demands were at one with the policy pursued by the AEU.[8]

Non-Communist reformers were equally anxious to open up links between JPCs and the Regional Boards. Alan Flanders, writing for the Socialist Vanguard Group, saw such links as the key to achieving 'an extension of real industrial self-government which can provide a counter-balance to the dangerous development towards economic totalitarianism involved in the growth of monopoly organisation.' PEP was no less anxious to integrate the JPCs fully into the Regional Board machinery, and G.D.H. Cole expected the issue of JPC relations with the Boards to figure prominently in ongoing struggles for worker participation in the war effort. J.T. Murphy, strategist of the shop stewards' movement in the First World War and now back at the bench in a London aircraft factory, believed that the absence of any reference to links with the planning machinery in the March 1942 JPC agreement represented a victory for employer conservatism over worker enthusiasm for production. As purely domestic institutions with no rights of appeal outside the factory the JPCs, he feared, would serve more to defuse and frustrate the drive to worker participation than to encourage it.[9]

One of the first tasks facing Norman Kipping when he took up his post as head of the Regional Division of the Ministry of Production in the spring of 1942 was to sort out the relationship between the Regional Boards and the JPCs. The Citrine Committee had recommended access by JPCs to the Boards, and the TUC believed that, by giving its emerging Trade Union District Production Committees (TUDPCs) power to refer disputes over production matters arising in JPCs to the Boards, they would be able to consolidate union authority over the JPCs. The EEF, however, strongly objected to the JPCs, which they had accepted as purely domestic arrangements, being integrated into either the district trade union machinery or the Regional Boards.[10] When Kipping confronted this problem in the summer of 1942 he was inclined to accept the union view, both because he wanted to strengthen the Regional Boards against the supply ministries, and because he was persuaded of the need to open up an alternative channel for the complaints with which shop stewards continued to deluge Whitehall. Kipping accepted Citrine's assurances that the TUDPCs would act as a filter, preventing 'hot heads on the workers' side' from abusing their right of appeal to the Regional Board.[11] Eventually, after several months of inconclusive discussions, the whole matter was referred to an emergency meeting of the National Production Advisory Council in September 1941. Overriding EEF protests that the Government had no right to interfere in a purely domestic arrangement between employers and unions, the Advisory Council agreed that Regional Boards should deal not only with matters referred jointly by both sides of a JPC, but also with one-sided references provided they were backed by employers' associations or trade unions, a clause which officials clearly intended to enable TUDPCs to take disputed matters to the Boards.[12] Conceding defeat on this issue by the combined pressure of the TUC and the Ministry of Production, the EEF secretary pessimistically concluded that further inroads into managerial authority were probably unavoidable.[13]

His discomfort was further increased by evidence that the emerging structures, far from *containing* pressure from below, were encouraging workers to increase their encroachments on managerial functions. The activities of Jack Jones, secretary of the Transport and General Workers' Union in Coventry, were especially worrying. Nowhere had the fight over JPCs been more intense during the winter of 1941–42. When in June 1942, the Coventry unions established the first TUDPC in the country, it was obviously going to provide something of a test case – not least because Jones was elected as its secretary.[14] While well aware that 'we have not the time to stop the war while we reorganise the social system', Jones nevertheless placed little faith in class harmony: 'Like the leopard, we haven't really changed our spots or our interests.'[15] The ambitious programme he set out for the TUDPC thoroughly alarmed the local engineering employers, who were not reassured by soothing words from London to the effect that Jones' speeches were 'little more than window dressing', intended to 'spike the activities' of the Communists.[16] The Coventry bosses remained unconvinced that an official movement run by Jack Jones was any improvement over an unofficial one run by Communists. The JPCs, accepted by employers as a way of containing tensions at plant level, were refusing to reach agreements without referring issues to the

TUDPC.[17] The employers' worst fears were confirmed when, in the autumn of 1942, Jones succeeded in persuading local Ministry of Labour officials to help him set up, under trade union auspices, a scheme to encourage engineering workers from several firms to volunteer to work temporarily in Coventry's major foundry, in order to break a bottleneck in the provision of castings which was holding up aircraft production.[18]

Although, at Bevin's insistence, employers and unions had agreed in national negotiations to permit the temporary transfer of labour between neighbouring firms in order to tackle bottlenecks, and the Ministry of Labour had actively promoted such transfers in other areas,[19] the Coventry employers were outraged by what they saw as a direct attack on managerial functions.   After pressuring the managements concerned to repudiate the whole idea, the director's assistant stormed off to sort out the hapless Ministry of Labour officials who had collaborated with Jones.   Why had they not consulted the Employers' Association before acting? Didn't they understand that sending highly paid men from nice clean factories to work in disgusting conditions alongside low-paid foundry labourers would be bound to stir up discontent over wages and conditions in the foundry? Insisting that the TUDPC, despite the TUC-headed notepaper that Jones had been careful to secure, was an 'illegal and irregular body', the employers' official 'pointed out ... that apparently the trade unions had pulled the wool over [their] eyes and were using the Ministry as a stalking horse for political kudos'. He concluded his lecture with a warning:

> He apparently did not appreciate the foolishness of what he had done, and I told him quite definitely that as far as I was concerned, having been here for 22 years, I knew the entirety of the working man better than he did, and that if he persisted in his attitude of leaving the Employers high and dry and simply negotiating with the labour representatives, he was going to get himself into serious difficulties.[20]

That this was not an idle threat is suggested by the fact that, nine months earlier, the Ministry of Labour's Welfare Officer in Coventry had been forced to resign, apparently for being too friendly with the unions.[21]

Despite the employers' intervention, Jones attempted to keep the idea alive, urging JPC members that the scheme would 'prove a flop and a set back' unless 'more effort is put into this campaign inside the factories.'[22]   As these remarks suggest, however, initial enthusiasm for the scheme had not been matched by the number of workers volunteering, and even those who had volunteered at the outset appear to have quickly changed their minds.[23] The employers could draw reassurance from this indication that ordinary workers were rather less inspired by visions of taking responsibility for production than their productivist leaders hoped.

The speed and vigour with which the TUDPC established its presence in Coventry was unusual, but over the winter of 1942–43 committees were set up in most engineering centres and the best of these committees played a major role in encouraging and supporting JPCs in individual factories.[24] The TUC published a short guide to the new machinery, showing how it created 'a production chain linking the men at the benches with the men in the War Cabinet', and it urged JPCs to make use of the hard-won right to refer matters to the Regional Boards.[25] As management explained their difficulties to the new JPCs, trade union activists increasingly recognised the role of factors beyond the control of the individual firm in causing production hold-ups.[26] The JPC at the General Aircraft factory in Feltham agreed to set up a special sub-committee responsible for taking all questions of delay in the supply of materials to the Regional Board with, it was reported, 'excellent results'.[27] This was, however, highly exceptional. Between January 1943 and the end of the war the total number of joint references (references agreed by both sides of a JPC) to all the Regional Boards was only 158.[28] The Northern Board received only eight references, five of them from two firms.[29] The East and West Ridings Regional Board commented that 'the matters referred ... by JPCs have been few in number and very trifling in character.'[30] One-sided references were even less frequent: by August 1943 the Boards had investigated only 45 cases brought directly to them by TUDPCs.[31] Although they had been forced to accept the possibility of direct union access to the Boards in 1942, the procedures involved were complex and time-consuming, and it was not difficult for the employers to frustrate union access in practice.[32] By claiming, however unreasonably, that any issue that the unions wished to refer to the Board lay outside the terms of the March 1942 agreement, employers were able to argue that the dispute concerned the interpretation of the agreement rather than substantive production issues and should therefore be handled not by the Board but through established collective bargaining procedures.[33] Both in Lancashire and the West Midlands employer representatives used this argument successfully to block TUDPC attempts to take issues to the Boards.[34] At the same time the employers were adamant in resisting pressure from the TUDPCs to negotiate directly on production issues with the local Employers' Associations or individual firms.[35] In March 1943 Citrine tentatively raised the question, writing to the EEF's Director: 'Don't you think we might at least say "how do you do" to one another at the district level so far as production matters are concerned.' He did not.[36] Despite renewed pressure from the engineering unions later in the war, the local Associations remained united in resisting a move which 'obviously aims at a share in the management and has much greater significance than mere recognition of JPCs.'[37]

In the absence of either employer recognition or effective access to the Regional Boards, many TUDCPs remained mere paper organisations meeting rarely and never convening conferences of local JPC members. Overworked full-time officials found it hard to make time for this new machinery, and shop floor activists were unwilling to devote their energies to an apparently powerless piece of union machinery.[38] Despite the procedures established in 1942 with the express intention of channelling production grievances through the Regional Boards, it was often easier to get things done by a direct approach to Whitehall. Thus trade unionists in Glasgow still found they could get more done about long-standing production grievances through an approach to the ex-shop steward MP, David Kirkwood, than through an official enquiry by the Board. Following this incident, Churchill had told Parliament that MPs could not be allowed to circumvent established procedures to get a hearing for unofficial delegations. But this was a difficult line to hold in practice.[39] In a number of cases trade unionists were able to secure Whitehall intervention over the heads of the Regional Boards to deal with recalcitrant problems in individual firms. In the autumn of 1942, for example, Whitehall responded to protests from the Armstrong Whitworth shop stewards in Coventry over material shortages and transfers of labour by dispatching high-level officials to meet jointly with union officials, shop stewards, the JPC and management to sort things out.[40] At Firth Brown (Doncaster) an official enquiry into shop steward allegations led to the appointment of a new Works Manager.[41] More dramatically, at the Fairey Aviation factory in Hayes long-standing complaints by the JPC about managerial incompetence were resolved when, in December 1942, Cripps went to the factory in person and replaced the existing managing director with his own appointee.[42] A few weeks later the chairman of Short Brothers in Rochester was replaced by a MAP appointee, and the firm, whose production record was extremely poor, was subsequently nationalised. In the Shorts case the Regional Board was not consulted at any stage.[43] Some militants were excited by the prospect of calling in the state to 'sack the management', but in practice the Government's emergency powers were used very sparingly.[44] Moreover the possibility of *ad hoc* crisis intervention of this type was no substitute for the day-to-day integration into planning procedures which the unions had hoped could be realised through the link between the JPCs and the Regional Boards.[45]

It was difficult to sustain interest in the Boards when they manifestly lacked the power to put things right, even if they could be persuaded to act on workers' complaints. The Ministry of Production made repeated efforts to persuade supply ministries to devolve more authority to their Regional Controllers.[46] Faced with widespread unrest over programme changes in 1943, the Ministry did succeed in establishing that JPCs could be given advanced warning about programme changes in their factory.[47] This top-down information flow was, however, no substitute for an effective system of communication in the other direction. When the run-down of war production from the summer of 1944 began to threaten large-scale redundancies, many JPCs and shop stewards' committees put forward proposals for the conversion of their factories to peace time production.[48] At Shorts, a sustained campaign by the JPC to keep the Rochester factory in business making flying boats after the war secured a pledge to this effect from Stafford Cripps: though in this case the JPC was careful to take its arguments against the idea that flying boats had had their day – a ridiculous and dangerous prejudice' – to the Regional Board as well.[49]   But, in general, the Regional Boards played little role in these initiatives; indeed the number of JPC references to Regional Boards declined substantially during 1944–45 from their already low levels.[50]   When, in February 1945, shop stewards in Coventry sought a hearing for their plans to convert the Shadow Factories to peacetime production, they turned not to the Regional Board but to Whitehall.   Just as they had done at the height of the production crisis three years earlier, the shop stewards dispatched a delegation to 'make a shindy' in the corridors of power.   Anxious notes passed up the bureaucratic hierarchy while angry shop stewards waited in the street.   The success of the 23 Coventry delegates in gaining access to six different ministries – resulting in a *Daily Worker* report exposing apparently contradictory responses from different departments – forced Whitehall to re-assess its gatekeeping procedures.   The Midlands Regional Board protested that 'it was useless to expect effective central control of workers organised by the TUC if official departments responded to approaches by irresponsible elements among workers.'[51]   Spurred on by Bevin, new instructions were issued to departments to be extremely careful not to give shop steward deputations any basis for claiming that their complaints had even been noted: nothing should be written down during the interview.   Instead they were merely to be informed of the proper procedure for raising their problems with the Regional Board.   At the same time the Boards were urged to make renewed effort to allay worker fears about redundancy.[52]

Without greater powers, however, there was little the Boards could do.   The AEU continued to press for a much more radical decentralisation of authority to the Boards, pointing out rather bitterly in 1944 that workers had quickly learned that there was not much point in taking issues to the Regional Boards as long as the Boards themselves continued to lack the executive authority to impose solutions.[53]   In the face of the blocking tactics of employers and supply ministries, the hopes of 1942 that the JPCs would operate as the lowest tier of the machinery of planning, integrating workers into the planning process, were largely disappointed. Consequently, the capacity of the JPCs to develop as instruments of worker participation at shop floor level was gravely restricted.

Challenges to the EEF's determination to restrict JPCs to a purely domestic role within the factory were not restricted to these frustrated attempts to activate the official machinery of TUDPCs and Regional Boards. At the same time activists sought to construct direct links between production committees in related factories. The SSNC encouraged JPCs to contact their equivalents in sub-contracting firms.[54] Members of the JPC at the Baginton AWA factory in Coventry floated the idea that they should be empowered to approach workers in any smaller firms which 'were felt to be in need of advice', because they were falling down on sub-contracted work.[55] Such suggestions were not always frowned upon by management: the JPC at the Fairey Aviation factory in Hayes (where the management had been replaced by Cripps after worker complaints) appointed a sub-committee responsible for chasing up sub-contractors.[56] In February 1942, a manager at Cossors, a Communist stronghold in North London, wrote to one of his suppliers in Liverpool supporting the request by the workers' secretary of the JPC to be put in touch with his counterpart in Liverpool. Such personal contact, he urged, would do more than the normal 'hackneyed priority and urgency phrases' to persuade workers to keep up their production effort.[57] A few months later John Hassal, the secretary of the Liverpool employers, was expressing alarm about the 'pure thoughtlessness' of those who encouraged reciprocal visits between JPCs from different firms. The JPCs, he wrote, 'have very dangerous possibilities ... there is no doubt but that the shop stewards' movement has no misconception about the possible uses to which they may be put. There is quite enough trouble being made in factories by shop stewards and other wolves in sheep's clothing, without taking them to other people's factories to get new ideas.'[58] Low thought he was exaggerating the prevalence of this practice, but nevertheless agreed to issue a national circular warning member firms about the danger of encouraging such visits.[59]

Hassal was, of course, right. Shop stewards were indeed under no misapprehension about the way in which links between JPCs could be used to build up their influence. One possibility was to use them to provide the basis for combine committees enabling shop stewards to negotiate with major firms at national level. Early in 1943, for example, JPCs at the Coventry and Lancaster plants of Armstrong Siddeley pressed for the establishment of a single JPC covering all the group's factories in the UK, and involving the firm's Directors. When the firm wrote to the EEF asking if there was any precedent for such an arrangement, Low urged them to reject the approach in the name of upholding the strictly domestic character of the JPCs.[60] When workers at firms in the London Aircraft Production group asked Cripps to help them secure recognition for a combined JPC, he replied that this was outside the terms of the March 1942 agreement.[61] In 1944 the SSNC was urging the establishment of firm-wide JPCs as essential to negotiating the process of conversion from war to peace production.[62] In Fairey Aviation and in the Vickers group, where combine committees were successfully formed – though not recognised by management – JPC issues were discussed alongside trade union questions.[63]

There were also attempts to establish structures linking firms working on the same product, whether or not they were directly supplying each other. Thus shop stewards at Harris Lebus, a (Communist-controlled) woodworking factory in East London employed on aircraft work, proposed the establishment of:

> a central Control of factories engaged on the same type of aircraft. Such Control to comprise representatives of the workers and management sides of JPCs, and of the Ministry of Aircraft Production. Its functions to include the Pooling of Ideas, the regulation of Material supplies, interchangeability of Labour, and other matters designed to promote the smooth running of production.[64]

The most sustained attempt to co-ordinate JPCs amongst factories working on the same product concerned the Lancaster bomber programme which involved at its peak up to one-third of Britain's industrial war effort.[65] In February 1943 the Coventry TUDPC asked the engineering unions to call a conference of JPC representatives in order to discuss transfer of labour within the group and 'the great disparity in methods of production, grading and rates at the various factories concerned'. Wages and conditions were clearly uppermost in their minds, but to make it easier for the national unions to respond positively they added that the conference would also be an opportunity to exchange information about methods of production. The national officials were reluctant to foster the kind of co-ordinated shop steward intervention in collective bargaining which the Coventry men had in mind, but they did agree to support a conference of the Lancaster JPCs if it could be shown that 'there was a substantial difficulty (apart from the question of rates of pay) in the production of this aeroplane'.[66]

Meanwhile JPC members in the leading firms were taking their own initiatives. In April delegates from Armstrong Whitworth in Coventry and Metro-Vickers in Manchester met to discuss the establishment of a Lancaster Group Council. There was little they could do without involving JPCs from the various plants of A.V. Roe, the Lancaster bomber parent company, and they decided to keep a low profile until this had been achieved. The next meeting, which did involve representatives from A.V. Roe, called on Cripps to convene monthly conferences involving both sides of the JPCs at which ideas about increasing production could be pooled. While JPC enthusiasts looked on this initiative as a promising new departure, the EEF was alarmed, viewing any such moves as 'the beginning of quite a dangerous deviation from the agreed functioning of works JPCs'. The Metro-Vickers management told the EEF that since the men were meeting in their own time there was nothing they could do, though they had stopped the works convener using the firm's headed notepaper to summon Lancaster Group Council meetings. Despite this, the impression formed by JPC representatives both at Metro-Vickers and AWA was that the management was not entirely hostile to their initiative and they in turn were careful to assure management 'that this group had no political backing and the only reason it was formed was in the interests of Lancaster production.'[67]

The A.V. Roe management, however, was made of sterner stuff. They already had experience of negotiating with a joint committee of shop stewards from their various plants in the Manchester area, an experience which led them to withdraw recognition from the joint committee in 1940.[68] Now they were determined not to allow the JPC initiative to draw them into negotiations which were bound, whatever their explicit objectives, to encourage leap-frogging wage claims amongst the different Lancaster plants, and they pressured their JPC members not to participate in the co-ordinating meetings. In this they appear to have had some success. At a meeting of Manchester factories engaged on Lancaster contracts in June 1943 the A.V. Roe delegates explained that 'we were elected to be Production Committee men in our own factory... and Avroes could not be represented at these meetings.' Shortly after this the A.V. Roe management provoked a major strike by unilaterally cutting piecework prices. This was seen by both employers and unions as a test case for the whole Lancaster programme, and the strike was prevented from spreading throughout the Manchester district only when, in August, the AEU Executive and the Ministry of Labour intervened to force the management to reverse the cuts.[69] But if A.V. Roe failed to control piecework earning, the shop stewards were unsuccessful in their campaign for a Lancaster Group Council. In July 1943 the engineering unions had finally agreed to support the Council, calling on Cripps to force the companies concerned to co-operate by calling a conference of the relevant JPCs. They did not press the case, and Cripps declined to act.[70] For a time the leaders of the Lancaster Council continued to seek official recognition, but, rebuffed by management and by MAP, and harried by the AEU Executive which opposed the establishment of combine committees outside normal collective bargaining procedures, the initiative seems to have faded away by the end of 1943.[71]

Denied effective integration of the JPCs with the state planning apparatus, the militants had little success in their efforts to build links between them on a purely trade union basis. Whatever potential the JPCs had for promoting worker participation and a measure of industrial democracy, therefore, would have to be fought out largely within the confines of individual factories. Here, however, the obstacles to a genuine process of democratisation were formidable.

NOTES

1. AEU, *Third Report on Production*, 1942, p. 9.
2. P. Inman, *Labour in the Munitions Industries*, 1957, p. 386; 'Making a success of the Joint Production Committee', *Business*, February 1943, p. 15. The section of Inman's history dealing with JPCs was drafted by J.B. Jefferys, an ex-LSE student whose postgraduate thesis provided the starting point for his official history of the AEU *(The Story of the Engineers*, London, 1945). During the war Jefferys had himself served as a JPC secretary while working at the Dunlop Wheel and Rim factory in Coventry. (J.B. Jefferys, *Trade Unions in a Labour Britain*, Fabian Society Pamphlet, 1947, p. 13.) He also helped PEP to prepare its account of the JPC experience.
3. Mark Benney, *Over to Bombers*, 1943, p. 178.
4. C. Riegelman, *British Joint Production Machinery*, Montreal, 1944, p. 88.
5. Riegelman was given considerable help by the unions, but cold shouldered by the EEF. Interview with Y. Kapp, June 1992; correspondence between Riegelman, Rollins and Low, 4, 5 August, 12, 20 October 1943, EEF 237/3/1/313 (W4, 108, File 6).
6. *Labour Research*, August 1941, p. 116, November 1941, pp. 215–16; Engineering and Allied Trades Shop Stewards' National Council, *Arms and the Men*, p. 6.
7. *Labour Research*, January 1942, pp. 7–8; Untitled typescript, notes on how to set up JPCs, n.d. (February 1942?), Len Powell Papers; R.P. Dutt, *Britain in the World Front*, 1942, p. 136; Len Powell, 'For a Real Ministry of Production', *Labour Monthly*, April 1942; *New Propeller*, April, June 1942.
8. AEU, Proceedings of Twenty-fourth National Committee, *Report*, June 1942, pp. 354–5.
9. A. Flanders, *The Battle for Production*, London, 1941; 'Production Clearing Centres', *Planning*, 191, 28 July 1942; G.D.H. Cole, 'Production Committees', *New Statesman*, 3 October 1942; Cole, 'Opinion in the Making', *New Statesman*, 15 August 1942; J.T. Murphy, *Victory Production*, London, 1942, pp. 113–14.
10. Committee on Regional Boards (Citrine Committee), *Report*, Cmd. 6360, 1942, paragraph 47; Kipping to Ramsay, 8 August 1943, Ramsay to Kipping, 28 August 1942, TUC 292/106.1/6.
11. Kipping, *Memorandum*, 29 August 1942, BT 168/20; Harries to Citrine, 24 August 1942, TUC 292/106.45; RO Circular 1/13, 30 September 1942, AVIA 15/2539; Eaton Griffith to Burns, 8 September 1942, BT 26/372.
12. NPAC, *Minutes*, 15 September 1942; *Minutes* of interdepartmental meeting, 2 September 1942; correspondence between Harries and Kipping, 19, 25, 26 June 1942, Harries to Siddall, 27 November 1942, TUC 292/106.412/5; Harries to Citrine, 24 August 1942, TUC 292/106.44/3; EEF Management Board, *Minutes*, 27 August 1942, EEF 237/1/1/39.
13. Low to Varley, 1 September 1942, EEF 237/3/1/312.
14. NACE&SI, *Minutes*, 25 June 1942 in TUC 292/106.451/2; AEU Coventry District Committee, *Minutes*, 28 April, 5 May, 2 June 1942.
15. *Midland Daily Telegraph*, 12 December 1941.
16. *Coventry Evening Telegraph*, 16 June 1942; Low to Varley, 19 June 1942, EEF 237/3/1/312.
17. Varley to Low, 1 July 1942, 7 August 1942, EEF 237/3/1/312; Low to Forbes 3, 14 July 1942, EEF 237/3/1/313; NACE&SI, *Minutes*, 14 July 1942, TUC 292/106.451/2; EEF Circular 170, 17 July 1942, LAB 10/213.
18. Varley to Low, 9 October 1942, correspondence between Evans and Low, 20, 23 November 1942, EEF 237/3/1/312; Scholes, 'Foundry Labour', 9, 10 October 1942, CEEA, 66/1/2/1.

19. AEU, Proceedings of Twenty-third National Committee, *Report*, 16–23 June 1941, pp. 101–2, 105; Argonaut, *Give Us the Tools*, 1942, p. 124; Jack Owen, *War in the Workshops*, 1942, p. 57.

20. Scholes, 'Foundry Labour', *loc. cit.*

21. In February the Coventry unions thanked a local Ministry of Labour official, who had been forced to resign, for 'his splendid work ... particularly his help to the trade unions': Confederation of Engineering and Shipbuilding Unions, Coventry District Committee, *Minutes*, 1 February 1942, TGWU 126/JJ/CS/1. Jones' ingenuity in using his friendly relations with local Ministry of Labour officials to promote trade union influence is discussed in S. Tolliday and J. Zeitlin (eds), *Shop Floor Bargaining and the State. Historical and Comparative Perspectives*, 1985, pp. 111–13. See also Jones' own testimony, J. Jones, *Union Man*, 1986, pp. 91, 92, 95, 114.

22. *Circular* from J. Jones to workers' side of JPCs, 12 October 1942, EEF 237/3/1/312.

23. Scholes, 'Foundry Labour', 10 October 1942, *loc. cit.*

24. *Labour Research* reported in February 1943 that 50 TUDPCs had been established; a further 20 had been set up by June 1943 ('Functions of TUDPCs', 28 June 1943, in TUC 292/106.44/1.) For an enthusiastic summary of the activities of the Manchester TUDPC during the war see Walker to Citrine, 4 June 1946, TUC 292/106.44/1.

25. TUC, Joint Production Committees: *Quiz*, February 1943; Harries to various shop stewards' committees, September 1943, in TUC 292/106.63/7; Harries to Siddall, 27 November 1942, TUC 292/106.412/5.

26. AEU, *Third Report on Production*, 1942, pp. 23, 31.

27. *Business*, February 1943, p. 17.

28. NACE&SI, *Minutes*, 6 August 1943, TUC 292/106.451/2.

29. NPAC, *Papers, passim*, TUC 292/106.1/8.

30. Northern Board, 21 June 1945; *Report* from East and West Ridings Board, 20 July 1945, BT 168/170.

31. 'Relationship of JPCs to Government Bodies', 1 August 1944, BT 168/169.

32. RO Circular 1/13, AVIA 15/2539; one irritated Glasgow employer remarked: 'if we get any more such language medleys ... we shall have to add a permanent resident lawyer to our staff to interpret the hidden meanings behind all the verbosity'. Miller to Low, 13 October 1942, EEF 237/1/1/312.

33. For example, at Standard Telephone And Cables in North Woolwich workers' attempts to refer a whole range of issues to the Regional Board were successfully resisted on these grounds, see AEU, *Third Report on Production*, 1942, p. 65 (case 758), and correspondence between Wright, Grindley, Margerum and Sargeant in October–December 1942, BT 168/169. For a very similar case at Ferranti in Manchester, where the management's interpretation of the March 1942 agreement was clearly perverse, see correspondence in April 1944, BT 168/169.

34. Belson to Pankhurst, 9 January 1946, BT 168/26; Mather to Kipping, 1 April 1944, BT 168/169.

35. EEF Circular, 1 March 1943, EEF briefing for negotiators, 21 February 1943 EEF 237/3/1/312. Many local associations asked the EEF for advice on how to handle approaches from the TUDPCs.

36. Citrine to Ramsay, 9 March 1943, Ramsay to Citrine, 13 April 1943, E. Harries, *Memorandum*, 4 June 1943, TUC 292/106.44/1.

37. York Conference, *Minutes*, 8 March 1944, EEF 237/1/13/70; EEF Management Board, *Minutes*, 31 August 1944, EEF 237/1/1/41; 'Summary of Local Associations' responses to Circular 194', 8/11/43, EEF 237/3/1/313 (File 6).

38. Thus Jack Jones, ingenious though he was, found it hard to find ways of using his position on the Midlands Regional Board to enhance the influence of the JPCs. Early in 1943 he was calling, rather desperately, on Coventry trade unionists to refer more

JPC issues to the Board 'which would either prove the benefit or the ineffectiveness of the organisation.' Coventry District Committee, Confederation of Engineering and Shipbuilding Unions, *Minutes*, 14 February 1943, TGWU 126/JJ/CS/1. See also Engineering and Shipbuilding Shop Stewards' Committee for Scotland, *Shop Stewards' Next Step*, n.d. (1944?), p. 14. The shop stewards' movement called for full-time officials to be seconded to run the JPCs (E&ATSSNC, n.d. (1945?), *Shop Stewards and the Future*, p. 9), but this was hardly feasible at a time when full-time officials were already desperately overloaded.

39. NPAC, *Minutes*, 5 February 1943, TUC 292/106.1/6; Bevin, 'Representations with regard to changes in production programmes and reallocation of labour', 22 March 1945, in BT 168/102; Stokes to Calder, 11 February 1946, in *idem*.

40. Coventry District Committee, Confederation of Engineering and Shipbuilding Unions, *Minutes*, 1 September 1942, TGWU 126/JJ/CS/1; Jack Jones, *op. cit.*, p. 110.

41. Industrial Panel Factory Investigations, 9 March 1943, BT 28/420.

42. *Labour Research*, February 1943, p. 23.

43. BT 28/426/IC/114/25 & 26; BT 28/1191/MISC/135; meeting of employer representatives on NPAC, *Minutes*, 2 April 1943, in FBI 200/F/1/1/145.

44. *Labour Research*, September 1941, p. 131; E&ATSSNC, n.d. (1945?), *Shop Stewards and the Future*, p. 8; W. Hannington, *The Rights of Engineers*, London, 1944, p. 96; S. Cripps, in Aircraft Conference, September 1943, *Report*, p. 18 in TUC 292/106.63/7. The unions were far from satisfied with the record of the Industrial Panel set up in April 1942 to investigate complaints about production: TUC, *Report*, 1942, p. 124; NACE&SI *Minutes*, 8 January 1943 TUC 292/106.451/2.

45. A point acknowledged by the Communist convener at Vickers' Openshaw factory when he admitted to fellow activists it had been a mistake to try to sort out a production problem in the factory by sending a deputation to the Minister of Production, rather than by using the channels provided by the TUDPC. Metro-Vickers Conference, *Minutes*, 21 November 1943, in Len Powell Papers; *Factory News* (Vickers Armstrong, Openshaw), November 1942. More generally, however, the shop stewards' movement encouraged militants to use all available channels, without excessive regard for 'due process': E&ATSSNC, *JPCs – How to Get the Best Results*, 1942, p. 15.

46. J.D. Scott and R. Hughes, *The Administration of British War Production*, London, 1955, p. 487; Lyttelton to Minister of Production's Council, 5 February 1943, BT 168/239.

47. 'Origins of JPCs', n.d. BT 171/210; 'Benefits from JPCs, Views of Regional Controllers', 1 August 1944, BT 168/169.

48. JPCs in several aircraft firms were already asking for manpower to be released to prepare for post-war production in September 1943 (TUC 292/106.63/7) and the Vickers Group combine committee was discussing conversion from armaments production to agricultural machinery in November 1943. (Metro-Vickers Conference, *Minutes*, 21 November 1943, in Len Powell Papers.)

49. Medway Towns District Full Employment Committee, *Minutes*, 20 February 1945, p. 3; Fred Crisp, report on Shorts, n.d. (1945?), in Michaelson Papers 233/3/3/5; E&ATSSNC, n.d. (1945?), *Shop Stewards and the Future*, p. 11.

50. NPAC, *Papers, passim*, TUC 292/106.1/8.

51. Brazendale to Pankhurst, 13 February 1945, BT 168/102; *Coventry Evening Telegraph*, 9 February 1945.

52. Deputations and Representations: Procedure for Dealing With, BT 168/102, *passim*; RO Circular 18/4, February 1945 in BT 168/239.

53. TUC, *Report*, 1943, pp. 205–6; *Memorandum*, on AEU's Southport Resolution, 11 November 1944, TUC 292/106/2; AEU National Committee, *Report*, 1943, p. 233.
54. Jack Owen, *War in the Workshops*, 1942, p. 57.
55. Giffiths to TUC, 17 September 1943. See also the Slough firm where the same thing was being proposed on the JPC in 1942: AEU, *Third Report on Production*, 1942, p. 30.
56. Fairey Aviation combine, *Minutes*, 16 May 1943, in Frow Papers, Working Class Movement Library.
57. Cossors to Wingrove and Rogers, 16 February 1942; White to Wingrove and Rogers, 21 January 1942; Marshall to Latter, 18 February 1942, Hassal to Low, 11 February 1942, EEF 237/3/1/312.
58. Hassal to Low, 12 June 1942, *ibid*.
59. Low to Hassal, 16 June 1942. Pye's of Cambridge was similarly 'thoughtless' in encouraging links between its own JPC and those of its sub-contractors: E. Wight to Telegraph Condensor Co, 17 July 1942, *ibid*.
60. *Correspondence* between Low and Preston EEA, 29 January, 2 February 1943, *ibid*. Significantly, Low did not reply that there was indeed a precedent – ICI's long-standing system of joint consultation.
61. Cripps to JPC at Express Motor and Body Works, 11 October 1943, TUC 292/106.63/7.
62. E&ATSSNC, *Shop Stewards and the Future*, n.d. (1945?).
63. Fairey Aviation combine, *Minutes*, 16 May 1943, in Frow Papers, Working Class Movement Library; Engineering and Shipbuilding Shop Stewards' Committee for Scotland, *Shop Stewards' Next Step*, n.d. (1944?), p. 14; E. and R. Frow, *Engineering Struggles. Episodes in the story of the shop stewards' movement*, Manchester, 1982, p. 420; Metro-Vickers Conference, *Minutes*, 21 November 1943, in Len Powell Papers. According to this last document, Vickers' management behaved obstructively to production committees in most of its plants.
64. Secretary of Harris Lebus shop stewards' committee to TUC, 16 September 1943, TUC 292/106.63/7.
65. D. Jay, *Change and Fortune. A Political Record*, 1980, p. 104.
66. NACE&SI, *Minutes*, 5 February, 5 March 1943 in TUC 292/106.451/2. Stokes to Harries, 4 March 1943, TUC 292//106.1/7.
67. Lancaster Group Production and Advisory Committee, Workers' Side, *Minutes*, 30 June 1943, in EEF 237/3/1/313; Low to Greenlagh, 2 June 1943, Duncan to Bissett, 3 June 1943, in *ibid*; *Daily Worker*, 20 April 1943; *Manchester Evening News*, 31 May 1943; *Lancashire Daily Post*, 31 May 1943; *Daily Sketch*, 31 May 1943; C. Reigelman, *op. cit.*, pp. 162–3; Edwards to Mares, 10 June 1943, BT 171/210.
68. R. Croucher, *Engineers at War, 1939–1945*, 1982, p. 85.
69. Lancaster Group Production and Advisory Committee, Workers' Side, *Minutes*, 30 June 1943, EEF 237/3/1/313; North West Regional Industrial Relations Officer, *Reports*, 30 July, 6, 13 August 1943, LAB 10/380. Subsequently the A.V. Roe management turned down requests for a joint meeting with the Metro-Vickers JPC: Questions for the Minister of Aircraft Production, September 1943, TUC 292/106.63/7.
70. NACE&SI, *Minutes*, 2 July, 6 August 1943, TUC 292/106.451/2.
71. Dixon to TUC, 14 September 1943, TUC 292/106.63/7; Bromsgrove Trades Council to TUC, 6 October 1943, TUC 292/106.45; AEU Manchester District Committee, *Minutes*, 19 December 1943.

6 Frontiers of Control

The evidence of what actually went on in JPCs is fragmentary. In 1945 the TUC official responsible for JPC matters, E.P. Harries, confessed that 'bewilderment at the results of setting up joint production committees is universal, and it is impossible to get a clear picture as to their value.'[1] The EEF, vigorously defending the purely 'domestic' character of the JPCs, was extremely resistant to attempts to collect and survey JPC minutes.[2] Only one such survey was carried out by Whitehall, for the MAP late in 1942, and this was based on the minutes of only two JPC meetings at each of 63 firms.[3] Other surveys were carried out by the AEU during 1942, the journal *Business* in 1943, the Industrial Welfare Society in 1944, and, much less systematically, by a Ministry of Production query to Regional Boards in the summer of 1945.[4] The TUC collected a substantial file of shop steward complaints about the functioning of JPCs in the aircraft industry which it forwarded to Cripps in September 1943.[5] Taken together with incidental material in the archives, these surveys provide sufficient evidence for some tentative conclusions about the experience of the JPCs themselves.

By the spring of 1943 most employers had lost their fear that JPCs would undermine managerial authority and were more or less satisfied with the way in which they were functioning.[6] The simple act of setting up a JPC could produce a boost in shop floor morale, and therefore in production. Those who had argued that, by taking the workers into their confidence about production problems, managements would be able to dispel allegations of incompetence had reason to feel well satisfied. The AEU Report showed that where JPCs existed shop stewards were more likely to blame idle time on unevenness in the flow of contracts than on the incompetence of their own management.[7] Where managements had the self-confidence to explain their difficulties openly to their workers, and the patience to listen, without over-reacting, to accusations of inefficiency from the workers' representatives, they

found that a little *glasnost* went a long way in allaying criticism and
unrest.[8] The major contribution of the JPCs to war production lay,
not so much in initiating specific changes in production techniques,
but in creating a climate for greater trust and co-operation between
management and workers.[9]

It was the view of the Ministry of Production's Regional
Controllers that JPCs had frequently acted 'as a spur to
managements to be more efficient in decisions and actions which are
to be judged by those who are in a good position to estimate
results'.[10] A degree of accountability to workers who knew far more
than any Board of Directors about what actually went on at shop
floor level, is likely to have enhanced the efficiency of management.
Certainly there were instances in which senior management learnt
about the ineptitude of front-line supervisors, and some even had the
confidence to encourage such tale-telling.[11]   This created alarm
amongst lower management, and sustaining the authority of the
foreman in the face of this direct access of workers to senior
management became a major concern.[12] Other authority relations in
the firm might also be challenged by the functioning of JPCs. It was
sometimes asserted by trade unionists that the existence of the JPC
made 'progressive' individuals in senior management more likely to
take on reactionary ideas among their colleagues, or the restrictive
attitudes of the Directors.[13]   Some left-wing theorists took things
further. G.D.H. Cole, defining himself as 'an unrepentant Guild
Socialist', saw in the JPCs, however limited their powers might be at
first, 'the thin edge of the wedge of ... industrial democracy'. By
providing 'fraternal leadership' to the workers in meeting the
production needs of the wartime state, progressive managers could
begin to free themselves from their subordination to an irresponsible
and functionless plutocracy.[14] Austin Albu, one of the few Labour
Party intellectuals with management experience, argued that the
experience of slump and war had created a potential sympathy for
socialist ideas among industrial managers. He urged trade unions to
respond to industrial inefficiency not with indiscriminate attacks on
'management', but by using the JPCs constructively to convince
conscientious managers that they would have more freedom to do
their jobs effectively in conditions of industrial democracy than they

had as servants of private capital.[15] Such ideas, however, met little response even among the more enlightened sections of management opinion.

Management literature, influenced by the Hawthorne Experiments and the 'human relations' belief that the key task of effective management was to meet the worker's psychological need to find fulfilment as a member of a small face-to-face functional team, frequently invoked the dawn of a new era of 'democracy' and 'participation' in industry: 'a conception of "factory democracy" by which the workers would share with management responsibility for turning the group into a happy and co-operative unit with some zest for production'.[16] In such writing, however, 'democracy' did not imply power-sharing, or a readiness to open higher-level decision-making to trade union negotiation. Indeed most management writers appeared unaware that workers already had their own democratically-elected leaders – shop stewards, preferring to disregard the structural conflicts of interest between labour and capital, and to work with a unitary conception of the firm in which the leadership role of management was beyond question. 'For human relations,' concludes the leading historian of the British management movement, 'the term "democratic" indicated a leadership style that was quite simply a means for the imposition of managerial command upon those who were led.'[17] Lloyd Roberts, the architect of ICI's labour relations, who was brought in to implement Bevin's JPC policy at the Ministry of Labour, argued that joint consultation involved 'a revolutionary change ... a new outlook on the function and place of the ordinary worker in the undertaking'. But the 'revolution' was strictly designed to promote worker loyalty to the firm and the legitimacy of private enterprise in general.[18]

The focus of 'human relations' thinking was on small work groups and the front-line management techniques needed to give such groups a sense of participation in the work of the firm. JPCs represented a challenge to this approach, since they operated at plant level, involved the democratic election of worker representatives and gave trade unions a central place in the process. But employers, well aware of the dangers of allowing collective bargaining to extend from wages and conditions to issues of production and commercial policy, were insistent on the advisory (not negotiating) nature of the committees.   Even the most enthusiastic advocates of joint consultation among employers were clear that their function was to legitimate, not to limit, managerial authority.   Thus Stanley Walpole, who published an influential book promoting JPCs in 1944, and whose public advocacy of joint consultation during the production crisis two years earlier had earned him the active hostility of the EEF, never suggested that the Committees should have more than advisory status.[19]   In fact, Walpole's first attempt to establish joint consultation at his own North London factory in the autumn of 1941 had been intended to break the hold of a troublesome group of left-wing shop stewards, and ran into determined opposition over the question of allowing non-unionists to participate.[20] Walpole learned from this experience. In his book he explicitly warned against using JPCs as a back-stairs way of undermining trade unionism, and dismissed arguments in favour of the involvement of non-unionists on the grounds that if people cannot be bothered to organise, they do not deserve representation.[21] Nevertheless he continued to deny his own JPC access to detailed production figures, and rebuffed worker attempts to raise issues of commercial policy by insisting that decisions on what contracts to take were purely a matter for the Directors.[22]

George Dickson, whose campaigns to extend the authority of the Regional Boards have already been discussed, liked to describe his own factory, Winget Ltd of Rochester, as a 'Laboratory of Industrial Democracy'. But he opposed suggestions that JPCs should develop beyond purely consultative status to interfere with the executive authority of management.[23] Despite his later adhesion to the pro-Labour 1944 Association,   Dickson's ideas about industrial democracy owed more to human relations management thinking than to any socialist sources of inspiration.[24]   Industrial leaders, he believed, should not be subject to democratic election: rather they would 'emerge'.   At Winget, leading hands were selected by management from nominations made by their fellow workers, just as members of Regional Boards were selected by Government from the nominations of employers' organisations and trade unions. In both cases, appointment from above after consultation, not democratic election, was seen as the proper means of creating legitimate industrial leadership. Nor did Dickson ever discuss the means by which workers might be enabled to remove industrial leaders who had ceased to enjoy their confidence. This was industrial democracy tempered by a strong sense of the leading role of management expertise in creating the conditions for effective worker participation.[25] The only example of the effective extension of joint consultation into a system of joint decision-making was at Glacier Metals, but even here management was careful to protect both day-to-day and top-level decision-making from the reach of the joint committees.[26]

If there were limits to the democratic intentions of even the most progressive firms, the great majority of employers had no time at all for the slippery language of 'industrial democracy'. Even among the enlightened members of the Industrial Welfare Society, many more were 'lukewarm' or 'sceptical' than were 'enthusiastic' about the JPCs' experience.[27] Many JPCs existed only on paper and rarely met: others were confined to dealing with absenteeism and listening to management harangues on need for greater effort.[28] Members found it hard to develop the potential of JPCs when, as frequently occurred, the management side refused to place items of their own on the agenda, or to give adequate details of production plans and achievements.[29] Workers frequently complained that criticisms of management were brushed aside and suggestions for improving production rejected without adequate investigation or explanation: 'The manager makes a point of ridiculing any feasible idea for increase of production.'[30] 'My idea is the JPCs are a waste of time,' said one labour manager responsible for several factories: 'My hope is to get the workers to take the same view'.[31] That this kind of attitude was widespread is clear from the flood of detailed complaints sent in by shop stewards in the aircraft industry in preparation for the national conference organised by Cripps in September 1943.[32] The EEF, though forced to tolerate JPCs for the duration, had no intention of allowing them to become an established part of industrial relations, and they rebuffed trade union efforts to discuss the post-war continuation of the committees.[33] Whitehall's reticence about surveying the activities of the JPCs reflected, in part, their fear that any official enquiry would jeopardise wartime relationships by provoking the employers into an open statement of their post-war intentions.[34] There could be little doubt that, left to their own devices, employers would move fast after the war to get rid of what most of them saw, at best, as a time-wasting encumbrance.[35]

Despite these obstacles much constructive work was done by JPCs. Extracts from JPC minutes reproduced in the AEU Report reveal a mass of detailed discussion of organisational and technical issues.[36] According to the *Business* survey carried out in 1943, 70% of managements thought that their JPCs had made a positive contribution to increasing efficiency and production, citing specific improvements in internal transport, machine tool maintenance, simplification of drawings, stores control, and the design of punchers and conveyors.[37] Where both sides were ready to co-operate there was no problem in finding detailed constructive work for the committees to pursue. What was much more difficult, however, was to sustain rank-and-file interest in the process.

In so far as they were effective in letting off the accumulated steam of the 1941–42 production crisis, the Committees did more to restore managerial authority, than to pave the way for a renewed offensive from below. As criticism of managerial competence subsided, workers became less anxious to show their bosses how to run the factory. After an initial period of enthusiasm, during which, as one employer put it, the committees served as 'a very useful "safety valve" in letting some of the communistic people believe they were taking a part in things', interest tended to fall away and the JPC 'became just another Shop Stewards' Committee and ... very rarely raised anything ... except grumbles and grouses such as the Shop Stewards raise at their own Meetings'.[38] James Jefferys, who drafted the section of the official history dealing with JPCs, and had himself been involved as a Communist shop steward in a major struggle to establish a JPC in a Coventry engineering factory, put the point perceptively:

everyone loves a fight: when there were prospects of the workers' representatives condemning the management roundly, but not necessarily soundly, interest and support on the workers' side ran high. With the growth of co-operation and the absence of fireworks, interest sometimes declined and counter criticism arose that the representatives had 'sold out to the management.'[39]

Using the JPC 'to explain innovations and difficulties' was all very well, one manager remarked: 'but ... when a workers' representative agrees too often without adequate explanation, the workers eventually regard him with suspicion as a "management man".'[40]

Late-coming and absenteeism – questions discussed by more JPCs than any other single production issue – raised especially tricky questions for the worker representatives. At worst the JPCs functioned simply as disciplinary courts, and several AEU District Committees initially reacted to this danger by trying to prohibit the JPCs from having anything to do with absenteeism at all.[41] Eventually, however, there was agreement to devolve the treatment of individual cases to small sub-committees, with the power to refer persistent offenders to the National Service Officer for prosecution.[42] In most cases, no doubt, such disciplinary powers were exercised with discretion, though the JPC representatives at the Bristol Aircraft Company went rather over the top when they asked Cripps to put pressure on local doctors who they accused of 'distributing medical certificates concerning absenteeism of persons who are not genuinely sick'.[43] The reward for responsibility could be substantial – as in the case of the Morris Radiator plant in Oxford where the management agreed to facilitate the unionisation of the women workers so that the union would be in a position to combat their undisciplined attitude to time-keeping.[44] Moreover discussion of the causes of absenteeism frequently enabled worker representatives to convince management of the need to improve transport facilities and working conditions.[45] Nevertheless, by taking such a direct role in the enforcement of work discipline JPC members laid themselves open to attack as bosses' men.[46]

A major obstacle to the maintenance of rank-and-file interest in the work of the JPC was the failure of many members to report back effectively.[47] As the shop stewards at the Cossor plant in Chadderton put it: 'There are very few occasions where workers' representatives are unable to find a solution of their difficulties in consultation with managements. The weak link lies in the inability of the workers' representatives to lay the whole case as they have seen it, before the general mass of the workers.'[48]   The EEF, anxious that details of domestic affairs of individual factories recorded in JPC minutes should not reach the TUDPCs or, indeed, Whitehall officials, advised employers to resist pressure to post the minutes on factory notice boards.[49]   Considerations of military security also inhibited full disclosure of matters discussed in the Committees.[50] Eventually the EEF and the unions agreed that JPCs should post short agreed summaries rather than the full minutes. This did not satisfy JPC enthusiasts like those at Armstrong Vickers' Openshaw works who complained that management refusal to post reports of the 'really useful work ... being done through the co-operation of the management and men' meant that 'half the workers don't know what is taking place and are not encouraged to raise their ideas with their Production Committee representatives.'[51]

Only a quarter of the JPCs surveyed by the AEU in autumn 1942 reported back to shop or factory meetings.[52]   Where they could, managements refused to allow such meetings, aware of the use that could be made of these when conflict arose. In August 1942, for example, the manager of the Standard Telephone and Cable plant in East London sought permission from the EEF to publish 'some kind of minutes of the JPC' on the grounds that 'this seems to be the only way we can withstand pressure for mass meetings, which we are fighting to do for fear of trade union and political propaganda.'[53] Management resistance to the use of works' canteens for mass meetings to report back from the JPC was a continuing source of tension in many factories.[54]

Such obstacles tended to leave JPC representatives isolated from their members. In the summer of 1943 a shop-floor versifier at Armstrong Vickers' Openshaw plant characterised the productionists as a small minority surrounded by a 'careless and idle' multitude of 'low and slinking jackals':

Of courageous honest purpose, we've just a little band
Who defiance roar to slip shod work and against it make a stand.

Conscientiously rebutting such pessimism about the qualities of the average worker, and blaming shop floor cynicism on the uncooperative attitude of the management, the editor of the shop steward paper, Frank Allaun, nevertheless admitted that 'there are rats and jackals in every factory. We should remember that we are living in the last years of a decaying society.... If we are brought up as wage slaves how can we all be expected to think like free men?'[55] And six months later he wrote, defensively:

> I can think of several really first class engineers – charge hands, Production Committee members, tradesmen, who attempted to improve the running of our factory with both ability and enthusiasm. Most of them have given it up as a bad job. They say it's banging their heads against a stone wall.... All credit to those few who, even if they are called fools for their pains, carry on the fight for better production, come what may.[56]

Meanwhile cynicism and hostility to productionist attitudes continued to be expressed in the factory.[57] Creating free men out of wage slaves was, it seemed, a thankless task.

Given these difficulties it is not surprising that many workers quickly lost interest in the JPCs. 'After the first burst of enthusiasm', wrote one employer in 1945, 'it is hard to get nominations for representatives', and the trajectory of turnout in JPC elections revealed by another company may not have been untypical:[58]

June 1942	58%
December 1943	28%
January 1945	20%

By the spring of 1944 the Shop Stewards' National Council was talking of the need to 'revive' the 'authority and leadership' of the JPCs.[59] According to a shop steward active in Coventry in 1944 only 15 of the 44 JPCs in the city were still meeting regularly: 'the remainder have tended to fade out after an initial burst of enthusiasm'. In two of Coventry's largest factories, the same man reported, the shop stewards had come to look on the JPCs as 'Gaffers' Committees'.[60]

Despite the evidence, cited above, from both sides of industry that JPCs made a significant contribution to solving production problems, there were in reality severe limits to the capacity of workers' representatives to contribute on technical issues. The Ministry of Production concluded, at the end of the war, that the JPCs had 'not played the large part that was expected of them in producing suggestions that have been useful to production'. Indeed, the number of usable suggestions was 'extremely small'.[61] The same point emerges clearly from the survey undertaken by the Industrial Welfare Society. However keen skilled workers were to enhance production, their understanding of the overall organisation of the factory was necessarily restricted, and, while they were well placed to point up practical problems in the implementation of production decisions, only the technical staff had the skills necessary to devise solutions.[62] Austin Albu put the point more harshly, commenting on the campaign for JPCs in the early months of 1942:

> In many cases the shop steward is a communist-inspired semi-skilled man with political acumen but with little real production ability or power to organise his fellows for constructive tasks. The competition for the job is unfortunately not great. The new type of socially responsible leadership among managers and workers has still to be created.[63]

While Albu was wrong about the typical Communist shop steward being semi-skilled, he was probably right to question the capacity of the stewards, or JPC members, to second-guess management on technical issues.[64] During the post-war attempts to revive JPCs some commentators called on trade unions to institute specific training programmes for JPC members, a proposal that had been raised by some baffled activists during the war. On neither occasion did the unions show any interest in providing this service.[65]

Summing up the JPC experience at the end of the war one trade union official in the Midlands produced a list of deficiencies on the workers' side of the Committees which probably reflects the reality more accurately than did the AEU's enthusiastic talk of a membership ready to take responsibility for production. They were 'diffident in front of executives', ill-prepared to present their case, relying too much on hearsay, lacking necessary information, and had only a 'weak conception of factory organisation'. Fearing victimisation by management and/or unpopularity on the shop floor, most JPC representatives lacked 'the self-discipline necessary for leadership' and used their positions to look after the bread-and-butter interests of their members rather than to pursue ambitious goals of worker participation.[66]   Outside the largest and best-organised factories, where shop stewards were certainly more forceful, this probably gives a more accurate picture of the position than does the AEU's optimistic talk of a membership 'awakened to their responsibility for production'.

The AEU, well aware that the ability of its own members to participate effectively in management decisions would be much enhanced by access to the know-how of the technical workers, fully supported the demands of white-collar unions to be permitted to nominate staff and technical workers to stand for election to the JPCs.[67] Members of the Glasgow TUDPC argued for the admission of technical staff on the somewhat confrontational grounds that 'they would be able to take the management down and at the same time feed the Workers' representatives with information that could be used against the management'.[68] Most of the pressure came from the Association of Engineering and Shipbuilding Draughtsmen (AESD), which saw the JPCs as a way to open up channels of communication between the drawing office and the shop floor, and an opportunity to break down 'the "bowler-hatted" superior attitude' traditionally attributed to their members.[69] The AESD campaigned 'to cement from below what employers were trying to prevent from above', urging members to set up unofficial factory-level meetings with manual shop stewards to shadow the work of the JPC, and to press their own managements for the right of representation on the JPC.[70] The March 1942 agreement permitted co-optees to attend for particular items, and the AESD appears to have been successful in widening this loophole to gain permanent representation for draughtsmen on up to a fifth of JPCs.[71] But all attempts to persuade the EEF to amend the agreement to permit the 'election [of draughtsmen] to a dignified and equal place beside the other workers', came to nothing,[72] Because the election of staff and technicians to the JPC would have involved wider questions of recognition of white-collar unions, the AESD was left protesting impotently that: 'The policy of keeping "white-collar" and "dungareed" workers apart is being placed before that of beating Hitler.'[73]

Given the difficulties placed by employers in the way of developing a sustained dialogue over production issues, it is not surprising that many activists saw JPCs more as a way of advancing ordinary trade union questions than of achieving a breakthrough into participation in production decisions.   Thus F.E. Walker, the Manchester AEU District Secretary, giving an enthusiastic account of the wartime work of the local TUDPC, chose to stress not its involvement with production issues as such but the inspiration it had provided to activists battling to establish a trade union presence in 'badly organised firms with out-of-date plant and factories whose earnings are low because of inefficiency; small firms that are anti-Union and use the big stick against trade union activities; firms that will not co-operate with the Works Production Committee in any real spirit of co-operation.'[74] In Southall, where the AEU had been quick off the mark in organising a local production conference intended to 'prove that our members are not alone interested in wages but in the real defence of democracy', a similar shift occurred away from concern with production issues to the use of JPCs as a means of advancing ordinary trade union goals. In the early months of 1942 local activists had been keen to stress that the emergence of the JPCs 'necessitates greater responsibility on the part of our members', appointing a sub-committee composed of shop stewards from the leading factories to share experiences about the solution of production problems.[75]   In later years, however, the Southall District's JPC work became largely concerned with establishing a union foothold in the small anti-union firms along the Great West Road. In such firms the JPC was often the first body to acquire effective negotiating rights.[76]

Although wage questions were in theory strictly excluded from the competence of the JPCs, over 40% of the establishments represented in the AEU survey reported that guaranteed piece rates and output bonuses had contributed to increases in production. In many cases long-standing grievances over these issues had been raised 'at the very first Joint Production Committee meeting'. Where a favourable response was forthcoming 'the work of the Joint Production Committee has not only proved more effective on other issues, but has enjoyed the wholehearted support of the mass of the workers on

these other issues.'[77] 'It was due to our efforts,' insisted the
secretary of the JPC at Armstrong Vickers' Openshaw works, that
guarantees were extracted from the management not to cut piece
prices or place limits on bonus earnings: 'If a man by his own
ingenuity improves the method of production he will receive the
benefits thereof and the time will not be altered.'[78] Wage questions
overlapped with production issues in other ways. It has been
suggested that in Coventry, where employers periodically sought to
reduce their exceptionally high wage bills, managements tried to use
the JPCs to convince workers that some wage restraint would be
beneficial to production. If so, such tactics had little success.[79]
Indeed at Armstrong Siddeley Motors JPC members turned this
argument on its head, blaming bottlenecks on the firm's use of out-
of-town sub-contractors to undercut the wages of its own skilled
workers. In this situation, they asserted, it was 'a sheer waste of
time to discuss the rhythms of production.'[80] Most JPCs had at least
one or two shop stewards among their members, and the precise
division of labour between the JPC and the established machinery of
collective bargaining could be worked out flexibly according to local
conditions, although conflicts of course occurred.[81] The handling of
redundancy and labour transfer issues often involved an overlap of
authority between the JPC and the shop stewards' committee, a fact
recognised by Whitehall which adopted a flexible position on
whether Regional Boards should approach JPCs or shop stewards, or
both together, to explain planned changes in production
programmes.[82]

If even the activists lacked the skills and knowledge necessary to
intervene effectively in managerial decision making, the mass of
ordinary workers were unlikely to be fired by visions of
participation. Despite her enthusiasm for JPCs, Yvonne Kapp, the
author of the AEU report, was aware that 'to the less advanced
sections, the idea of participating in the actual organisation of
production is very new and not entirely welcome ... they tend to see
only the disadvantages of such a shift in responsibility and to view
with suspicion the JPC and all its works'. The key to arousing and
sustaining workers' commitment to the JPC, she argued, was to

combine production with welfare and other issues which affected the immediate material interests of the workforce:

> Where a very advanced body of workpeople, elected to a JPC, concentrated wholly upon the higher spheres and technicalities of production, losing sight, if it may so be phrased, of the lavatories in their enthusiasm to support the Eighth Army and offensive action everywhere, they tend to isolate themselves from all but their most faithful adherents.[83]

It was quite natural for JPCs to deal with welfare issues, since such things as canteens, sanitation, ventilation, transport and lighting often had direct implications for production.[84] Although the MAP survey of late 1942 showed that JPC agendas contained more than three times as many items dealing with technical and production matters, as they did with welfare issues, it seems likely that, however they started out, most JPCs came increasingly to concentrate on welfare issues.[85] Impressed by the degree of shop floor concern over health and welfare issues revealed by the production enquiries, Kapp initiated a follow-up enquiry into health and welfare issues. She received little encouragement from the union hierarchy, although there was an (unsuccessful) attempt by the Coventry TUDPC to establish health sub-committees of the JPCs on the same lines as the absenteeism committees.[86]

This slippage from production to welfare issues highlights a further weakness of the JPCs: women played very little part in them.[87] That this was not initially a matter of great concern to the AEU (which did not, in any case, admit women into its own ranks until 1943) is clear from the way in which Jack Tanner, negotiating the original JPC agreement in March 1942, explained to the employers why it was essential to have a skilled worker as joint secretary of the committee:

> A fellow, with the best intentions in the world – or a girl, may come along with a suggestion which she thinks is very fine. She brings it to one of the workers' representatives and he will tell her she is well up in the air, that it is a foolish suggestion which could not be considered. If you have got a Secretary on the management side, he may be a clerk or somebody who has no technical knowledge, and he may accept the suggestion, and when it comes before the full Committee there will be a burst of laughter, and he will look very ridiculous, whereas, when she went to the workers' Secretary he would

simply cut it out; he would sift or weed out all the impractical suggestions before they went before the Committee.[88]

The arrogance of the craftsmen gained plausibility to the extent that the JPCs were indeed dealing with technical issues which only skilled workers would have the knowledge to handle. As, however, JPCs came increasingly to focus on welfare obstacles to production, the marginalisation of the women became increasingly irrational. Because of the 'dual burden' of housework and wage labour that most women carried, welfare issues played a critical role in limiting the productivity of women.[89] According to the AEU enquiry, however, of the welfare issues discussed by the JPCs in the autumn of 1942 only 6% concerned matters specifically applying to women – despite the fact that these issues were 'generally recognised as one of the most vexed problems in industry today'. Well over half of the 48 JPCs for which the AEU had full membership lists had no women members at all.[90]

Denigrating women no doubt helped to sustain the confidence of the craftsmen, but it provided no solution to their own problems in getting to grips with the larger issues of management and production planning. The problem was not that some 'fellows' were no better than Jack Tanner's 'foolish girls', nor was it to be solved by empowering an elite of intelligent craftsmen at the expense of the workforce as a whole. The problem was that all the workers were, to a greater or lesser degree, trapped by the hallmarks of their subaltern status – lack of knowledge, lack of ambition, lack of confidence, and a tendency to react to the fact of their relative powerlessness by eschewing visions of responsible self-government in favour of a narrow defence of immediate economic interests. As the relentlessly realistic Midlands trade unionist quoted earlier put it: 'Sectarian in outlook. £.S.D. dominated thoughts and actions'.[91]

The poverty of desire induced by this subaltern status is nicely illustrated by a futuristic fantasy written by one of the fitters at the Armstrong Vickers' Openshaw works in 1944:

An Engineer's Dream

Along the broad white concrete ribbon of Ashton Old Road glide the streamlined Astro-buses, they pull up ... and disgorge their loads of overalled workers. There in front is a massive concrete and steel structure towering to the sky. The huge Neon Sign blazes forth the words:

State Factory No. 2706
Heavy Industry
North-West Region

There is no clocking in. As each worker passes through the gate a photo-electric eye takes an impression of his face and number stitched to his overalls. And so to the workshops. Beautifully clean flooring of a noiseless composition. Walls tastefully decorated in delicate pastel shades with friezes depicting workshop life.... All the machines have plastic gears and are enclosed in a soundproof casing.... At the corner of each bay is a collection of automatic machines fixed to the wall from which various articles can be obtained: morning, afternoon and evening papers, chocolates, cigarettes, and concentrated food tablets.... As time wears on 10 a.m. is approached and exactly on the minute, streamlined noiseless wagons appear through the various doors, drawn by lovely female attendants who serve out hot and cold snacks and liquid refreshments.

And so it goes on. The heading 'Glamour Girls Again' introduces the 2-hour dinner break during which 'a beautiful 4-course luncheon cooked by expert chefs is served by lovely, glamorous waitresses.' After which there is ample time for a swim and a rest on the indoor imitation beach, or a visit to one of the 'special little rooms, cosily furnished and extremely private' supplied for the use of 'courting couples'.

Apart from a workers' committee which fixes the extremely generous piece prices – 'there are no ratefixers' – there is no hint of democratic participation in this vision. Utopia, as imagined by Jack Myers, was a state of privileged passivity, serviced by endlessly willing – but noiseless! – females.[92] That Jack Myers was not entirely unrepresentative is suggested by the novelist Mark Benney's complaint about his fellow engineering workers: 'when any of these men tried to think seriously about the future, their imagination worked almost exclusively in terms of Wellsian fantasy. "Science", an impersonal, uncontrollable force, and not themselves, was the agent of change.'[93] There were mountains to move in the popular psyche before productionist participation could be made a reality. Given the vigorous resistance mounted by employers against even minor encroachments on their autocratic powers it should not be surprising that industrial democracy remained a dream of the few rather than a reality of every-day life in the war factories.

The JPC experience did not create a self-sustaining practice of worker participation in British industry capable of opening the way to popular empowerment in a planned economy. For those who had hoped that it would, the essential relationship was between workers and the state. They sought to create a framework within which workers would no longer abandon their citizenship at the factory gate, and the power and autonomy of the capitalist firm would be subordinated to the disciplines of the planned economy. Workers, it was hoped, would gain the confidence to demand greater participation through the discovery that they could, in the wartime conditions of planned economy, call in the state to redress the power of the bosses.

At first the militants' strategy seemed to be working. The employers were forced to retreat in the face of workers' pressure from below and state pressure from above. For reasons of their own various parts of the state apparatus and trade union bureaucracy put their weight behind the Left's demands. At the Ministry of Labour, Bevin used the threat of compulsion to force employers to come to terms with the JPC movement. Ministry of Production officials promoted JPC access to the Regional Boards as part of their strategy of outflanking the sectional power of the rival supply ministries. Similarly, Citrine's bureaucracy at the TUC promoted the TUDPCs as part of its own attempt to whittle away the sovereign independence of its constituent unions whose inability to co-operate did so much to create the space for unofficial movements.

By the summer of 1942 employer fears for the integrity of 'managerial functions' were matched by triumphalism among the militants: witness the shop stewards at one London factory who explained to their members that the candidates for election to the JPC 'have behind them a powerful organisation with influence extending through every Government Department to the Cabinet itself, whereby they can force their decisions on the Management for better production'.[94] Thereafter, however, the employers recovered their confidence, and for the remainder of the war they were generally successful in resisting any extension of the democratising implications of the JPCs. By effectively keeping the TUDPCs and the Regional Boards at arm's length from domestic joint consultation, the employers limited any capacity the JPC experiment might have had to initiate a genuine transformation of attitudes among workers. The point was well made by one commentator in 1944:

> Many of those who enthusiastically urged the setting up of JPCs were looking to Russia where regular hierarchies of committees play a definite part in national, local and industrial organisation, being at the same time an educative force and a check on inefficient management.... [In practice, however, while JPCs] can be channels for the exchange in either direction of information and opinion between management and rank and file ... they do not form an effective link in a chain of committees ranging from factory through regional committees to national committees.... On the whole ... too much was expected of the JPC, at any rate from the employees' side.[95]

It may be that, however closely JPCs had been integrated into the machinery of production administration, the mass of ordinary workers would have remained uninterested in participation. We do not know. What is clear is that, during the winter of 1941–42, the reformists were able, often in the teeth of employer resistance, to build at least the beginnings of a structure for shop floor participation in economic planning. This advance towards industrial democracy was possible only because, in the special conditions of war economy, industrial militants were able to find allies in powerful places. The limits of the advance were set, partly by the EEF's strenuous defence of managerial prerogative, and partly the reassertion of voluntarist values in the state's approach to industrial relations once the employers had been forced to accept JPCs as a means of restoring managerial legitimacy. What was not yet clear, in 1945, was whether the election of a majority Labour Government would open up the possibility of a more decisive shift towards industrial democracy than had been possible within the political context created by the Churchill Coalition.

NOTES

1. E.P. Harries, 'Joint Consultation. A Trade Union Point of View', *Industrial Welfare*, July-August 1945.
2. EEF Management Board, *Minutes*, 17 December 1942, 25 July 1943, EEF 237/1/1/40; Low to Varley, 18 December 1942, Low to Latter, 22 March 1945, EEF 237/3/1/312.
3. M.H. Locks, 'JPCs in the Aircraft Industry', 7 January 1943, AVIA 9/57.
4. AEU, *Third Report on Production*, 1942; C. Chisholm, 'Joint Production Councils' Business*, June and July 1943; the Industrial Welfare Society survey is summarised in *Trade Union Report*, Mass Observation, 'Industry' Topic Collection, n.d. (1946?); the results of the Ministry of Production enquiry are in BT 168/170.
5. TUC 292/106.73/1. 75 JPCs responded to the TUC invitation despite being given only one week in which to do so.
6. Summary of replies from local associations, April 1943, EEF 237/1/1/312. This survey, however, covered only 36 of the 50 local associations, and among those omitted was Coventry, where the employers may well have been less reconciled to the new machinery. C. Riegelman, *British Joint Production Machinery*, Montreal, 1944, pp. 99, 185; 'Making a success of the Joint Production Committee', *Business*, February 1943.
7. AEU, *Third Report on Production*, 1942, pp. 23, 31.
8. C. Riegelman, *British Joint Production Machinery*, Montreal, 1944, p. 186; 'Benefits from JPCs. Views of Regional Controllers', 1 August 1944, BT 168/169; *Statement* by the joint (employer) chairman of Southern Regional Board, 24 July 1945, BT 168/179; *Summary* of replies to Midland Regional Board circular re JPCs, 27 July 1945, p. 3, BT 168/170.
9. 'Benefits from JPCs. Views of Regional Controllers', 1 August 1944, BT 168/169; Industrial Welfare Society survey, *loc. cit.*, p. 113–4; AEU, *op. cit.*, p. 15.
10. 'Benefits from JPCs. Views of Regional Controllers', 1 August 1944, BT 168/169.
11. *Summary* of enquiry into JPCs in the Radio Industry (Philco), EEF 237/3/1/313 (W4/108/File 6); G.S. Walpole, *Management and Men*, 1944, pp. 35, 56, 98. See also *Joint Consultation in British Industry*, National Institute of Industrial Psychology, (sponsored by the Human Factors Panel of the Committee on Industrial Productivity), London, 1952, pp. 74–5.
12. C. Riegelman, *op. cit.*, pp. 187–8; P. Inman, *Labour in the Munitions Industries*, 1957, p. 385; R. Lloyd Roberts, 'Development of Joint Consultation in Factories', n.d. (January 1942?) LAB 10/213; AEU, *op. cit.*, pp. 72–74; C. Chisholm, 'Joint Production Councils', *Business*, June 1943; F. Zweig, *Productivity and Trade Unions*, Oxford, 1951, p. 239.
13. *Memorandum* on AEU Resolution to TUC 1943, 11 April 1944, TUC 292/106/2.
14. G.D.H. Cole, 'Plan for Living', in Fabian Society, *Plan for Britain*, Routledge, 1943, pp. 28–31.
15. A. Albu, *Management in Transition*, Fabian Society Research Series, 68, London, 1942, *passim*.
16. *Trade Union Report*, Mass Observation, 'Industry' Topic Collection, n.d. (1946?), p. 104; John Child, *British Management Thought. A Critical Analysis*, London, 1969, p. 126.
17. Child, *op. cit.*, p. 127. One of the few management thinkers to recognise that democratic leadership of the work-group required election and already existed in the form of the shop steward was himself an ex-shop steward. J.J. Gillespie, *Free Expression in Industry. A Social-Psychological Study of Work and Leisure*, London, 1948, pp. 56–7, 106, 108.
18. Lloyd Roberts, 'Development of Joint Consultation in Factories', n.d. (January 1942?), LAB 10/213. The historian of ICI shows clearly how Lloyd Roberts' ideas

about 'human relations in industry' were designed to uphold the authority of his employers: W.J. Reader, *ICI, A History*, Vol. II, 1975, pp. 64, 67–70, 301.

19. G.S. Walpole, *Management and Men. A Study of the Theory and Practice of Joint Consultation at all Levels*, 1944, *passim*. The EEF press officer put pressure on *Picture Post* to tone down an article on Walpole's JPC published during a delicate stage of the national negotiations in February 1942: Lewcock to Sheffield EEA, 27 February 1942, EEF 237/1/1/312 (Sheffield); Lewcock to Hassal, 2 March 1942, EEF 237/1/1/312 (Liverpool). Low to Rollins, 20 October 1943, EEF 237/3/1/313 (W4, 108, File 6).

20. Correspondence between Walpole and Low, 18, 19, 22, 24, 25 September 1941, EEF 237/3/1/264 (81); 'Masseley Joint Works Council', n.d. 'Masseley Matters!', 30 January 1942, various correspondence, TUC 292/106.45.

21. G.S. Walpole, *op. cit.*, pp. 42, 132–3.

22. *Idem*, pp. 69–70; E.P. Harries, JPC meeting at Masseley, *Report*, 13 April 1943, TUC 292/106.45.

23. Dickson to Mayhew, 6 October 1946, 1944 Association, Correspondence, Labour Party Archive; *Winget Life*, March 1939.

24. Although Dickson read widely he seems to have had no knowledge of socialist writing about industrial democracy. His gurus were Urwick and Karl Manheim: G. Dickson *Already Our Children Sneer*, 1941, pp. 92ff; Dickson to Young, 9 October 1940, BT 168/120.

25. G. Dickson, 'Evolution in Management', in J.R.M. Bramwell (ed.), *This Changing World*, 1944, pp. 105, 109; Dickson, *Already Our Children Sneer*, 1941, pp. 9–10. *Winget Life*, March 1942, Autumn 1947, Christmas 1947; G. Dickson, *Industrial Democracy*, Talk given to British Institute of Industrial Administration, Waldorf Hotel, 20 November 1946.

26. J. Kelly, *Is Scientific Management Possible?*, Faber, London, 1968, p. 54; Child, *op. cit.*, p. 149; A. Flanders and H.A. Clegg, *The System of Industrial Relations in Great Britain*, 1954, pp. 355–6; W. Brown, *Exploration in Management*, Heinemann, London, 1960; E. Jacques, *The Changing Culture of a Factory*, Tavistock, London, 1951; E. Jacques, *Employee Participation and Managerial Authority*, London, 1968.

27. Industrial Welfare Society survey, *loc. cit.*, p. 109.

28. AEU, *Third Report on Production*, 1942, pp. 41–2; Metro-Vickers Conference, 21 November 1943, *Minutes*, in Len Powell Papers.

29. *Idem*; AEU Report, *op. cit.*, pp. 33–4, 41–3; letters from shop stewards at A.V. Roe (Yeadon) and Standard Telephone and Cables (Leicester) to TUC, September 1943, TUC 292/106.63/7. But see defence of this reticence: 'It would be so easy for management to flood the agenda with technical details.' C. Chisholm, *op. cit.*, p. 26.

30. AEU Report, *op. cit.*, pp. 24, 33, 71; letters from shop stewards at Mullards Radio Valves and Cossor (Chadderton) to TUC, September 1943, TUC 292/106.63/7; E.P. Harries, 'Joint Consultation. A Trade Union Point of View', *Industrial Welfare*, July–August 1945.

31. C. Reaveley and J. Winnington, *Democracy and Industry*, London, 1947, p. 54.

32. TUC 292/106.73/1.

33. EEF Management Board, *Minutes*, 30 May 1945, EEF 237/1/1/41.

34. Pankhurst to Garro Jones, 1 August 1944, BT 168/169.

35. See, for example, the heartfelt plea of one Hampshire employer: 'I do not think it has ever been appreciated, the extraordinary amount of work which these JWPC Meetings have thrown on to Works' Managers and Executive – who have had probably the most difficult of all jobs to do throughout the War and I feel they are now entitled to call it a day so far as spending their evenings arguing with a lot of

Shop Stewards ... about things which do not improve production anyway!' (Howlett to Eyston, 25 July 1945, BT 168/170.)

36. AEU, *op. cit.*, pp. 53ff: 'In the full Minutes of many of the committees which we have examined it is found that entire meetings are devoted to the discussion of improvements to existing machine tools and their more productive use' (*idem*, pp. 52–3).

37. C. Chisholm, *op. cit.*, p. 27.

38. Howlett to Eyston, 25 July 1945, BT 168/170.

39. P. Inman, *op. cit.*, pp. 286–7; Coventry and District Engineering Employers' Association, *Works Conferences*, 25 May 1942, CEEA 66/1/2/1/113.

40. Industrial Welfare Society survey, *loc. cit.*, p. 110.

41. AEU, *op. cit.*, p. 52; Riegelman, *op. cit.*, pp. 175–6; AEU Manchester District Committee, *Minutes*, 14 May 1942; Berry to Cameron, 2 July 1942, EEF 237/1/1/312 (North East); Local Conference, *Minutes*, 30 July 1942, *idem* (North West); Low to Maloney, 2 June 1942, EEF 237/3/1/312 (AEU); Confederation of Engineering and Shipbuilding Unions, Coventry District Committee, *Minutes*, 12 May 1942, TGWU 126/JJ/CS/1. The SSNC also took this line in 1942: E&ATSSNC, *JPCs – How to Get the Best Results*, 1942, p. 5; Riegelman, *op. cit.*, p. 108.

42. 65% of the JPCs surveyed by *Business*, June 1943, reported that absenteeism was dealt with in this way. In 1943 AEU and EEF agreed this was the best way to deal with absenteeism: York Conference, *Minutes*, 12 March 1943, EEF 237/1/13/66. See also AEU, *Third Report on Production*, 1942, p. 20.

43. Secretary of BAC JPC to TUC, September 1943, TUC 292/106.63/7.

44. A. Exell, 'Morris Motors in the 1940s', *History Workshop*, 9, 1980, pp. 94–5.

45. AEU, *op. cit.*, p. 38.

46. E.g. the case discussed by AEU Manchester District Committee, *Minutes*, 5 August 1943.

47. AEU, *Third Report on Production*, 1942, p. 42 shows 40% of JPCs as having no satisfactory means of reporting back, except to shop stewards' meetings or 'by verbal reports to interested individuals'. See also C. Riegelman, *op. cit.*, pp. 134–5.

48. Letter from shop stewards at Cossor (Chadderton) to TUC, September 1943, TUC 292/106.63/7.

49. EEF Management Board, *Minutes*, 27 August, 17 December 1942, 25 July 1943, EEF 237/1/1/39; Low to Varley, 18 December 1942, EEF 237/3/1/312 (Coventry).

50. Riegelman, *op. cit.*, p. 132; Abraham to Bacon, 3 January 1944, BT 168/169. Some employers invoked the Official Secrets Act to prevent representatives from disclosing details of matters discussed in JPCs to 'outside persons': Western Regional Controller to Grindley, 25 February 1943, BT 168/169; Coventry EEA response to EEF circular 194, 8 November 1943, EEF 237/3/1/313 (W4/108/File 6).

51. NEJTM to EEF, 3 July 1943, EEF 237/1/1/312 (W4/108/4); Tanner to Harries, 7 July 1943, TUC 292/106.45; *Factory News* (Armstrong Vickers, Openshaw), April, July 1943; Metro-Vickers Conference, 21 November 1943, *Minutes*, in Len Powell Papers.

52. AEU, *Third Report on Production*, 1942, p. 42.

53. Miles to Handicar, 31 August 1942. The JPC was pressing on both issues: 'lack of mass meetings in canteen and non-availability of minutes prevent the creative energy of our workers being utilised to best advantage', AEU, *op. cit.*, p. 19.

54. E.g. complaints from shop stewards at De Havilland (Hatfield), Standard Telephone and Cables (Leicester) and Cossor (Chadderon) to TUC, September 1943, TUC 292/106.63/7. On the importance of canteens in factory social relations see R. Price, *Labour in British Society*, 1986, pp. 193–4.

55. *Factory News* (Armstrong Vickers, Openshaw), August 1943.

56. *Idem*, January 1944.

57. *Idem*, October 1943.
58. *Statement* by the joint (employer) chairman of Southern Regional Board, 24 July 1945, BT 168/179; *Memorandum*, 14 February 1945, BT 168/166.
59. 'Millions Like Us', Report of a Conference called by the SSNC, 12 March 1944, p. 23.
60. *Trade Union Report*, Mass Observation 'Industry' Topic Collection, n.d. (1946?), pp. 112, 122.
61. 'JPCs. Debate on the Adjournment', 'Benefits from JPCs. Views of Regional Controllers', 1 August 1944, BT 168/169.
62. *Trade Union Report, loc. cit.*, pp. 113–14; Mary Bountflower, Joint Consultation, *Industrial Welfare and Personnel Management*, September/October 1994; AEU, *op. cit.*, p. 53.
63. *Tribune*, 24 April 1942. See also A. Albu, *Management in Transition*, Fabian Society Research Series, 68, London, 1942, p. 23.
64. It was sometimes suggested that the more technically competent craftsmen were unlikely to volunteer for election to the JPCs because 'craftsmen often feel that it is a waste of time taking part in "just talking", which appears to them to be the main task of the Committee.' F. Zweig, *op. cit.*, p. 239.
65. *Socialist Commentary*, April 1946, p. 316; Communist Party, *Britain's Plan for Prosperity*, 1947, pp. 108, 110; J.B. Jefferys, *op. cit.*, p. 3; N. Barou, *British Trade Unions*, Gollancz, 1947, p. 236; BAC shop stewards to TUC, September 1943, TUC 292/106.63/7; Albu, *op. cit.*, pp. 18–19; P. Inman, *op. cit.*, p. 386; AEU National Committee, *Minutes*, June 1947, pp. 276–7; A. Flanders and H.A. Clegg, *op. cit.*, p. 360; A.P. Young to J.C. Little, 5 July 1944, Young Papers, C/1/140.
66. *Summary* of responses to MRB circular, 27 July 1945, p. 4, BT 168/170.
67. *Memorandum* on AEU Resolution to TUC 1943, 11 April 1944, TUC 292/106/2: the absence of the scientific and technical staff 'nourishes the contention of the more reactionary types of employer seeking to discredit the value of the JPCs who argue that the workers' side has not the necessary knowledge to formulate practical proposals.'
68. Miller to Low, 14 June 1943, EEF 237/1/1/312 (North West).
69. *The Draughtsman*, September 1943, p. 139; York Conference, Minutes, 19 November 1942, EEF 237/1/13/65.
70. *The Draughtsman*, September 1943, p. 139; TUC, *Report*, 1943, p. 203.
71. *The Draughtsman*, March 1944; C. Riegelman, *op. cit.*, p. 124; correspondence between Low and Cameron concerning admission of AESD to JPC at Reyrolle between June 1942 and January 1944, EEF 237/1/1/312 (North East); EEF Management Board, *Minutes*, 6 January 1944, EEF 237/1/1/41. In many cases, of course, technical staff sat on the JPCs as part of the management representation.
72. *The Draughtsman*, September 1943, p. 139.
73. *The Draughtsman*, May 1944, p. 68. See also T.W. Agar, 'Towards Industrial Democracy' in Fabian Society, *Can Planning be Democratic?*, 1944, p. 27. The indifference – or even hostility – of many members to JPCs also weakened the draughtsmen's campaign: J.E. Mortimer, *A History of the Association of Engineering and Shipbuilding Draughtsmen*, 1960, p. 215.
74. Walker to Citrine, 4 June 1946, TUC 292/106.44/1. In the 1920s Walker had led the Minority Movement in Manchester: R. Croucher, 'Communist Politics and Shop Stewards in Engineering, 1935–46', Warwick PhD, 1977, Appendix. By the 1940s, however, he was leading the anti-Communist majority on the District Committee: AEU Manchester District Committee, *Minutes*, 29 June 1941, 7 May 1942. In 1942 he had taken a strong line against employers who refused to establish JPCs, commenting: 'we will have to settle with our local fascists after the war': AEU Manchester District Committee circular, n.d. (early 1942), in EEF 237/1/1/312.
75. AEU Southall District Committee, *Minutes*, 19 March 1942.

76. N. Fishman, 'The British Communist Party and the Trade Unions, 1933–1945', London PhD, pp. 466–7; Inman, *op. cit.*, p. 387.

77. AEU, *Third Report on Production*, 1942, p. 47. One-fifth of the JPCs covered by the AEU survey discussed output bonuses and guaranteed piece prices: *ibid.*, p. 52. But only 11% of all respondents cited grievances in relation to earnings as a factor retarding production: *ibid.*, p. 22. The MAP survey showed 6.2% of items on JPC agendas dealt with wages and hours: C. Riegelman, *op. cit.* p. 179.

78. *Factory News* (Armstrong Vickers, Openshaw), May 1943. At another Vickers' plant the same agreement was elaborated to include provision for revision of the basis time (but with no loss of earnings) if innovations suggested by the men involved the company in expenditure on new machinery: AEU, *Third Report on Production*, December 1942, p. 38.

79. R. Croucher, *Engineers at War, 1939–1945*, pp. 158–9. Such arguments may have played a part in securing reductions in piece rates at the Standard.

80. Armstrong Siddeley Motors shop stewards to TUC, September 1943, TUC 292/106.63/7. Relations had long been strained at the factory, the workers' side of the JPC alleging that: 'The management are quite clearly opposed to the whole idea of production committees and do their best to pour cold water on practically every idea we bring forward.' AEU, *op. cit.*, pp. 33, 24, 25, 29 (firm 17/33).

81. Inman, *op. cit.*, pp. 387–8; Riegelman, *op. cit.*, pp. 104, 181, 262; W. Hannington, *The Rights of Engineers*, 1944, pp. 98–9. For examples of conflict see *Factory News*, August 1943; AEU Coventry District Committee, *Minutes*, 31 July 1945 (BTH).

82. Riegelman, *op. cit.*, p. 105; E&ATSSNC, 'England National Acting Committee Meeting', 17 October 1943, MRC Mss 233/3/3/5; Metro-Vickers Conference, 21 November 1943, *Minutes*, in Len Powell Papers; E&ATSSNC, n.d. (1945?), *Shop Stewards and the Future*, p. 10; RO Circular 18/4, in BT 168/239.

83. AEU, *Third Report on Production*, December 1942, p. 47.

84. *Ibid.*, p. 47; *Trade Union Report, loc. cit.*, p. 113. All the topics listed in the text had been discussed by more than 25% of JPCs surveyed by the AEU: C. Riegelman, *op. cit.*, p. 180.

85. *Idem*, p. 179; *Summary* of responses to MRB circular, 27 July 1945, pp. 1, 3, BT 168/170.

86. Interview with Y. Kapp, June 1992; AEU Coventry District Committee, *Minutes*, 17 April, 11 September 1945.

87. Women, many of whom were new to the war factories, were disproportionately excluded by the rule that members of JPCs must have at least two years service. In practice, however, this rule seems to have been interpreted flexibly: NUGMW National Woman Officer to Harries, 4 November 1942, TUC 292/106.45.

88. York Conference, *Minutes*, 18 March 1942, p. 38, EEF 237/1/13/62.

89. P. Summerfield, *Women Workers in the Second World War*, 1984, *passim*.

90. AEU, *Third Report on Production*, December 1942, p. 44; C. Riegelman, *op. cit.*, pp. 125n, 180. Matters may have improved slightly – the *Business* survey in summer 1943 showed women on just over 50% of the committees, *loc. cit.*

91. *Summary* of responses to MRB circular, 27 July 1945, p. 4, BT 168/170.

92. *Factory News*, December 1944.

93. Mark Benney, *Over to Bombers*, 1943, p. 100.

94. Handicar to Low, 3 July 1942, EEF 237/1/1/312 (London).

95. Mary Bountflower, *op. cit.*

7 Reconstruction and the Regional Boards

In 1944, as minds turned towards reconstruction, the long-term future of the Regional Boards became an issue of debate. Their supporters argued that the degree of state intervention necessary for conversion from war to peace could only function effectively with the help of authoritative tripartite bodies at regional and local levels. At the same time they pointed out that the Regional Boards had a key role to play in sustaining social harmony – a much more problematic objective once the wartime pressures for national unity were removed. The constituency of support for the maintenance of Regional Boards with significant powers was a wide one, including some Whitehall officials, many of the employer members of the Boards and their District Advisory Committees, the unions, Communists and other left-wingers.

This chapter focuses on the activities of the employer members of this coalition, in particular of Norman Kipping and George Dickson. Kipping, who began the period as head of the Ministry of Production's Regional Division and ended it as Director General of the FBI, fought hard against the opponents of regionalism, both in Whitehall and amongst his fellow employers. Kipping's desire to build up the Regional Boards had more to do with protecting employers against state interference, than it did with any more generous definition of democracy. But, as long as he accepted the post-war necessity of high levels of state intervention in industry and of direct trade union involvement in the structures of production administration, his advocacy of 'self-government in industry' could help to provide a sympathetic environment for much more left-wing projects of participatory economic planning. Meanwhile George Dickson, as impatient to plan for peace as he had earlier been to organise for war, set out to improvise decentralised planning from below. Just as in 1940–41, when he had invented the Capacity

Clearing Centres, Dickson's combination of imaginative local improvisation with irrepressible energy in expounding his visions in every nook and cranny of the tripartite power structure, helped to keep the issues of decentralisation and democratisation on the agenda of debate about Britain's post-war economic reconstruction.

During the final year of the war, members of the Regional Boards became increasingly exasperated by the failure of Government to give any clear indication of what role the Boards would be expected to play in the organisation of post-war reconstruction.[1] Behind this reticence lay a bureaucratic struggle between the Ministry of Production currently responsible for the Regional Boards, and the Board of Trade, its designated post-war successor. Despite endless talk and several interdepartmental committees neither the civil servants nor the Coalition Government were able to resolve these differences before the end of the war. Norman Kipping, whose main task as head of the Ministry of Production's Regional Division had been to persuade the various supply departments to devolve authority to the regions, was convinced that further measures of devolution would be essential in handling the complexities of the transition to peace. 'The sheer volume of detail to be collated will, we think, enforce a considerable measure of decentralisation'.[2] In the future, Kipping envisaged, agreements arising from national discussions between trade associations and Whitehall could be made subject to review by the Regional Boards.[3]

Through the Regional Boards, the regional controllers of particular departments were able to take full account of the views both of other departments, and of the unofficial members of the Boards representing the two sides of industry, thus enabling national industrial policy to be adapted to meet the needs of particular areas. 'This form of interdepartmental delegation to a concerting body,' Kipping argued, 'constitutes an extension in administrative technique which should be retained and developed in the post-war relations of Government and Industry'. The wartime experience of the Ministry of Production – a co-ordinating department with virtually no executive powers – had reinforced Kipping's belief in the superiority of persuasion over coercion in dealing with difficult conflicts of interest. During the war years the regional representatives of rival

Whitehall departments had learned to make use of Regional Board
Chairmen, despite their lack of executive authority, to arbitrate their
disputes.[4] For Kipping, the Regional Boards were equally important
as focal points for the construction of tripartite consensus.   They
were not only 'the most obvious of all answers to criticisms of
remote bureaucratic control from Whitehall'; they also facilitated a
meeting of minds between employer and trade union representatives
which did much to ameliorate the antagonisms characteristic of
every-day industrial relations.[5]

Kipping's decentralist philosophy had little appeal to the Board of
Trade, whose relations with industry had traditionally been
conducted through national trade associations, without involving
trade unions.[6]   In response to Kipping's plans for the Regional
Boards, Board of Trade officials raised a whole series of objections.
Wartime national unity, they argued, had made it possible to admit
employers and trade unionists to executive decision-making in ways
that could not be sustained in post-war conditions.   As partisan
politics returned, employer and/or trade union members of Regional
Boards would be likely to find difficulty in loyally executing
Government policies of which they disapproved.   Moreover, the
revival of competition between firms would make it much more
difficult than it had been in wartime for employer members of
Regional Boards to separate their private interests from their public
duties.   Particular embarrassment was anticipated over the access of
members of Regional Board Executives to commercially sensitive
information about rival firms.[7]   A final worry was that if Regional
Boards were given too much authority, departmental officials
outposted to the regions would tend to 'go native', enabling local
authorities and the two sides of industry to manipulate them for
parochial or sectional purposes.[8]

It was this potential parochialism of the Regional Boards which led
Hugh Dalton, the Labour President of the Board of Trade, to mount
the sharpest attack on the authority of the Boards since their
struggles with the supply ministries in 1941–42. Dalton was an
unashamed centralist, and his major objective at the Board of Trade
was to lay the basis for a strong location of industry policy, ensuring
that the state took power to prevent the re-emergence of the inter-

war depressed areas.[9] Having won the authority to use wartime controls to influence post-war industrial location, Dalton proceeded to set up special regional committees to deal with location issues, committees composed exclusively of officials from the various ministries concerned.[10] Effectively this meant excluding unofficial members of the Regional Boards from any direct voice in decisions which would clearly be of central importance in the reconstruction of the local economy.[11] The TUC objected, seeing this as an attack on their wartime entry into the corridors of power.[12] George Dickson tried to persuade his fellow employers to join with the TUC, as they had done once before, in 1942, to defend regional tripartism against Whitehall centralisers. But the main employers' organisations, impressed by the potential clash between public duty and the individual commercial interests of employer members of the Boards and keen to limit trade union access where possible, were happy to endorse the Board of Trade's determination to restore the distinction, deliberately blurred in the wartime Regional Boards, between the executive powers of the officials and the advisory status of employer and trade union representatives.[13] The leadership of the FBI had no long-term interest in the survival of the Regional Boards: 'we feel that when peace-time conditions prevail, we should rely on the Trade Associations'.[14] In the spring of 1945 the FBI resisted pressure from Dickson and others to call a general meeting of employer members of the Regional Boards, since such a meeting could be expected to support their continuation.[15]

In December 1944 Kipping secured a minimalist commitment to decentralisation with simultaneous parliamentary statements from Lyttelton and Dalton endorsing the post-war devolution of authority from Whitehall to the regions 'on all matters not of major importance'.[16] But the quarrel over the involvement of the Regional Boards with location of industry decisions remained unresolved. When, in February 1945 ministers discussed the report of the Official Reconstruction Committee on Regional Machinery, it was agreed that, in the long term, the Boards would lose their quasi-executive wartime powers and become purely advisory bodies. It was accepted, however, that the transition to a purely advisory status would have to be a gradual one,[17] both because trade union (and to some extent employer) members of the Boards were certain to resist any such weakening of their powers,[18] and because Whitehall would be unable to handle the complexities of the change-over to peace without devolving substantial powers to the Boards. To enable the Boards to deal with these issues, representation would have to be extended to industries apart from engineering, and some kind of relationship would need to be established between the Boards, the Ministry of Town and Country Planning and the local authorities.[19] Ministerial endorsement of the long-term objective of reducing the Boards to a merely advisory status was not too much of a set-back for the decentralisers, since, as every good administrator knows, what can be postponed can possibly be prevented altogether. Moreover, the line between 'advisory' and 'executive' functions had never been very clear and Kipping's hope was that, once the real problems of reconstruction had to be faced, experience would teach the Board of Trade what they had failed to learn from reasoned argument.[20] In a summary of the Ministry of Production position in May 1945 Kipping foreshadowed post-war Boards continuing to provide the main machinery for interdepartmental co-ordination in the regions, having authority to deal with problems unforeseen in Whitehall, and being run by strong independent part-time chairmen, not officials but 'prominent and experienced men of standing, likely ... to be able to exert a Chairman's influence upon the departmental Regional Officials'.[21] Here was a most elastic definition of the word 'advisory'!

While Kipping prepared his positions, knowing that nothing would be settled until the political character of the post-war Government was decided, outside Whitehall a significant groundswell of opinion had emerged in favour of adapting wartime tripartism at regional and local levels to the needs of post-war economic planning. The growing problem of redundancies as arms production ran down following D-Day, together with the publication of the White Paper on Employment in May 1944, helped to stimulate debate within the Regional Boards about their post-war role. To George Dickson it seemed obvious that the wartime practice of district-level co-operation between employers, unions and the local officers of Whitehall departments – itself partly a product of his own initiative with the Capacity Clearing Centres in 1940 – would provide a basis on which to build local economic planning after the war. The wartime objective of maximum arms production would now be replaced by 'our common objective of sustaining full employment, under fair wages and conditions, for the employable population of the district'.[22] To this end, in May 1944, he launched a Medway Full Employment Council. Alongside trade unionists and employers, the Council included the Admiral in charge of the dockyard, and representatives of the chamber of commerce, the master builders' association, the local bank managers, the transport concerns, the water, gas and electricity undertakings, and each of the four local authorities in the Medway District. To the chagrin of their superiors in Whitehall, Dickson also managed to draw in the local officers of three Government departments – the district tax inspector, the manager of the local labour exchange and the Ministry of Production's district manager.[23] The Council's work was financed by two or three local employers and, as with the Clearing Centre in 1940, run from Dickson's company office.[24]

There was nothing parochial about Dickson's intentions. He aimed to stimulate the setting up of similar bodies throughout the country, able to function, eventually, as 'self-governing local units inside the national plan.'[25] He viewed the Medway Council less as 'an engine for pushing purely local interests' than as a launch pad for an agitation designed to transform the national machinery of economic planning.[26] As with Clearing Centres in 1941, he intended to save Medway by his exertions and the nation by his example.[27] From the outset, Dickson went to some lengths to inform the rest of the world about his initiative, firing off a characteristic note to 'My Dear Norman' (Kipping): 'The last thing I want to do is to embarrass you unnecessarily, particularly when I am so proud of my friendship with a man doing his job so well in such difficult circumstances.... I am anxious that you should know how I feel towards you personally, just in case any sparks should fly'.[28] Then, without informing Kipping, he sent copies of a booklet describing the Medway Council, to all the Regional Boards and their District Committees, forcing Kipping, when he found out, to issue instructions that the booklet had no official status and should not be further distributed.[29] When, in June 1944, the *AEU Monthly Journal* printed an article boosting the Medway experiment, Robert Burns, Kipping's close adviser, anticipated a rash of similar initiatives in other areas.[30]

In the Eastern Region chairmen of a number of District Committees got together to press Whitehall to permit them to link up with broader unofficial bodies interested in post-war full employment. The Regional Controller warned Kipping that unless he went some way to meet this demand, many of the people currently serving on District Committees would 'be inclined to set up a parallel organisation', proliferating 'movements such as those sponsored by Dickson in the Medway towns'.[31] In July the Ministry of Production's Chief Executive, meeting a deputation of employers from the Eastern Region, was taken aback by the fervour with which their spokesman, G.R. Barclay from Watford, talked about perpetuating the wartime subordination of private interests to 'the spirit of National service'. When challenged, Barclay hastened to reassure his listeners that he did not see such local organisation 'as an alternative to free enterprise. They had no ideas that it would control industry, but would supplement the official machine and co-ordinate the unofficial approaches to post-war questions'.[32] In fact Barclay's rhetoric of service before profit was seriously intended: he was at this time, not only a close ally of Dickson's, but also actively involved in setting up the 1944 Association – a group of businessmen sympathetic to the Labour Party.[33] By the autumn of 1944 the Eastern Regional Controller was proposing that the Medway-style organisations springing up in his region should be allowed to affiliate to the Regional Board, acting as its local advisers, and being permitted to co-opt relevant departmental officials operating in the district.[34]

It is not clear, in the absence of systematic local research, to what extent the Medway example was imitated outside the circle of Dickson's friends and contacts.[35] Nor is it clear how far it appealed to employers outside the small group of Christian Socialists and Labour sympathisers that Dickson and Barclay belonged to. Even in the Medway towns themselves there were limits to the inspirational power of Dickson's advocacy. Formally the Full Employment

Council was a non-partisan body, welcoming representatives of local interests regardless of their party affiliation. Although it had Conservative members from the outset, and worked closely with the local Tory MPs, the dominant mood on the Council owed less to a genuine all-party consensus, than to ideas of 'progressive unity' rooted in the fact that anti-Tory sentiment was still denied a partisan outlet. Dickson's leading ally, Wal Blackmore, was a Transport and General Workers' Union official and Labour councillor who had worked closely with Dickson in establishing the first Capacity Clearing Centre in 1940. Other trade unionists were initially more suspicious, afraid that the Council 'might ... tend to confuse the workers and divert their attention from the political problem' of winning the post-war election. The Communist shop stewards from the Shorts aircraft factory – 'a tough bunch' – doubted the possibility of creating full employment in a capitalist society. They quickly came round, however, comforting themselves with the thought that 'if, in open collaboration with other interests concerned, it was proved that the existing capitalist control of the means of production and distribution could not provide adequate opportunity for full employment, then the political issue would be quite clear'. Subsequently the Communist Party gave its support to Dickson's Council.[36] At least two of the trade union representatives on the Council were Communists, and one of them, A.J. Gayner, played a central role as co-chair (alongside the manager of the local Westminster Bank) of the economics sub-committee.[37] For the CP's policy of 'progressive unity', Dickson was a natural ally, not only because of his attitude to economic planning, but also because he had no more time than they had for orthodox party politics; and he went out of his way to publicly welcome Communist support for the Council.[38]

The Conservatives, who controlled all four of the local authorities involved, were rather less susceptible to Dickson's charms.[39] Not only did Dickson have little place for geographically elected local government in his functional plan of social reorganisation, he was also openly contemptuous about the competence of the local councillors.[40] Moreover, he allowed the Medway Council to be closely associated with a political initiative that did nothing to appease Tory worthies. Within weeks of founding the Full Employment Council, Dickson agreed to chair a debate organised by the local Communist Party between their district organiser and the rector of Chatham, Rev. Joseph McCulloch – himself a Dickson disciple.[41] McCulloch was happy to support a resolution declaring that 'this meeting of the citizens of the Medway Towns considers that there is no fundamental incompatibility between the immediate social objectives of Christianity and Communism' and calling for 'an alliance between the progressive sections of the people' to realise these objectives.[42] At the same time Dickson and McCulloch launched a non-partisan 'Use Your Vote Society' intended to encourage political participation. Although a Communist attempt to turn this into an explicitly anti-Tory front was rebuffed,[43] few local Conservatives can have been in any doubt about what this sinister duo of radical priest and radical capitalist had in mind. Tory anger was further provoked by a follow-up meeting on Conservatism and Christianity, organised by the Use Your Vote Society in the interests of balance. At this meeting, according to an indignant correspondent in the local paper 'the motion that a common ground for action could be found between Christians and Conservatives had to be withdrawn in face of an amendment proposed by the secretary of the local Communist Party'.[44] While some local Conservatives fulminated against the 'offensive, misleading and mischievous' attempt of the rector to drag Christ into politics, others deplored the failure of Party members to attend the meeting to support the Central Office speaker, a Miss Howieson, leaving her 'to be devoured by the lions while they were getting over their Sunday dinners'.[45] The resulting correspondence inspired one local satirist to verse:

> The shameless impropriety
> Of the Use Your Vote Society
> Disturbed the Conservative Association's
> Sunday meditations...
> They passed the time with pot and tankard
> Read their Punch but not their Hansard
> (Unlike a Certain Element
> Whose Sunday Afternoon was spent
> In manner far less indolent)
> The Tories drank their beer and port
> And left a woman to hold the fort[46]

At its first meeting in May 1944, the Council agreed to organise its work, in accordance with Dickson's 'Star Plan', around four functional sub-committees. The Council protested against Whitehall's decision, announced in the Employment White Paper, to run down the Ministry of Production after the war, and called for the setting up of parallel district–regional–national structures to manage consumption, finance and development planning.[47] Pointing out that firms 'were bewildered by the lack of information' about consumer demand, Dickson argued that, at least for the transition period, market forces would have to be replaced by a co-ordinated national machinery 'to assess, co-ordinate and direct all consumer needs'.[48] 'Circumstances' he added, 'won't yet permit the old peacetime salesman's order book method of discussing these questions'.[49] To enable it to play its part in this assessment of demand, the Council launched a household survey of consumer needs with help from the WVS, trade union branches and other voluntary organisations.[50]

Despite their acquiescence in Dickson's schemes for reorganising the national economy, most members of the Council were no doubt mainly interested in the more parochial goal of securing jobs for the Medway towns. The local economy was dominated by Admiralty work at the Chatham Dockyard, and warplane production at Shorts' Rochester works. After the First World War unemployment had been a major problem,[51] and there were bitter local memories of councillors going 'cap in hand to London begging for more work to be given' to the dockyard.[52] Dickson had a theory that the employment of around 20% of the local population in the production of goods or services exported across the district boundary would be sufficient to pay for necessary imports and to sustain employment in the local service sector, and he used this figure to establish a target for the number of manufacturing jobs needed in the area.[53] After collecting information from local employers about their post-war intentions the Council calculated that little more than half of the estimated 30,000 'export' jobs required were assured, even on optimistic assumptions about the future of Shorts and the Dockyard.[54] Convinced that Whitehall was steering interested firms away from Medway to the development areas, and worried by the implications of Dalton's Distribution of Industry Bill, the Council set itself 'to prove factually the perhaps surprising news that there was a serious problem of a potential "development" area right here on the London doorstep in a district for which the Government as employers and industrial owners had particular responsibility'.[55]   In March 1945, however, the Board of Trade turned down their request for development area status under the new Bill, arguing that their proximity to London meant they would have no difficulty in attracting new industry after the war.[56] After further attempts by the local MPs to intervene at the Committee stage of the Bill came to nothing, Dickson turned to the Regional Board for help in steering new industry to Rochester.   Even there, however, there was considerable feeling that Rochester was less deserving than some other parts of the region.[57]

After Labour swept to power in the November 1945 municipal elections, the Medway Council became less influential, and leadership of the local search for employment passed to the local authorities.[58] The major post-war initiative taken by the Council was a campaign, led by the Communist, Gayner, and fully backed by the Chamber of Commerce and the Trades Council, to attract new industry by establishing a local Trading Estate: but this collapsed when it became clear that there was no land available.[59] When the big blow came in June 1946, with the announcement that Shorts was to be moved to Belfast, it was Dickson who chaired the initial protest meeting.   The Government decision to move Shorts was acutely embarrassing to the local Labour Party, not least because the MP for Rochester held a junior post in the Ministry of Supply and was therefore unable to distance himself from the decision. Among the slogans carried by protesting Shorts workers was: 'We put you in. You put us out'.[60] In fact, the removal of Shorts, which occurred gradually over the next two years, created the necessary factory space for new industry to move in, as the Board of Trade had all along argued that it would. The future prosperity of the Medway towns, however, owed more to office and commercial development, and an influx of commuters – all dependent on the proximity of the metropolis – than to any realisation of Dickson's project of a cohesive 'self-governing local unit inside the national plan' rooted in manufacturing industry.[61]

Unlike his earlier Capacity Clearing Centre initiative, Dickson's Medway Council did not set the pattern for the local articulation of national production planning. In the summer and autumn of 1944, as we have seen, it aroused a good deal of interest, and some anxiety in Whitehall. The Medway Council may not have been the wave of the future, but it was symptomatic of a broader current of discontent apparent in Regional Boards and their District Committees at the failure of Whitehall to come up with any coherent structures for the involvement of the public-spirited employers and trade union officials who staffed the Regional apparatus in the planning of post-war economic reconstruction.[62] In January 1945 Dickson visited the US, where he was delighted to discover a proliferation of local voluntary groupings similar to the Medway. He was particularly taken by a Department of Labor initiative to encourage such groups on the grounds that 'the proper division of responsibility between local, state and national government cannot be determined accurately unless local groups first stake out the field, examine the reconversion and re-employment problem in their communities, and indicate the type and extent of assistance they will require from state and national authorities'.[63] It is hard to imagine a Whitehall department approaching reconstruction from such an essentially federalist perspective. As Dickson complained to the London Regional Board in May 1945, Whitehall seemed determined to make it impossible to establish 'a straight line through from the local districts, where the citizens are becoming increasingly bewildered', to link their own contribution to post-war full employment national economic planning.[64] A few months later Dickson gave vent to his frustrations in the local press:

> From their wartime experience of the Government control of industry most manufacturing employers and organised trade unionists realise that the democratic situation is worse than ever. Unless our local democracy really becomes alive ... and insists that the international and national industrial problems are broken down into the districts where we spend our working lives, and where we can build up our real democratic strength on the facts that only we local citizens can know fully, democracy as we have fondly dreamed about it, and fought for it, is doomed.[65]

At the root of these frustrations was the fact that Dickson's premise – 'there can be no sensible overall planning done nationally for Full Employment unless it is based on the co-ordination of local interests in every district'[66] – was not shared by those responsible in Whitehall for location of industry policy. To Dalton and his officials, planning for full employment was a national question to be decided by national criteria. Far from seeking a 'straight line through' from local initiative to national planning, the Board of Trade was anxious to preserve as much distance as possible between planning decisions and the grinding of parochial axes, whether these were wielded by local authorities, Regional Boards or bodies like the Medway Full Employment Committee.[67] The Board of Trade view was informed by a scepticism about the capacity of representatives of industry and local electorates to subordinate sectional interests to higher national purposes which cut across Dickson's optimistic conviction that participation in an open and coherent structure of national planning would induce all parties to act in a spirit of co-operation and service to the public good. In this the Board was fully supported by the FBI which, as we have seen, resisted pressure from Dickson and others to mobilise support for the continuation of the Regional Boards, and rebuffed Dickson's decentralist ideas on the grounds that it was absurd to suppose that national policies could 'emerge from a mosaic of local decisions and actions'.[68] There was no place for 'self-governing units within the national plan' in the centralised structure of government/industry relations favoured by the FBI and sponsored by the Board of Trade in its every-day relations with the trade associations. However much Dalton's socialism might put him on a potential collision course with the leaders of private capital, neither he, nor his civil servants had any more sympathy than the FBI for the attempts of Dickson or Norman Kipping to carry over the wartime experiments in decentralisation into the planning of post-war reconstruction.

After the war there was a significant shift in this pattern of alignments. Stafford Cripps, who replaced Dalton at the Board of Trade in the new Labour Government, had considerable sympathy with Kipping's regionalism: 'While main decisions of policy must remain at the centre, we must, in my view, increasingly decentralise the detail of administration'.[69] He also inherited Kipping himself when Attlee, implementing plans agreed by the Coalition Government in 1944, shut down the Ministry of Production and transferred its Regional Division to the Board of Trade. Cripps endorsed Kipping's proposals to appoint independent part-time chairmen for the Boards, drawn from industrialists, trade unionists or other 'prominent and experienced men of standing'.[70] At the same time he dissolved the purely official Distribution of Industry Committees, which Dalton had established in his effort to keep the unofficial members of the Boards out of policy-making. In future it would be the Regional Boards, not a separate committee excluding the unofficial members, which advised the Minister on recommendations made by his regional officials concerning the distribution of industry.[71]

Despite their defeat at the Board of Trade, Whitehall critics of the Regional Boards found powerful new support in the Lord President's Office, responsible, under Herbert Morrison, for overall co-ordination of economic policy. Morrison's advisers quickly rumbled Kipping's attempt to smuggle through a continuing executive function for the Boards. Picking up Kipping's phrase about the new Regional Board chairmen having sufficient standing 'to exert a Chairmen's influence upon the Departmental Regional officials', Professor Dennison asked: 'Does this mean that the Regional Controller of, say, the Board of Trade, is to disregard his instructions from headquarters at the behest of the independent Chairman?... It is difficult to visualise a Minister accepting a condition in which the policies of his department were to be changed by decision of a Regional body'. For Morrison's advisers, decentralisation meant devolving authority to departmental officials in the regions, not to people outside the Government machine – and such officials did not need the help of Regional Boards to consult one another across departmental frontiers. The critics' main concern was to bring to an end the wartime practice of blurring the distinction between 'matters proper to a Government department and those which might be discussed with representatives of outside bodies'.[72]

In line with this advice the Lord President's Committee reaffirmed the strictly advisory functions of the Boards, and agreed that formal machinery for interdepartmental consultation among officials in the regions should be maintained in future quite independently of the Boards. Subsequently a working party was set up, under Treasury chairmanship, to report on what were now to be seen as the quite distinct issues of departmental decentralisation and the future of the Regional Boards.[73] The report of this working party, agreed by ministers in January 1946, spelled out that 'the restriction of the Boards to advisory functions makes a fundamental change in their place in the regional system; they will no longer direct any executive work'. Kipping's Regional Division was reduced to dealing with procedural questions only, while the general process of decentralisation within departments became the responsibility of a new Committee on Regional Organisation located in the Treasury.[74] As these decisions took shape, Morrison's advisers remained unhappy, believing that measures agreed to ensure that the Boards were kept sufficiently informed of official activity to be able to comment before final decisions were taken gave them a dangerous foothold for ongoing encroachments on the proper independence of the state: 'Now that the war is over and party government resumed there may be the strongest objections to placing all kinds of details of government policy in front of employers and trade unions'. The Treasury officials, however, thought that nothing more could be done for the time being to clip the wings of the Regional Boards; meanwhile Cripps and Kipping would need to be carefully watched.[75]

At this point, abandoning his losing battle against the Whitehall centralisers, Kipping quit to return to his business career. Within months he had re-emerged as Director General of the FBI, providing the gospel of regionalism with a new power base. Kipping immediately set in motion a regionalisation of the FBI's internal structures which, among other things, helped to create a more concerted and authoritative employer presence on the Regional Boards.[76] In May 1946 the employers' side of the National Production Advisory Council summoned the first – and, as things turned out, the only – meeting of employer members of Regional

Boards.[77] Many of the delegates were demoralised, frustrated by the powerlessness of the Boards and the lack of respect with which they were treated by Government officials. Instead of giving up, Kipping urged, they should go all out to reverse the sidelining of the Boards:

> An outstanding feature of current Government administration was its continual growth and increased complexity. This was happening irrespective of what Government was in power. Unless there was decentralisation there would be complete administrative breakdown, and decentralisation was likely to go a great deal further as the proper technique was developed.[78]

Kipping's own experience left him with little faith that Whitehall would be capable of accomplishing its own decentralisation. Pressure from industry was therefore the key – no less than in the production crisis of 1941–42 – to avoiding the slow strangulation of the economy by an over-centralised and undercoordinated Government machine. The FBI followed up the meeting of Regional Board members with a paper to the National Production Advisory Council warning that industrialists would be unlikely to continue to give their time indefinitely to the Boards unless departmental Regional Controllers did more to make use of 'the accumulated knowledge and experience represented on the Boards and District Committees, rather than ... regarding them as the passive recipients of information as to decisions or actions already made or taken'. The memorandum also reasserted the wartime role of Boards as 'a valuable piece of machinery whereby the activities of the various Government Departments in a Region can be harmonised' with one another, as well as with the views of the two sides of industry.[79]

Historians have disagreed about the attitude adopted by the FBI during the early years of the Attlee Government. Stephen Blank argues that FBI leaders initially pursued a non-confrontational strategy, accepting the verdict of the electorate and seeking a *modus vivendi* between private capital and what they generally assumed would be a long-term involvement of the state in economic life. It was not until 1948 that relations between Government and business turned sour, partly as a result of Government plans for Development Councils and steel nationalisation, but more fundamentally because the very success of Labour's reconstruction policy opened the way for the re-emergence of neo-liberal attitudes in the business community. Helen Mercer, by contrast, has argued more recently that the notion of a 'honeymoon period' in government–industry relations immediately after the war cannot survive the opening of the records.[80] The evidence surveyed in this chapter lends weight to the older interpretation. Of course the FBI was at all times determined to defend free enterprise. But they accepted in 1945 that reconstruction required economic planning, and they sought to defend the autonomy of business within, rather than against, the apparatus of state intervention. Traditionally, business had conducted its industrial diplomacy with Whitehall through national trade associations which, among other things, effectively excluded trade unions from participation in industrial policy-making. Norman Kipping used his authority, both in Whitehall and, subsequently, in the FBI to keep alive the possibility of using the Regional Boards to introduce a measure of decentralisation into industrial planning. Kipping's resistance to the centralist doctrines of the Board of Trade reflected a desire to foster 'self-government in industry' within the limits set by reconstruction planning.[81] He was not attempting to promote participatory planning as an end in itself. Nevertheless Kipping's battles served to keep open the door for the more radical enthusiasms of George Dickson, and to set the scene for left-wing advocates of the link between Regional Boards and JPCs as a key to participatory planning to use the mounting economic crisis of 1947 in order to re-open the agenda of 1941–42. The reactions of trade unions to that crisis, however, can only be understood in relation to their determination to gain access to decision-making about the post-war reconstruction of their industry at a national, as well as a regional, level. However much engineering trade unionists shared Dickson's or Kipping's belief in the potential of the Regional Boards, they were also well aware that without the admission of the unions into the heart of business–government relations at the national industrial level, they would only be scratching at the edge of the problem of participation.

NOTES

1. See notes 15 and 62 below.
2. Kipping to Brook, CAB 124/348.
3. Kipping, 'Future Regional Organisation Committee Report', 3 November 1943, Stokes Papers 180/MRB/3/4.
4. The same was true of Kipping's own work in Whitehall: N. Kipping, *Summing Up*, 1972, p. 8.
5. Kipping, 'Future Regional Organisation Committee Report', 3 November 1943, *loc. cit.*; Brook, memorandum for War Cabinet, 2 February 1945 in CAB 124/348.
6. R. Roberts, 'The Administrative Origins of Industrial Diplomacy: an Aspect of Government–Industry Relations, 1929–1935', in J. Turner (ed.), *Businessmen and Politics*, 1984. The Board remained weakly articulated in the regions: Kipping to Coleridge, 11 November 1944, CAB 124/348; in October 1944 a senior official told the Reconstruction Committee that they 'had not yet decided the form and scope of their post-war field organisation. It was accepted that there would have to be some such organisation, but it might not be comprehensive, either in territory or subjects; it might cover only development areas'. *Minutes* of 18th meeting of Reconstruction Committee, 24 October 1944, in CAB 124/348.
7. Johnson to Brook, 2 October 1944; N. Brook, memorandum for War Cabinet, 2 February 1945, CAB 124/348.
8. 'There has been a tendency for the outlook of some Regional officials to be unduly influenced by local conditions.' (Reconstruction Committee, *Minutes*, 24 October 1944, CAB 124/348.) The Cabinet Committee on the Machinery of Government dismissed this fear as groundless: *Minutes*, 18 May 1945, in CAB 124/348.
9. B. Pimlott, *Hugh Dalton*, 1985, pp. 400–7.
10. The Board of Trade, Ministry of Labour, Ministry of Production, Ministry of Town and Country Planning. White Paper on Employment Policy, Cmnd. 6527, 1944, p. 13.
11. Among the duties of the Distribution of Industry Committees was 'to advise the Regional Boards about the requirements of civil production, as capacity and labour is released from war production'. (Reconstruction Committee *Minutes*, 13 December 1944, in CAB 124/138).
12. NPAC, employers' side, *Minutes*, 3 November 1944, FBI 200/F/1/1/145. See also NPAC, *Minutes*, 3 November 1944, TUC 292/106.1/6; Confederation of Engineering and Shipbuilding Unions, *Conference Report*, 1945, pp. 116–17.
13. NPAC, employers' side, *Minutes*, 3 November 1944; Barclay to Ramsay, 27 October 1944, Locock to Nelson, 7 February 1945, Locock to Mathew, 2 March 1945, FBI 200/F/1/1/145. Earlier, Dickson had deprecated the FBI preference for trade associations over the Regional Board structures which involved trade unions: NPAC, employers' side, *Minutes*, 3 March 1943; MTFEC, *Minutes*, 14 November 1944, p. 2, BT 168/214.
14. Locock to Mathew, 2 March 1945; Locock to Nelson, 7 February, 1945, FBI 200/F/3//S2/29/36/b.
15. King to Gordon, 7 March 1945, Gordon to Walker, 12 March 1945, Gordon to Locock, 29 March 1945: *idem*. NPAC employers' side, *Minutes*, 3 November 1944, 31 May 1945, in FBI 200/F/1/1/145. Instead they concerted policy with the BEC at a meeting specially convened to exclude the Regional Board representatives. Locock to Gough, 12 April 1945, FBI 200/F/3//S2/29/36/b. The BEC agreed with Locock, in line with the views of the EEF which 'would be only too pleased to see [the Regional Boards] die of inanition'. Walker to Kipping, 29 July 1946, FBI 200/F/3//S2/29/36/c.
16. Brook, memorandum for War Cabinet, 2 February 1945, CAB 124/348.

17. Reconstruction Sub-Committee on Industrial Problems, *Minutes*, 12 February 1945, CAB 124/348.
18. Reconstruction Committee, *Minutes*, 24 October 1944; Brook to War Cabinet, 2 February 1945, CAB 124/348.
19. *Ibid.*; NPAC, *Minutes*, 2 March 1945, TUC 292/106.1/6.
20. See also the decision of the Ministry of Production Regional Controllers to avoid pushing the Distribution of Industry question: 1 March 1945, Stokes Papers 180/MRB/3/4.
21. Kipping, 'Future of Regional Boards', 7 May 1945, CAB 124/348. Since 1942 the Boards had been chaired by the Ministry of Production Regional Controllers. It was not possible to replace these with Board of Trade controllers, since the latter had little standing in the business community. (*Idem*; Dibben to Locock, 21, 24 and 26 October 1944, FBI 200/F/3/S2/29/36/b; NPAC, *Minutes*, 25 September 1944, TUC 292/106.1/6)
22. *Chatham, Rochester and Gillingham News*, 5 May 1944.
23. *Ibid.*, 18 August 1944; Dickson, 'What means Sin in the Twentieth Century', *Copartnership*, January–February 1945. Other organisations came in later, including the Co-op (MTFEC. *Minutes*, 14 November 1944, BT 168/214, p. 4) and the British Legion (*Chatham Observer*, 15 June 1945); J. McCulloch, *Medway Adventure*, London, 1946, p. 105; Wood to Pankhurst, 26 April 1946, BT 168/214.
24. Interview with Mr. G. Dickson, 11 December 1944, Cole Papers, B3/4/f6.
25. *Chatham, Rochester and Gillingham News*, 17 November 1944.
26. Interview with Mr. G. Dickson, 11 December 1944, Cole Papers, B3/4/f6. Firms approached the Council for help in finding factory space, but according to this interviewer, Dickson was not very interested in helping them.
27. *Chatham, Rochester and Gillingham News*, 5 May 1944.
28. Dickson to Kipping, 12 May 1944, BT 168/214. Some members came to feel that the Council was better known elsewhere than it was in the Medway Towns themselves: *Chatham, Rochester and Gillingham News*, 17 November 1944.
29. Kipping to Regional Controllers, 6 June 1944, BT 168/214; Minutes of Regional Controllers' Conference, 12 July 1944, BT 168/151. Kipping went to some pains to conciliate Dickson, inviting him to lunch with the Permanent Secretary and the PPS in July: 'I know that you will perfectly understand (the refusal to circulate his booklet officially) ... and will not misinterpret our viewpoint as in any way a damper upon your keen and constructive endeavours'. (Kipping to 'My Dear George', 7 July 1944, JIP to Woods, 17 July 1944, BT 168/214).
30. Burns to Kipping, 27 June 1944, BT 168/214; *AEU Monthly Journal*, June 1944.
31. Howard to Kipping, 6 June 1944, BT 168/214. Some had already started to do so: e.g. St. Albans (meeting with Sir Robert Sinclair, *Minutes*, 28 June 1944, BT 168/214). Barclay, in October, was holding up the formation of a Full Employment Council in Watford in the hope that something could be won from Whitehall. (Barclay to Dickson, 28 October 1944, FBI 200/F/3/s2/29/36/b). By December 1944 there were fully-fledged Medway-style organisations in Watford, St. Albans, Luton and Colchester ('Regional Views on Future of District Committees', n.d. (late 1944), Stokes Papers 180/MRB/3/4), as well as the neighbouring Kentish towns of Erith, Crayford and Tonbridge (Full Employment Council *Minutes*, 14 November 1944, p. 1, BT 168/214).
32. *Minutes* of meeting with Sir Robert Sinclair, 28 June 1944, BT 168/214.
33. In 1946 he was responsible for recruiting Dickson to the Association. (1944 Association, *Minute Book*, 3 May 1946, Labour Party Archive.) In 1946 the Chairman of the Regional Board, Weston Howard, also joined the 1944 Association (*idem*, 1 February 1946). For Weston Howard's views on joint consultation see *Industrial Welfare*, July–August, 1947.

34. 'Regional Views on Future of District Committees', *idem.*
35. There was some interest in the Medway experiment in Wolverhampton. *Express and Star* (Wolverhampton), 18 July 1944; J.W. Smith, 'Planning Full Employment', *AEU Monthly Journal*, October 1945.
36. *Chatham, Rochester and Gillingham News*, 5 May 1944; Interview with Mr. G. Dickson, 11 December 1944, Cole Papers, B3/4/f6; E&ATSSNC *Shop Stewards and the Future*, n.d. (1945?), p. 11; H. Pollitt, *Answers to Questions*, 1945, p. 36. The local Communist Party welcomed the Council as an opportunity to discover 'whether it is possible for a community to live and develop in an orderly and constructive manner, instead of by the rather chaotic and haphazard methods of the past'. *Chatham, Rochester and Gillingham News*, 19 May 1944.
37. *Idem*, 18 August 1944. Gayner, a clerical worker, was secretary both of the JPC at Shorts, and of the Kent District Committee of the Communist Party. (*Idem*, 26 January 1945, 30 November 1945, 26 April 1946.) As secretary of the Shorts JPC, Gayner played a leading role in getting Cripps' guarantee, and pressing management to set up a market research and sales organisation to develop the civil aviation market, and perhaps alternative production as well (*idem*, 26 January 1945) – as Shorts had done successfully between the wars. (J.M. Preston, *Industrial Medway: an Historical Survey*, 1977, p. 197.) After the war he was nominated for membership of the Regional Board. (Taylor to Harries, 20 January 1948, TUC 292/557.4/2.)
38. *Chatham, Rochester and Gillingham News*, 26 May 1944. He saw party politics as a diversionary argument over the issue of ownership and an attempt to 'stampede the electorate emotionally' (*idem*, 27 April 1945). He liked to counterpoise the ineptitude of politicians to the hard practical understanding of the practical men in industry: 'Politically we will again hear the deluding lie about muddling through somehow. Industrially we cannot afford to listen to that nonsense' (*idem*, 12 May 1944).
39. *Chatham, Rochester and Gillingham News*, 13 July 1945.
40. Interview with Mr. G. Dickson, 11 December 1944, Cole Papers, B3/4/f6. Dickson pointed to the failure of the local authorities, embroiled in long-running disputes about whether or not to amalgamate, to give any coherent thought to the industrial future of the district as a whole, *Chatham Observer*, 22 December 1944; see also local Communist Party views on the amalgamation issue, *idem*, 6 April 1945; *Chatham, Rochester and Gillingham News*, 30 November 1945.
41. McCulloch, *op. cit.*, *passim.*
42. *Chatham, Rochester and Gillingham News*, 23 June 1944.
43. *Idem*, 23 June, 7 July 1944.
44. *Idem*, 21 July 1944. But a report in another local paper says it was passed – *Rochester, Chatham and Gillingham Journal*, 19 July 1944.
45. *Chatham, Rochester and Gillingham News*, 21 July 1944.
46. *Idem*, 4 August 1944. The Use Your Vote Society held a further debate, on Christianity and Labour, which passed off without incident, *Rochester, Chatham and Gillingham Journal*, 16 August 1944.
47. *Chatham, Rochester and Gillingham News*, 12 May 1944, 9 June 1944.
48. *Idem*, 12 May 1944. Dickson elaborated on the need for a Ministry of Distribution in a leaflet issued in October 1944, TUC 292/79M/19.
49. Dickson to Gardner, 24 October 1944, TUC 292/557/1; Dickson, 'Evolution in Management', in J.R.M. Bramwell (ed.), *This Changing World*, 1944, p. 98; Dickson, *Already Our Children Sneer*, 1941, p. 64. He was familiar with such methods having spent 10 years as a salesman and sales manager himself.
50. *Chatham, Rochester and Gillingham News*, 18 August 1944; MTFEC, *Minutes*, 14 November 1944, pp. 4–5, BT 168/214.

51. Preston, *op. cit.*, p. 197.
52. Minutes of Full Employment Council, 20 February 1945, p. 7, BT 168/214.
53. Robert Burns, Kipping's friend and adviser in the Ministry of Production, was interested in the 20% rule, which Dickson believed would apply to any industrial area, and he asked the resident economist, Kahn, to comment. Kahn was sceptical. Kipping to Dickson, 27 March 1945, Kahn to Burns, 21 March 1945, Burns to Kahn, 16 March 1945, Burns to Kipping, 26 March 1945, BT 168/214.
54. Under pressure from the JPC at Shorts, Cripps gave a guarantee that the firm would remain part of the nucleus of British aircraft production after the war supplying at least 4000 jobs in Rochester. MTFEC, *Minutes*, 20 February 1945, p. 3, BT 168/214; Report from Brother Crisp of Shorts to E&ASSNC, n.d. (early 1945), in Michaelson Papers 233/3/3/5; *Chatham, Rochester and Gillingham News*, 26 January 1945.
55. MTFEC, *Minutes*, 20 February 1945, pp. 2, 7. BT 168/214.
56. *The Times*, 28 March 1945.
57. *Chatham, Rochester and Gillingham News*, 20 April 1945, MTFEC, *Minutes*, 10 April 1945, pp. 2, 4–5, FBI 200/F/3/S2/29/36/b; London Regional Board, *Minutes*, 25 May 1945, BT 168/214.
58. *Chatham, Rochester and Gillingham News*, 7 June 1946, 2 November 1945.
59. *Idem*, 11 January, 26 April, 7 June, 5 July 1946; MTFEC, *Minutes*, 8 January 1946.
60. Also: 'Food is going to Germany. Work is going to Belfast. We are going to Hell fast', *Chatham, Rochester and Gillingham News*, 4 April, 14 June, 21 June, 5 July 1946.
61. H. Rees, 'The Medway Towns – their settlement, growth and economic development', London PhD, 1954, p. 296; J.M. Preston, *op. cit.*, pp. 204–5. There was, however, some serious unemployment in the late 1940s: London Regional Board, *Minutes*, 7 July 1948, in BT 168/214.
62. See, for example, the fury expressed by a Midlands businessmen active in the Regional Board at Whitehall's failure to make – or communicate – coherent reconstruction plans. Lancaster to King, 20 September 1944, Stokes Papers 180/MRB/3/4
63. MTFEC, *Minutes*, 10 April 1945, pp. 2–4, in FBI 200/F/3//S2/29/36/b.
64. Dickson to Wright, 2 May 1945, BT 168/214.
65. *Chatham, Rochester and Gillingham News*, 27 July 1945.
66. Dickson to Wright, 2 May 1945, BT 168/214.
67. Memo by Wood, 26 April 1946, BT 168/214. For a statement of the fear of local authority parochialism, see the Yorkshire Regional Controller in April 1945, BT 168/214.
68. FBI secretary to Dickson, April 1945, FBI 200/F/3//S2/29/36/b.
69. Cripps to Lord President's Committee, LP (45) 145, BT 171/301.
70. Some of the Trade Union representatives misinterpreted the shift to part-time chairmen as a downgrading of the Boards and opposed this innovation. Dickson, on the other hand, understood the real implications and backed Cripps at the NPACI. NPACI, *Minutes*, 24 August 1945, TUC 292/106.1/6; H.A. Turner to Woodcock, 27 August 1945, TUC 292/557/1.
71. Lord President's Committee, *Minutes*, 24 August 1945, BT 171/301.
72. Dennison to Lord President, 23 August 1945, CAB 124/349. Dennison also opposed the retention of NPACI.
73. Sheepshanks to Kipping, 28 September 1945, BT 171/301.
74. 'Future of the Regional Boards', pp. 6–7, LP(46)17, 22 January 1946, CAB 132/2; Chairmen of Regional Boards' Conference, *Minutes*, 15 February 1946, BT 168/225.

75. Johnson to Fraser, 1 November 1945, CAB 124/349.
76. Kipping, *Summing Up*, pp. 23–4; Minutes of meeting of employer representatives on Regional Boards, 21 June 1946, FBI 200/F/1/1/145. For FBI regionalisation see S. Blank, *Industry and Government in Britain. The FBI in Politics, 1945–65*, 1973, pp. 48–9.
77. Dickson to Kipping, 24 May 1946, FBI 200/F/3//S2/29/36/c.
78. Meeting of employer representatives on Regional Boards, *Minutes*, 21 June 1946, FBI 200/F/1/1/145. Kipping also attacked exaggerated Whitehall anxiety about secrecy: as did the TUC, where Harries points out that even when Regional Board members were informed they were not allowed to pass on information, turning the Boards into 'a small charm circle' with little impact in the real world. (Harries to Pankhurst, 12 June 1946, TUC 292/557.4/1.) And see Wal Blackmore, trade union vice-chair of the Medway Towns Full Employment Council on the same: Blackmore to Harries, 4 October 1946, TUC 292/557.4/1.
79. Sir Clive Baillieu, Regional Boards and District Committees, September 1946, NPACI papers, TUC 292/557.12/1. The TUC agreed. NPACI, trade union side, 3 October 1946, TUC 292/557.1/1.
80. S. Blank, *op. cit.*, pp. 75–6, 83, 108; H. Mercer, 'Labour and Private Industry, 1945–51', in N. Tiratsoo (ed.), *The Attlee Years*, 1991, pp. 73–4, 84.
81. N. Kipping, *Summing Up*, pp. 76–83.

8 Plan for Engineering

When, in 1943, Hugh Dalton launched the Board of Trade enquiries into the problems of post-war reconstruction faced by specific industries, he made clear his intention to proceed in the spirit of tripartism: 'arrangements will be made for consultation with the trade unions concerned.'[1] In engineering, however, this was easier said than done. Despite the relative homogeneity of the industry's skill base, the fragmentation of its markets encouraged employers to organise themselves for commercial purposes in a multitude of sectoral trade associations. Each trade association conducted its own relationship with Whitehall, leaving relations with the trade unions entirely in the hands of the EEF whose brief excluded it from discussing anything other than labour policy.[2] There was, therefore, no obvious forum within which tripartite consultations about the commercial future of the industry, or its various sectors, could take place. Matters were further complicated by disunity among the unions themselves. Acting on TUC advice, Dalton refused to meet representatives of the Confederation of Engineering and Shipbuilding Unions, since two of the major unions organising in the industry – the Foundry Workers and the AEU – remained outside the Confederation.[3] Ideally the TUC would have liked consultation to have been arranged through the National Production Advisory Council, on which all the unions were represented, but this was a non-starter since this was primarily a Ministry of Production affair with a brief for war production not for post-war reconstruction.[4] Instead they urged the unions to use the National Joint Engineering Trades Movement, re-established by the three unions in May 1942 to co-ordinate bargaining strategy with the EEF, to make a joint approach to the Board of Trade. Gavin Martin, the Confederation General Secretary, resisted a joint approach, and for some months the inter-union deadlock prevented any movement.[5]

Eventually agreement was reached to set up a sub-committee of the Joint Trades Movement to decide on a concerted approach to

post-war reconstruction.[6]   When this committee met in February
1944, Jack Tanner resisted proposals for an immediate deputation to
Dalton.   Instead the meeting asked the AEU research department to
prepare a list of questions to put to the Board of Trade as the
beginning of what Tanner saw as a 'slow and laborious job' of
gathering information: 'it would be necessary to evolve all the data
possible, and get answers to all the questions which the movement
felt necessary, until the time arrived when the sub-committee could
deal with the matter on the basis of fundamentals'.   A further reason
for delaying positive proposals was that the TUC was working on its
own Interim Report on Reconstruction, and until this was finalised,
it would be difficult to concert the approach of the engineering
unions with that of the movement in general.[7]   In the spring of 1944
union leaders presented their questions at a series of meetings with
the Principal Industrial Adviser to the Board of Trade, but they got
no satisfactory answers.   Tanner wondered whether this was because
the Board was being secretive, or because it had no reconstruction
plans to disclose.[8]   In fact, the union approach was so much at odds
with Board of Trade assumptions about future industrial policy, that
there was little constructive dialogue to be had.

The unions were not demanding nationalisation, which had
received only token support in trade union circles in the 1930s.[9]
Rather they wanted the Board of Trade to take over, and strengthen,
the co-ordinating role played by the wartime Ministry of Production.
In line with TUC proposals for the post-war control of industry they
called for the establishment of a tripartite Control Board for the
industry, closely integrated with Regional Boards and Joint
Production Committees.   Through this Board the Government should
lay down priorities, manpower and output targets for the various
sections of the industry during the transition period, and take power
to enforce its plans on industry.[10]   Shortly before the end of the war
the Joint Trades Movement published a detailed memorandum on the
state of the engineering industry in which they argued that the future
of Britain 'as a first-class industrial nation' depended on
comprehensive planning designed to modernise industrial plant,
boost exports and meet the pent-up demand for housing and
consumer goods.[11]   When they discussed this with the man in charge

of industrial reconversion at the Board of Trade he made it clear that while the Board was 'closely in touch with these matters ... it had no controlling or directive powers.' Not surprisingly the unions concluded that no 'proper long-term planning was being made in the reconstruction of the Engineering Industry'.[12]

After the Labour victory, the unions produced a supplementary report, putting forward much more ambitious claims. While accepting that the Government had no mandate to nationalise the industry, the unions 'were not prepared to allow the industry to drift ... to limp along in the old uncoordinated way.'[13] In contrast to the logic of the Board of Trade's traditional close relations with trade associations, the unions argued that the sectoral organisation of the engineering industry should itself be an object of planning:

> Presumably, the Government's broad plan for the economy as a whole will set given tasks and targets for the engineering industry (and its various branches) as for other industries. To fit into the master plan the industry will be required to make adjustments in manpower, the capacity devoted to given products and groups of products. It may be called upon to make a special effort to enhance output per head in various sectors because of manpower shortage; to pursue a policy of sharp expansion or concentration to meet changing needs and so on. To operate such a plan it is clearly necessary that an all-engineering Council be set up – engineers are engineers, no matter what section they are working in and a manpower budget may call for their skills to be used in different and changing directions.[14]

Wartime mobilisation had demonstrated the transferability of skills and machinery from one product to another, and the desire of individual firms to return as fast as possible to their pre-war specialisms was not, in the union view, a sensible basis for deciding the most appropriate use of engineering skills and capacities. During the next two years they complained repeatedly that engineering firms were being permitted to put short-term profit before the needs of national reconstruction with the result that scare resources were being wasted on the production of inessentials. In particular, the unions argued, the production of the capital goods necessary to re-equip British – and foreign – industry was being starved of capacity and manpower in order to make inessential luxury goods. Coal-mining machinery, electrical-generating plant, and other essentials remained in short supply, while resources were squandered on cars, radios, and household electrical goods.[15]   While this issue was sometimes pressed with a fervour that had more to do with productionist puritanism than with any careful assessment of the actual balance of industrial output, it nevertheless had a rational core. As Harold Wilson – drawing on his experience as President of the Board of Trade from 1947 –   was later to point out, the dependence of Whitehall on trade associations served to freeze the industrial structure, preventing radical innovation.[16] The structural evolution of the engineering unions on the basis of skills rather than products predisposed them to a more flexible view of the future of the industry than was possible for many of their employers, locked as they were into particular product markets and organised in product-specific trade associations.

To ensure that 'first things come first' the unions demanded the elaboration of detailed controls which would effectively transfer the initiative in deciding 'types and quantities of engineering products' from individual firms to the planning apparatus.[17]   One favoured means of control was through monopoly purchasing by the state – a control technique which, a few years later, Harold Wilson was to complain had been sadly neglected by the Labour Government.[18] The guaranteed market for standardised goods provided by state orders was seen by the unions as an important method of providing the stability favourable to mass production and technical progress in the industry. Bulk-buying, they argued, should be extended from defence and housing equipment to some capital goods and (with the aid of bilateral trading arrangements) leading export products: 'so that the manufacturer can proceed on the basis of full capacity mass production without fear of being unable to dispose of the output'.[19]

More generally, the unions argued, the aim of planning should be to elaborate targets applicable at sectoral, regional, firm and workshop levels, targets against which workers and managers could measure their own performance.[20] Merely giving priority to certain kinds of production was quite inadequate, if only because of the difficulties of transferring priorities for the finished goods back along the chain of component manufacturers involved in most engineering production. Moreover, as Gavin Martin put it, 'the vague priorities technique is incapable of mobilising the drive and initiative in the workshops, which is essential if the level of production is to be raised substantially. For essential requirements there must be a concrete detailed plan or programme. To be effective the programme must be capable of being broken down to specific tasks for individual factories. Everyone concerned should know exactly what he is asked to do'.[21] In response to criticism that the engineering industry was too diverse and complex for any such target setting, the unions stressed the need to articulate any industry-wide planning body at sectoral and regional levels.[22] They also pointed to the dominant role of large firms in most sectors of the industry as a potential aid to planning – 'by influencing the plans of [the dominant few] the industry can be moulded into the national plan'.[23] As a civil servant noted at the time, this was 'a surprising piece of political theory from the trade unions', and one that they failed to follow up – though others, from Harold Wilson to Tony Benn were later to do so.[24]

To oversee the industry the unions demanded the establishment of a tripartite Engineering Advisory Board. They did not challenge the constitutional fiction of parliamentary sovereignty, which Whitehall invoked to deny any executive powers to the proposed Board, and they usually remembered to stress that the function of the Board would be to 'assist the Minister' in planning the engineering industry.[25] As the prime source of 'planning', however, the Board was to have a full-time independent chairman 'preferably unconnected with the industry', and its own staff, independent of any Government department.[26] Whitehall officials believed that it would in practice be impossible to prevent a Board charged with the detailed planning functions envisaged by the unions from acquiring de facto executive powers. Full implementation of the union plan would mean corporatist self-government for the engineering industry, in which the independent chair and staff of the Board became servants of the two sides of industry rather than of the state.[27] This was not the union intention – they were more interested in securing the kind of close supervision by the state believed to be involved in the pre-nationalisation Board established for the iron and steel industry.[28] In the ambiguous language of Labour's 1945 manifesto, the 'constructive supervision' of private industry was, for the unions, a phase in the process by which their industry (or parts of it) would eventually become 'ripe for public ownership'.[29] The fact that many Labour ministers were coming to see the Iron and Steel Board as an alternative, rather than a stepping stone, to nationalisation, would have given union leaders pause for thought had they known it.[30]

Alongside the National Board the unions called for the strengthening of both Regional Boards and the JPCs. Only through a fully participatory system of planning, they argued, could 'the boundless enthusiasm, drive and initiative of the men and women on the job ... be won for the economic aims of the Labour Government.'[31] One objective of union policy was to entrench and strengthen wartime advances in the status of their shop floor organisation. The problems of inter-union rivalry, which had held back a coherent trade union response to the JPC agitation in 1941, were now less acute. The affiliation of the AEU to the Confederation finally took effect in December 1946, after years of strenuous negotiation. Well before this, however, the Confederation and the AEU had adapted their district machinery to accommodate joint shop steward organisation in the factories, and the unions were now committed to obtaining full recognition of joint shop steward committees within the procedure agreement with the EEF.[32] At the same time they reversed their earlier policy of insisting on the separation between collective bargaining and joint consultation over production issues, seeking instead to re-negotiate the JPC agreement to permit complete fusion between JPC and shop steward organisation.[33] This was a major departure from the wartime policy of seeking to fence off productionist collaboration with employers from established collective bargaining procedures, and while the reasoning behind it was probably pragmatic, its achievement would have represented a new level of shop floor challenge to the EEF's defence of managerial functions.[34] So also would the establishment of the planning machinery proposed by the unions, as the Whitehall briefing for the ministerial response to the trade union demands clearly explained:

> It is known that the unions would like to see the system of JPCs develop into a participation of trade unions in the organisation of production ... [The

proposed Engineering Board] would not be a mere extension of the JPCs.
JPCs have not participated in *planning* strictly so-called. The setting up of an
Engineering Advisory Board therefore would have a reflex action on JPCs and
would increase their specific gravity in factory affairs.[35]

When it had been announced in May 1944 that the Ministry of
Production was to be closed down at the end of the war, it had been
generally assumed that responsibility for the engineering industry
would revert to the Board of Trade. Instead, Attlee amalgamated
MAP into the Ministry of Supply, and gave the latter responsibility
for engineering in general, not just defence procurement. Because
Supply did not command a seat in the Cabinet the engineering unions
found themselves pressing their arguments about planning at some
remove from the central levers of power, and their situation was all
the more depressing since John Wilmot, the new Minister, was an
undistinguished politician prone to accept the views of his civil
servants and the business lobby.[36] Indeed it took the pleas of his
press officer to persuade him to stop his habit of wandering around
factories, after a good lunch with the bosses, flicking cigar ash on
the floor – not the kind of behaviour likely to endear a Labour
minister to ordinary workers.[37]

Wilmot and his officials were unimpressed by the trade union
ideas, which involved 'a far closer and more rigid degree of
planning than the Government contemplates':

They seem to have in mind a detailed plan which will enable Government for
example to say what type of product shall be made by a particular factory and
the quantities and delivery dates and to give instructions accordingly. This is
very different from the strategical approach which aims at painting in broad
outline a picture of the engineering industry appropriate to the national
economy as a whole and then devising administrative techniques for creating
the conditions in which such an industry will develop or for more positively
guiding industry towards that end.[38]

Within this 'strategic' approach planning, however, Wilmot did see a
role for an advisory body covering engineering as a whole, and he
used the union pressure to overcome Board of Trade objections that
any such forum was unnecessary.[39]

Wilmot finally approached the employers at the end of July 1946,
nearly six months after the first approach from the unions.

Representatives of engineering trade associations, convened by the FBI in August, were generally hostile to the proposal, fearing that it would provide the Government with new means of interfering in the industry.[40] There were also strong objections to the unions' claim to be equal partners in discussing questions of industrial policy with the Government, and the EEF Director, Sir Alexander Ramsay was said to be 'unable ... to see any good reason why the trade unions should extend their interest in engineering outside the field of labour wages and conditions'.[41] The employers delayed their response, awaiting the report of a joint FBI–BEC committee previously set up to clarify policy on tripartite machinery in general.[42] While reasserting the FBI's established policy that trade associations should ideally be the sole channel of communication between particular industries and the Government, this report acknowledged that simply standing pat was likely to provoke legislative intervention. Where, as in engineering, no organisation capable of speaking for the industry as a whole was in existence an Advisory Council might be needed and, if so, trade union participation could not be avoided.[43] In October the FBI agreed to support an Engineering Advisory Council provided it remained a purely advisory body. The employer members, to be appointed by the Minister from nominations submitted by the major employers' organisations, were not to be seen as representative of industry nor were they empowered to enter into agreements on its behalf. Moreover the Council would address only general questions affecting the industry as a whole and have no brief for the affairs of particular sectors, where the existing direct links between trade associations and the Ministry would remain the normal method of communication.[44] Where sectoral Advisory Committees already existed these were to remain entirely separate from the new Council. By thus cutting the Council off from sectoral questions, the employers' conditions undermined a major purpose of the union approach, which had been to reorientate Government relations with engineering from a sectoral to an all-industry basis. Wilmot, however, refused to countenance the unions' argument for the subordination of sectoral advisory bodies to the Council.[45] On this basis the Engineering Advisory Council was established in December 1946.

After nearly a year of discussions, it was clear to the unions that they had gained only the form, not the substance of their demand, and subsequent events fully confirmed that the Council could provide neither direction to the industry nor effective trade union participation in relations between business and the Government.[46] The Minister, Gavin Martin complained bitterly, had capitulated to employers who 'were only prepared to come in on this Council if it were rendered impotent through executive power remaining with' themselves. Wilmot's response strikingly revealed his insensitivity to the arguments for participation in private industry presented by the unions: 'The engineering industries were privately owned; this was a fact which as they knew, was unlikely to be changed within the lifetime of the present Government. Ownership carried with it executive functions'.[47] Just as Dalton's Board of Trade had no time for the divided sovereignties involved in George Dickson's schemes for local autonomy, or the milder devolution favoured by Norman Kipping, so Wilmot ruled out any possibility that power in industry could effectively be shared. There was no room within his bald formulation for the project of a democratising alliance against employer autocracy which, however tentatively, had been struck between productionist trade unionism and some Whitehall departments during the war – and which the unions had hoped to revive and extend under a Labour Government. Wilmot had persuaded the employers to co-operate in a toothless Advisory Council, but on their autocratic powers in industry he encroached not one inch.

NOTES

1. AEU National Committee, *Report*, 1943, p. 123.
2. In 1945 the engineering unions asked the EEF to join them in a joint approach to Whitehall. (Confederation of Shipbuilding and Engineering Unions, *Report*, 1946, p. 111.) The EEF, who had no wish to encourage the unions to engage with issues of industrial policy, declined. (EEF Management Board, *Minutes*, 26 July 1945, EEF 237/1/1/42.) Earlier the unions had brushed aside a tentative proposal for informal talks made by Low to Tanner, fearing that they would be blinded with science and suborned to the plans of the monopolists. NEJTM Sub-Committee, *Minutes*, 6 April 1944, TUC 292/615/2.
3. Cronyn, memoranda, 2, 12 July, 1943, 2 February 1944; ? (indecipherable) to Meeres, 16 March 1944, BT 64/3099.

4. O'Donnell to Cronyn, 1 June 1943, BT 64/3099. But the TUC *was* able to use the NPAC in the autumn of 1944 to pressure Whitehall to release research and development capacity for post-war production, a question on which it saw eye to eye with the employers. NPAC, *Minutes*, 1, 25 September, 3 November 1944, TUC 292/106.1/6; Harries to Citrine, 13 November 1944, TUC 292/557/1; TUC Economic Committee, *Minutes*, 5 November 1944, TUC 292/560.1/3.
5. O'Donnell to Woodcock, 15 November 1944, TUC 292/557/1; BT 64/3099, *passim*; J.B Jefferys, *The Story of the Engineers*, 1945, p. 263.
6. AEU National Committee, *Report*, 1944, pp. 96–8, 254.
7. NEJTM Sub-Committee on Post-War Reconstruction, *Minutes*, 2 April 1944, TUC 292/615/2. Tanner argued that they would need to pay for expert economic advice if they were serious. In fact Yvonne Kapp of the AEU research department did most of the work, with some help from the TUC officials: Gardner to Citrine, 5 October 1944, Martin to Turner, 9 October 1946, TUC 292/615/2.
8. AEU National Committee, *Report*, 1944, pp. 96–8.
9. 'Nationalisation of Engineering Industry', TUC 292/615.2/4, *passim*.
10. NEJTM, *Post-war Reconstruction*, 1945; Martin to Citrine, 13 September 1944, TUC 292/615.2/4; B. Bellairs, 'The Ministry of Production Must Stay', *AEU Monthly Journal*, January 1945; AEU National Committee, *Report*, 1944, p. 98; E&ATSSNC, *Shop Stewards and the Future*, n.d. (1945?), p. 7.
11. NEJTM, *Post-war Reconstruction*, 1945, p. 8; Confederation of Shipbuilding and Engineering Unions, *Report*, 1946, p. 112; AEU National Committee, *Report*, 1944, p. 220.
12. Confederation of Shipbuilding and Engineering Unions, *Report*, 1946, p. 112.
13. NEJTM to Wilmot, 9 January 1946, SUPP 14/137; Meeting between MOS and NEJTM, 13 February 1946, TUC 292/615.2/5.
14. 'Need for an Advisory Board', NEJTM memorandum to Ministry of Supply, 28 February 1946, TUC 292/615.2/5.
15. 'Engineering and the Crisis', 8 December 1947, TUC 292/615.2/5; Jack Tanner, Economic Planning Board Minutes, 30 October 1947, TUC 292/567.13/1; Gavin Martin in *Labour Monthly*, June 1947; Tanner to AEU National Committee, *AEU Monthly Journal*, August 1947; Tanner at York Conference, 3 March 1947, EEF 237/1/13/80.
16. A.A. Rogow and P. Shore, *The Labour Government and British Industry*, 1955, pp. 66–7.
17. Meeting between MOS and NEJTM, 13 February 1946, TUC 292/615.2/5; NEJTM, *Memorandum on Post-war Reconstruction in the Engineering Industry*, 1945, p. 9.
18. H. Wilson, 'The State and Private Industry', 4 May 1950, CAB 124/1200. pp. 11–13.
19. NEJTM, *op. cit.*, pp. 7–8; AEU National Committee, *Report*, 1948, p. 77. In 1947 pro-Labour businessmen in the 1944 Association – including George Dickson – urged Government intervention in the export trade along similar lines. Crittall to Cripps, 17 December 1947, SUPP 14/137.
20. NEJTM, 'Engineering Advisory Board', 29 October 1946, p. 3, SUPP 14/137; NEJTM, 'Engineering and the Crisis', 8 December 1947, p. 2, TUC 292/615.2/5.
21. *Labour Monthly*, June 1947.
22. Tanner to AEU National Committee, *AEU Monthly Journal*, August 1947; NEJTM, *op. cit.*, 1945, pp. 9, 11; NEJTM, 'Engineering and the Crisis', 8 December 1947, p. 2, TUC 292/615.2/5; Meeting between CSEU and MOS, 5 April 1948; NEJTM, 'Engineering Advisory Board', 29 October 1946, SUPP 14/137.
23. NEJTM to Wilmot, 28 February 1946, TUC 292/615/2.
24. Brief for Minister, February 1946, SUPP 14/137; H. Wilson, *op. cit.*, p. 17. See also G.D.H. Cole, *Guide to the Elements of Socialism*, Labour Party, 1947, p. 20.

25. 'Need for an Advisory Board', NEJTM memorandum to MOS, 28 February 1946; Meeting between MOS and NEJTM, 13 February 1946, TUC 292/615.2/5.

26. NEJTM, 'Engineering Advisory Board', 29 October 1946, SUPP 14/137. In later versions, the idea of an independent staff was dropped: instead there was to be 'a small permanent full-time committee' which would 'play a leading part ... in constant consultation' with both Whitehall and sectional committees, in working out the broad lines of the engineering plan: NEJTM, 'Engineering and the Crisis', 8 December 1947, p. 2, TUC 292/615.2/5.

27. Brief for Minister, 18 November 1946, SUPP 14/137.

28. Draft Brief for Minister, November 1946; NEJTM meeting with MOS, 10 December 1946, SUPP 14/137; AEU National Committee, *Report*, 1946, p. 253.

29. Labour Party, *Let Us Face the Future*, 1945, p. 6.

30. K.O. Morgan, *Labour in Power, 1945-1951*, Oxford, 1984, pp. 113-14.

31. 'Need for an Advisory Board', NEJTM memorandum to Ministry of Supply, 28 February 1946, TUC 292/615.2/5; NEJTM, *Memorandum on Post-war Reconstruction in the Engineering Industry*, 1945, p. 9; AEU National Committee, *Report*, 1947, p. 275.

32. *Idem*, p. 60; *New Propeller*, January, June 1946, April 1947; York Conference, *Minutes*, 23 October, 17 December 1947 EEF 237/1/13/82.

33. NACE&SI, *Minutes*, 24 January 1946, TUC 292/106.451/2; York Conference, *Minutes*, 30 April 1946, EEF 237/1/13/84; EEF Policy Committee, *Minutes*, 20 November 1946, EEF 237/1/9/3; AEU National Committee, *Report*, 1946, p. 99.

34. J.B. Jefferys, *Trade Unions in a Labour Britain*, 1947, p. 3.

35. Bower, Briefs for Minister, 8 February 1946; 28 February 1946, SUPP 14/137.

36. Morgan, *op. cit.*, pp. 85, 112.

37. R. Williams Thompson, *Was I Really Necessary?*, 1951, p. 99.

38. Bower, Brief for Minister, 8 February 1946; 28 February 1946; Downey, notes on planning, 18 November 1946, SUPP 14/137. Privately, however, Downey acknowledged that *ad hoc* tactical intervention designed to sort out particular bottlenecks would continue to be necessary during the transition period, and might well prove permanent, given the rigidities likely to be created by full employment.

39. Wilmot to Bowen, 14 February 1946; Wilmot to Cripps, 11 March 1946, SUPP 14/137. Cripps would have preferred a sub-committee of the NPACI: Turner to Woods, 15 July 1946; Brief for Minister, 31 July 1946, SUPP 14/137.

40. Meeting of Engineering Industry Associations, 15 August, 1946, FBI 200/F/3/S1/46/1.

41. Memorandum by Bowen, 24 May 1946, SUPP 14/137. Sir Lyndon Macassey wanted to limit union initiative on any Council by restricting the right to raise issues to the Minister: Meeting of Engineering Industry Associations, 23 October 1946, FBI 200/F/3/S1/46/1.

42. Meetings of Engineering Industry Associations, 15 August, 3 October 1946, FBI 200/F/3/S1/46/1; Meeting of FBI and MOS, 25 September 1946, SUPP 14/137. S.Blank, *Industry and Government in Britain. The FBI in Politics, 1945-65*, 1973, pp. 86-7.

43. S. Blank, *op. cit.*, pp. 86-7.

44. Maginness to Wilmot, 24 October 1946, SUPP 14/137; memo (unsigned) to Kipping, 2 August 1946; Meeting of Engineering Industry Associations, 23 October 1946, FBI 200/F/3/S1/46/1.

45. NEJTM, 'Engineering Advisory Board', 29 October 1946, SUPP 14/136. Moreover the unions were highly critical of the existing sectoral advisory councils because they gave unions a less than equal role: Tewson to Wilmot, 5 July 1946, TUC 292/615.61/1; NEJTM to Wilmot, 28 February, 1946, TUC 292/615/2.

46. In 1950 the CSU complained that the EAC served 'mainly as a sounding board for employers complaints', and that the Minister of Supply had shown himself

indifferent or hostile to trade union ideas about the future of the industry. (E&SINAC, *Minutes*, 1 March 1950, in TUC 292/615.2/5.) See also below p. 201.

47. Meeting between MOS and NEJTM, 10 December 1946, SUPP 14/137.

9 Crisis, 1947

The engineering unions did not lack constructive proposals about economic planning to offer to the Labour Government, as the evidence reviewed in the last chapter makes clear. But confronted with a right-wing and ineffective minister in their sponsoring department, there was little the unions could do to open a meaningful dialogue with the Government. When the coal crisis of January and February 1947 shut down large parts of British industry and threw 1.5 million people out of work, the unions tried again to press their proposals. At the same time members of the Regional Boards, from both sides of industry, seized on the opportunity created by the Boards' enhanced authority during the coal crisis to press for a revival of the JPCs, which had withered away in most factories since the end of the war. During the summer of 1947 a vigorous argument developed at national level over the relationship between the Regional Boards and any JPC revival. The Ministry of Labour's traditional concern to foster joint consultation in the factories in a spirit of conciliation and free from external pressures was challenged by productionist voices which looked to the JPCs as the key to securing positive shop floor participation in tackling Britain's economic crisis. This productionist challenge gained heavy-weight political support from Stafford Cripps who, as President of the Board of Trade, had inherited responsibility for the Regional Boards from the wartime Ministry of Production.

In the aftermath of the sterling crisis of August 1947, when Cripps became Minister of Economic Affairs, he took the Regional Boards with him. For a brief moment it seemed that the productionists might be given their head. Proposals were floated to merge the tripartite consultative machinery of the National Production Advisory Council with that maintained by the Ministry of Labour. As with the agitation for an overlord Ministry of Production in 1941–42, these developments called into question that institutional separation between industrial relations and economic policy which stood like a road-block in the path of attempts to mobilise a productionist alliance between Government and the shop floor. But reform of the Whitehall machine, especially when such sensitive interests were involved, was not on the agenda of the Attlee Cabinet. After Cripps replaced Dalton as Chancellor of the Exchequer in November 1947, the potential threat to Treasury authority represented by his fledgling Ministry of Economic Affairs was contained. At the same time Cripps acquiesced in a compromise settlement of the argument over Ministry of Labour stewardship of joint consultation in the factories. Deprived of his leadership, the productionist challenge quickly ran into the sands, if only because the dominant groups on both sides of industry remained fully committed to the politics of voluntarism. TUC leaders saw their special relationship with the Ministry of Labour through the National Joint Advisory Committee as an anchor for free collective bargaining – their most profound commitment. The continuing devotion of employers to the separation of commercial and labour issues in their dealings with Government was apparent from the failure of efforts to negotiate a merger of the two peak organisations responsible for these areas, the FBI and the BEC.[1] In the absence of powerful political support at the apex of Government, the productionist visions of a handful of public-spirited employers and a rather larger number of trade union leaders and activists were easily subordinated to the voluntaristic codes implicit in the established structures of state/industry relations. The breakthrough to a more positive relationship between the British state and its shop floor citizens would have required institutional upheavals which the Attlee Government – immersed in the politics of nationalisation, welfare reform and crisis management – had neither the energy nor the imagination to initiate.

It was not only at elite level that productionist enthusiasm ran into obstacles. The shop floor citizens themselves were not easily aroused to embrace their own responsibilities. Underpinning all the discussions between Government, employers' organisations and trade unions during 1947, was a shared recognition that Britain stood on the edge of an economic precipice. While they disagreed, often fundamentally, about the measures needed to secure it, all parties to these top-level discussions agreed that a new production effort equivalent to that achieved during the war would be essential to averting catastrophic economic collapse. In contrast to the early war years, however, this sense of crisis among the elites was not met by an answering commitment from below. However acute, problems of economic survival could never have the same mobilising impact as the threat from Hitler. Moreover, the election of a Labour Government in 1945 had done much to defuse one central component of the popular mobilisations of 1940–42. No-one could any longer argue convincingly that the Men of Munich, the Blimps, 'the old and the silly' remained in charge. There was, therefore, no widely perceived need for popular revolt to enforce change at the top. The planners and the progressives now held the levers of power, and the need of the hour was not to attack them, but to respond loyally to their demands. The belief, shared by Beaverbrook and the Communist Party in 1941, that the aim of responsible leadership should be, not to dissipate popular discontent, but to direct the energies it released into constructive channels, would have appeared to post-1945 Labour ministers as not only distastefully populist, but also entirely irrelevant. The task facing political leaders in 1947 was not to respond to popular anger at elite complacency and inefficiency but the much more complex task of convincing workers that the situation was indeed desperate, without, at the same time, sowing the seeds of apathy, cynicism and despair.

For the first eighteen months of peace there was little popular understanding of the depth of the economic problems facing Britain. When, in March 1946, a poll asked: 'What do you think should be done to persuade people in this country to step up production', the response revealed a massive unsatisfied desire for higher consumption, but very little idea about how it was to be achieved. The overwhelming majority of respondents suggested that the key to greater production lay in providing material incentives – more money, more goods in the shops, extra food and clothes for production workers, better working conditions. But where was this cornucopia to be found? The possibility that increased productive effort might have to be the precondition, rather than the result, of greater consumption was clearly not a thought that was widely entertained. Less than 10% of those questioned saw the key as lying in more effective Government efforts to persuade workers of the need for greater output, and a similarly small proportion believed that increased production required structural changes – more (or less) state intervention in industry, more industrial democracy, and so on.[2]

In the face of such attitudes it is not surprising that most surviving Joint Production Committees withered away during the early post-war months.[3] A minority of activists made brave efforts to defend the Committees against employer hostility and rank-and-file indifference, but even in the Communist Party, the productionist visions of the leadership were hard to sustain among shop floor activists. Writing early in 1947, one militant bemoaned his comrades' inability to understand that:

> Success in this period depends on how much the workers gain a controlling voice in the economy, in production ... government control of engineering with direct workers' control in ever-increasing whacks in the factories. We see Party members of long standing, some with steward's tickets, fighting valiantly for a penny increase in the bonus, while the whole production of the factory is in a state of chaos. Brand spanking new machine tools coming in for luxury production, while the pits cry out for machinery.... I am convinced that the biggest job we have in the next few months is to win first our own cadres in the factories for the policy of the Party in relation to production and Britain's economic future, before we can get any real basis in the factories at all.[4]

Other sources told the same story: 'There is no fervour for production, and JPCs ... have largely disappeared. Those that remain are more dead than alive.'[5] Such impressions are confirmed by the responses to an AEU circular to North London factories in 1947: less than 20% had JPCs, and those that survived dealt with a narrower agenda than in wartime.[6] A survey conducted by the Midland Regional Board in the summer of 1947, found only 194 firms with any kind of arrangement for joint consultation, compared with over five times as many at the height of the wartime mobilisation.[7]

By the autumn of 1947 popular attitudes to production had undergone a major change. Few were now unaware of what was known simply as 'the crisis', and, surprisingly perhaps, more people supported Government plans to re-introduce direction of labour than

opposed them.[8] This shift in public perceptions may have owed
something to intensive propaganda campaigns designed to raise
public awareness that the fulfilment of material aspirations depended
on increased production: 'We Work or Want'. But the major
educator was life itself – above all the disruption of everyday life
caused by the coal shortages of the early months of 1947. If the
public was now much more aware of the dangers of Britain's
economic situation, most remained unconvinced that there was
anything they personally could do about it. Thus a Social Survey
report on the effects of the 'Work or Want' campaign found that
80% felt that they were already doing everything they could.[9] A
study of three small London factories conducted in the summer of
1947 showed that while most of the workers 'fully realised the
importance of the production drive', and were willing, indeed
anxious, to help, they were unconvinced that their firms were
producing what was needed for national economic recovery. As one
worker explained: 'I think [the production drive] is terribly
important and I feel it affects me just as much as anyone else. But
what can you do about it? ... I think a lot about it – I read the paper
every day and listen to the wireless, hoping I'll hear someone with a
brilliant solution, but I've never found it yet.'[10] Most, no doubt,
were rather less conscientious. Nevertheless, compared with the
immediate post-war period, by 1947 workers had come to
understand the seriousness of Britain's economic position. The
Government, however, was failing to turn this growing
understanding into a positive production effort. The workers felt
powerless in the face of the crisis: apathy and cynicism in the
workshops was the result.

Nothing revealed this more clearly than response to the
Government's productivity campaigns. The 'Work or Want'
campaign was deemed by the Social Survey to have had little
positive effect: 'Public statements of urgency unaccompanied by
evidence of urgent public action are not likely to effect large changes
in public attitudes.'[11] But its negative effects may well have been
more substantial. An irate meeting of Midlands employers reported
that 'workers themselves were deriding such propaganda'. The
campaign relied heavily on official speakers – 'well-dressed, well-

fed ... obviously not workers' – who toured the factories 'telling other people to work harder'.[12] As one trade unionist put it: 'One group of people has always worked and wanted – another group has never worked, and never wanted.' The invasion of 2,000 factory canteens by such speakers over the summer of 1947 probably did more to stir up class resentment than productive effort. The campaign had been launched without any prior consultation with the trade unions, and they were quick to condemn it. Worst of all was the timing of the campaign, launched while the effects of the coal crisis were still widely felt in industry. The combination of the implied threat in the slogan 'We Work or Want' with the constant disruption of production by fuel and raw material shortages beyond the control of workers or individual firms, served not to mobilise workers, but to reinforce feelings of 'bewilderment and helplessness'. 'What was the use of appealing for more work when materials were in short supply?', asked the Midlands employers. The main effect of the campaign was probably to trigger deep-rooted fears that the Government might be unable to prevent the much-anticipated post-war slump.[13] 'It was impossible' members of the Northern Regional Board explained, 'to stir a man to greater effort if he saw that supplies were so low that he would simply work himself out of a job very quickly.'[14] Workers no longer needed to be told there was a crisis. But neither the Government's propaganda nor its management of the economy was doing much to create the climate of opinion in which a productionist alliance could be built.

The leaders of the engineering unions believed that the coal crisis clearly vindicated the arguments they had put, unavailingly, to Wilmot. In February 1947 the employers, forced by selective electricity cuts to reorganise the working day, sought to suspend existing agreements on nightshift and overtime pay. The unions responded with a forceful re-statement of their arguments:

> We do not think that the workers should be called upon to foot the entire bill for something which was not of their making.... For nearly two years now we have been stressing the fundamental role of engineering in the tasks of reconstruction. We have repeated over and over again the obvious fact that the nation's needs ... cannot be obtained unless the engineering industry supplies the machinery and equipment. If, since the end of the war, our industry had been concentrating on the equipment most needed – coalmining

machinery and supplies, plant for electricity generation, distribution, etc, locomotives, rolling stock and other transport equipment – then the crisis might never have happened.... For what has been happening?.... There has been a scramble to get back to the production of the most profitable products regardless of national needs.

Instead of cutting wages, the unions appealed to the employers to join them in 'a statesman-like approach ... to take a national, rather than a sectional or selfish view'. Getting back to normal was not what the industry needed; rather the unions were ready to co-operate in a

selective re-starting of firms and section ... on a basis of first things first.... Something must go; and among the things sacrificed may well be a seemingly prosperous engineering business which will not or cannot switch from the less essential to the more essential products.... In our opinion, any engineering employer with any patriotic spirit at all should be consulting his trade association and pestering the Government to find out how he can help most

to redirect the activity of his firm to the meeting of national needs.[15] While not wishing to stress the point in the context of a negotiation about limiting workers' sacrifices, it is clear that Tanner and the Communists were prepared to face the problems of redundancy and transfer of labour that would have been involved in a systematic programme of shifting resources out of inessential production.[16]

When Jack Tanner put these proposals to the employers, they were happy to agree that the Government had failed to plan effectively, but the EEF deflected any suggestion of a joint approach to Government by arguing that such matters were the province of the newly established Engineering Advisory Council.[17] The Council, however, was a disappointment – 'just another advisory body'[18] – and union offers of 'loyal co-operation' with its directives were futile, since no such directives were forthcoming.[19] In 1946 a Ministry of Supply official had meanly suggested that the real driving force behind union demands for an Advisory Council was the leaders' search for well-paid part-time jobs like those available to their colleagues on the Iron and Steel Control Board.[20] While such motives should not be altogether discounted, it is clear that the activists (who had no prospects of such perks) were as keen on 'responsibility' and 'statesmanship' as were the national leaders.[21]

An attempt by right-wing delegates at the AEU National Committee in June 1947 to remove demands for detailed planning and trade union participation from the resolution on reconstruction was defeated by 36 votes to 14.[22]

It was on the shop floor that activists would have to make a reality of their constructive attitudes to the economic crisis. Before he left Whitehall, Norman Kipping had done what he could to entrench JPCs in the post-war production machinery, reminding the Regional Boards of their responsibility for handling shop floor grievances,[23] and urging the TUC to use its newly established Regional Advisory Committees to filter and pass on to the Boards shop floor complaints about production.[24]   But, while in January 1946 Cripps could heartily agree with a deputation of Coventry trade unionists that the JPCs were as relevant to peace as to war, his officials were wary of antagonising employers by acceding to demands for a new campaign on the issue.[25] When, in the summer of 1946, the Regional Boards were given responsibility for organising 'production drive' meetings,[26] some of the employer members were convinced by trade union arguments that, without effective JPCs in the factories, production propaganda was a waste of breath. In January 1947 the Chairman of the South Western Regional Board, an employer, called on the National Production Advisory Council to launch a new drive to establish JPCs in all industries, arguing that elected representatives would be better placed than 'professional speakers' to convince workers of the need for greater output.[27] The Regional Boards, many of their members felt, would be better employed promoting a JPC revival, than in arranging possibly counterproductive factory visits for speakers supplied by the Central Office of Information.[28]

It was the 1947 coal crisis which created the opportunity for the Regional Boards to recapture some of their wartime importance. During an earlier fuel crisis, caused by the miners' strike of 1944, the Boards had used their powers to ration supplies to industrial users. In 1946, as the fuel situation deteriorated, Whitehall again turned to the Boards for help.[29] In the crisis months of early 1947 the Boards became, according to a rapturous article in the *Board of Trade Journal*, 'the focal point of the nation-wide battle to overcome a menace which threatened to bring industry to a standstill', responsible for allocating coal from regional pools to individual firms, and for arranging to stagger working hours in order to reduce peak electricity demand.[30] For a moment, the coal crisis revived the wartime atmosphere of co-operation as management and shop stewards struggled to keep factories open: 'Emergency joint meetings were called. The management procured petrol generators and people worked all night to install them. Some workers with motor cycles contributed a part of their petrol ration.... This is only one example of similar experiences in other firms visited.'[31] In the South West, where the Regional Board encouraged the establishment of special fuel-efficiency committees in the factories, nearly 500 firms responded positively. This initiative had the enthusiastic support of the shop stewards' movement – indeed the Bristol Communist Party claimed to have been working with the local Ministry of Fuel and Power Controller to promote such committees ever since December 1945.[32]

For George Dickson, who had managed to get himself appointed acting chair of the London Regional Board, the coal crisis was 1940 come again. Euphorically he wrote to Norman Kipping: 'If we moved very fast and used the goodwill and understanding there is about the fuel and power situation ... we could get the basic structure [of joint consultation in the factories, and tripartite planning at local, district, and regional levels] into shape by March 1st'.[33] Kipping was unimpressed, but the shop stewards' movement enthused over Dickson's call for production targets to be agreed in every factory: 'He makes it clear that he does not expect such a drive to be successful without an overall plan for each industry, but there is much to be said for stimulating pressure in the shops as this will help to force action at the top.'[34]

The experience of the coal crisis helped to consolidate support for the revival of JPCs and in April the chairmen of the Regional Boards called for an urgent statement of Government policy on the issue.[35] In the Midlands, the AEU Divisional Organiser Billy Stokes, who had vied with the Communists to take the initiative on JPCs in the autumn of 1941, returned to the issue, this time as Chairman of the Regional Board. Production conferences were organised throughout the region and, reversing the position it had taken under employer pressure at the end of 1945, the Board agreed to a request from Coventry to circulate all firms in the town asking them to establish JPCs.[36] But when, in March 1947, the Eastern Regional Board (whose Chairman, Weston Howard, was a member of the pro-Labour 1944 Association) proposed a similar initiative, it was warned off by Whitehall on the grounds that any such move might adversely affect negotiations currently underway between the peak organisations.[37]

In the autumn of 1946 the TUC had circulated a position paper on the problem of 'Production under Full Employment' in which it argued that the removal of what the Webbs had called 'the whip of starvation' made the general extension of joint consultation a necessary basis for effective management.[38] When, in February 1947, the Chairman of the South West Regional Board urged the National Production Advisory Council to support the establishment of JPCs on the engineering model in all industries, he was enthusiastically backed by Tanner and the other trade union delegates.[39] The British Employers' Confederation, which had already consulted its members about the TUC paper, responded with a proposal that employers and unions in each industry should be encouraged to open national negotiations for the establishment of joint consultative machinery. Apart from insisting that any such machinery should be voluntary, advisory and quite separate from normal collective bargaining arrangements, the employers' proposal made no recommendations about the form joint consultation should take. In some industries, it suggested, it might be more appropriate to introduce joint consultation at district or regional levels rather than at the workplace. Significantly, no mention was made of the principle established in engineering that all JPC members should be members of trade unions.[40] These proposals were endorsed by the National Production Advisory Council in April 1947, firmly placing the promotion of joint consultation, however modestly defined, on the official agenda for the first time since the war.

As the worst of the coal shortages receded, and Regional Board members had time to reflect on the experience, they voiced their discontents with increasing vigour. Despite official gratitude, the

Boards themselves were far from happy about their role during the coal crisis. Lacking the executive authority necessary to impose their recommendations on individual firms, most Board members seem to have experienced the crisis as a frustrating exercise in responsibility without power.[41] The leader of the Labour Group on Birmingham City Council declared that he 'was very much afraid that the authority of the Regional Boards ... would be fatally weakened if schemes for the staggering of the electricity load, which had been prepared after long hours of consultation, broke down because recalcitrant firms were not forced to comply.' The Government's decision to launch its ill-conceived 'Work or Want' campaign in the immediate aftermath of the crisis, without consulting the Boards, was a further provocation. When, in June 1947, Hilary Marquand, the Paymaster-General, toured the country listening to the grievances of the Regional Boards, he found that the frustrations expressed at the FBI conference a year earlier had by no means diminished, and that they were fully shared by trade union members of the Boards. He brought back a bleak picture of civil servants treating Board meetings as a tedious chore, failing to participate in discussion, and, when challenged by their unofficial colleagues, stressing the extent to which they were bound by rules of confidentiality and instructions from Whitehall. 'The goose is cooked' remarked one trade unionist, 'before it is brought to the Regional Board.' Unless something was done, Marquand reported (unconsciously echoing Harold Macmillan's words after a similar investigation in 1941), the Boards were in danger of becoming:

> not a source of strength to the Government but a focussing point for discontent and irritation.... Here we have an organisation, containing leaders of both sides of industry, which is prepared to take responsibility and do unpopular things. We should regard them as a protection, not a nuisance.[42]

The discontent in the Regional Boards was widely reflected among trade union activists more generally. Thus the minutes of a meeting of Midlands' trade union officials in June 1947 show successive speakers calling for the reconstruction of the wartime link between JPCs and the Regional Boards, and the granting of executive authority to the Boards themselves. Within the existing structures, an AEU official from Wolverhampton complained, trade union officials could hope to do no more than pour oil on troubled waters: they lacked the power to do anything positive about the production problem. They looked to the TUC and the Government to take the necessary initiatives to get JPCs off the ground, in co-operation with the Regional Board.[43] These sentiments were fully shared by the shop stewards' movement and the Communist Party. It was through reviving and extending the JPCs, Communists argued, that the workers would be able to 'lead the drive for efficiency, for improved methods of production and for a reasonable labour discipline.'[44] By linking factory production committees to the Regional Boards, argued Harry Pollitt, 'the JPCs and shop stewards can become the Governments' main organised force for carrying through the plan.... We need to break down the bureaucratic idea that planning means doing everything from Whitehall'.[45] Within the factories, it was argued, shop stewards should concern themselves with commercial and pricing policy as well as with production as such and they should be given full access to the company's books. Where firms were pursuing short-term profit in inessential production at the expense of the national plan, JPCs should take the initiative in demanding the transfer of plant and labour to essential work.[46]

This ambitious programme, however much it appealed to the militants, meant little at a time when active JPCs had virtually ceased to exist in the factories. Well aware of this, the Left renewed its calls for legislation to enforce JPCs on reluctant employers. Articles in the *New Propeller* drew attention to Czech, French and Scandinavian legislation on workers' rights to joint consultation.[47] In Coventry, the local Labour Party and Trades Council backed local AEU demands for legislation to make JPCs compulsory, adding that they should 'be empowered to inspect the records and stocks, and to have access to all other information relevant to the successful carrying out of production processes in the establishment.' They also demanded the right to refer disputed issues directly to the Regional Board, and warned that 'without the mentioned authority the JPCs are useless and would be ineffective' in the fight to increase production.[48] At the AEU National Committee in June 1946 a resolution demanding statutory intervention had been withdrawn, but a year later the Left pushed the issue to a vote and won by a majority of 46 to four.[49]   Within two months, even the TUC leadership, provoked by the refusal of employers to give anything more than lip service to joint consultation, was ready to back compulsion.

When, in June 1947, Morrison met chairmen of the Regional Boards and their District Committees he went out of his way to praise the production campaign mounted by the activities of Stokes and the Midlands Regional Board. Rising to the occasion, Stokes laid out his demands for the integration of JPCs with the Boards:

> something had been missing with regard to JPCs both during the war and at the present time. JPCs were isolated units with no relationship outside their individual establishments. The formal agreement in the engineering industry only went as far as setting up a JPC and there was no provision for any relationship with other JPCs. The Regional Board could correct this situation and arrange, for example, quarterly meetings of JPCs within a district to discuss matters of mutual interest and compare methods of working.[50]

Marquand's report on the Regional Boards, written a few weeks later, also called for a strengthening of the link with JPCs: 'I regard this as my principal proposal', he wrote to Stafford Cripps.[51]

Morrison's support for the reformists produced a sharp response from the employers. At the National Joint Advisory Committee in July they ruled out the idea that Regional Boards should be permitted to convene meetings of JPC representatives.[52] At the same time they slapped down a modest proposal from the Ministry of Labour that they should be allowed to facilitate the various ongoing national negotiations in particular industries, by establishing a National Joint Advisory Committee sub-committee to monitor best practice and draw up a (purely optional) model constitution. The most the employers would accept was that conciliation officers should be allowed to assist in the establishment of joint consultative machinery after – but only after – a national agreement had been freely negotiated in the industry concerned.[53]

In taking such a tough line at the National Joint Advisory Committee, the employers came close to over-reaching themselves. Infuriated by their obstructiveness, TUC leaders toyed with the idea of pressing for compulsion, as they had done at a critical moment in the original JPC negotiation of 1942.[54] Cripps was probably more willing than Bevin had been in 1942 to respond, and early in September he delivered a public threat that unless more rapid progress was made in establishing JPCs 'we shall be obliged to take steps to enforce their constitution.'[55] At the TUC Congress a few days earlier, however, the engineering unions' annual demand for compulsion had been referred back to the General Council, after the shopworkers' leader warned that compulsion could pave the way for company unionism in weakly organised industries like his own.[56] Militants ridiculed this argument, arguing that if membership of JPCs was restricted to trade union members, as in the engineering agreement, there would be no such danger.[57] But such a demand – legislation to enforce trade union recognition – represented a breach in the traditions of voluntarism too fundamental for most trade union leaders to contemplate. Despite continued pressure from the engineering unions the TUC reverted to its traditional stance of opposition to compulsion.[58]

Though the threat of compulsion receded, neither Cripps nor his officials in the Regional Division were happy about the employer veto on strengthening the links between JPCs and the Regional Boards. In mid-October, attending a meeting of the Midlands Regional Board, Cripps stressed his commitment to devolving power to the Boards, and declared his determination to involve them in developing the JPCs.[59] Pankhurst, who had replaced Kipping in charge of the Regional Division, was unimpressed with the Ministry of Labour's record in encouraging JPCs – two years of inactivity followed by the thoroughly unsatisfactory National Joint Advisory Committee agreement of July 1947.[60] Pankhurst believed that the time had come to transfer the main responsibility for promoting JPCs from the Ministry of Labour to the Regional Boards, where the urgent question of mobilising productive effort would take priority over the traditional tenderness of the Ministry of Labour towards the susceptibilities of employers.[61] In addition he pressed the Ministry of Labour to accept the right of the Boards both to communicate with JPCs directly, and to call meetings of JPC representatives 'to give the current facts of the economic position'.[62] Convinced that Regional Board intervention would undermine all their patient work in reassuring employers that JPCs posed no threat to their authority,

Ministry of Labour officials accepted no more than a marginal shift from the National Joint Advisory Committee position, allowing Regional Boards to make general propaganda in favour of JPCs and to help to promote them in industries where a national agreement had already been negotiated.[63]   Unwilling to precipitate an inter-departmental confrontation over the issue, Cripps and his officials settled for this – 'if this is the most we can get agreed we had better accept it and get on with the job'[64] – and told the Regional Board chairmen that more direct access to the JPCs had been ruled out by the Ministry of Labour.[65] They had not, however, abandoned hope of circumventing Ministry of Labour obstruction by other means.[66]

Underlying these administrative squabbles lay a major issue about the nature of the relationships between state, business and labour in the British polity. When Dickson wrote, so excitedly, to Kipping in January 1947 he identified the key issue as being to break down the separation between Board of Trade and Ministry of Labour approaches to industry, starting with the fusion of the local advisory bodies attached to the two Ministries: the Regional Boards' District Advisory Committees, on the one hand, and the Ministry of Labour's Local Employment Committees, on the other. To this end, somewhat overestimating his friend's powers, he appealed to Kipping: 'Could you not get John Henry [Woods] and Godfrey Ince together', so that Dickson could explain his scheme. Characteristically Dickson assumed that if only he could get face to face with the decision-makers – in this case the permanent secretaries of the two departments – his own conviction and enthusiasm would be sufficient to make them see the light.[67]

The meeting Dickson requested never occurred, nor would it have produced results had it done so. In the summer of 1947 Hilary Marquand, reporting on the mounting frustration in the Regional Boards, proposed the same solution – the two Ministries should be given joint responsibility for the Boards and their local advisory committees merged.[68] Herbert Morrison, whose Lord President's Committee would decide what to do about the Marquand Report, was urged by his civil servants to back these proposals, pointing out that such a move would open the way to merging the tripartite structures not only locally, but also at national level – the National

Production Advisory Council and the National Joint Advisory Committee. They warned Morrison not to allow ministers to refer the issue back to the officials to sort out: 'This would lead nowhere. All kinds of interdepartmental rivalries and jealousies are at stake and this is pre-eminently a question on which ministers must take a decision.'[69]   In disregard of this advice the Lord President's Committee asked Marquand to conduct further consultations with officials in the departments concerned before any decisions were taken.[70]

The Cabinet reshuffle that followed the convertibility crisis momentarily opened the way to a more fundamental attack on the central structural problem identified by the reformers.   The translation of Stafford Cripps from President of the Board of Trade to Minister of Economic Affairs, responsible for overall co-ordination of the production programme and equal in authority to the Chancellor of the Exchequer, appeared to create the kind of production overlord that reformers had been pressing for ever since the debates of 1941–42.   Cripps took the Regional Division with him, thus going some way to reconstitute the wartime Ministry of Production.   Not surprisingly, Billy Stokes chose Cripps' new appointment as the moment to reopen the question of forcing the Ministry of Labour to share responsibility for the JPCs with the Boards.[71]   Cripps had for some time been exercised by the overlapping jurisdiction of the National Production Advisory Council and the National Joint Advisory Committee.[72] Harold Wilson, who replaced Cripps as President of the Board of Trade, told TUC leaders in October 1947 that Cripps 'strongly sympathised' with the view that the division of responsibility for tripartite consultation between the Ministries of Labour and Supply and the Board of Trade, was irrational and should be replaced by a single co-ordinated system of consultation.[73] When the official committee on Government Organisation met to review what changes were necessary following Cripps' appointment as Minister of Economic Affairs they noted that it would be necessary to reconsider the responsibilities of all three Ministries concerned.[74]

The threat to Whitehall traditionalists represented by a Ministry of Economic Affairs was, however, shortlived.   Within six weeks,

Cripps had been moved on to the Treasury, and thoughts of a radical recasting of the state apparatus faded away. When the leaders of the engineering unions met Cripps to protest against emergency measures which cut back on capital expenditure and, once more, to press for 'an effective machinery for democratic planning designed to draw the organised workers into partnership', they came away disappointed. The Labour Government had weathered its deepest crisis, and the reformers were no closer to their goal of 'a definite and well-organised programme of production' capable of mobilising 'workshop enthusiasm and initiative'.[75]

Writing in October 1946, George Dickson complained that the absence of any coherent planning machinery was frustrating 'the efforts of hundreds of thousands of intelligent and eager to help citizens ... who cannot get into the action.' What was missing, he lamented, was any equivalent to the 1918 Haldane Report on the Machinery of Government. 'Today everyone puzzled by the problems, from the Prime Minister to the intelligent shop steward, has his own ideas of how the machinery of government should be changed to suit our 1946 needs. But there is no official public study on the subject. Perhaps it is too late for that study now.'[76] Dickson's frustrated sense of a lost opportunity for radical administrative reform has been echoed by recent historians.[77] The fundamental re-thinking of the machinery of government that would have been essential to the institution of any system of participatory planning was not undertaken by the Labour Government. There was no Haldane Committee, and Cripps, the man most interested in rationalising the Whitehall apparatus, was too involved in the day-to-day management of economic policy to have the time to confront the forces of passive resistance to radical change. As Hilary Marquand had written at the height of the coal crisis: 'one more illustration of the fact that our governmental system in Britain never thinks ahead. All through the war, every Minister and every senior official was taken up with the crisis of the moment.... Just the same since the war.... Always thinking hard about to-day, sometimes about to-morrow, never about next year.'[78]

NOTES

1. S. Blank, *Industry and Government in Britain. The FBI in Politics, 1945–65*, 1973, pp. 38–40, 130–6; President's Morning Meetings, *Minutes*, 3 June 1947, BT 13/200.
2. G.H. Gallup (ed.), *The Gallup International Public Opinion Polls, Great Britain, 1937–1975*, Vol. 1 (1937–1964), New York, 1977.
3. EEF Policy Committee, *Minutes*, 25 September 1947, EEF 237/1/1/44.
4. *World News and Views*, 15 February 1947. For an example of sustained attempts to keep a JPC going see the file of Trade Union News and Tatler (Fergusson Pailin Ltd) in the Working-Class Movement Library, Manchester. In Coventry the AEU rejected moves to abandon JPCs as 'incompatible with [post-war] conditions wherein the Employers are fighting for profits and the worker for his existence', (Coventry AEU District Committee, *Minutes*, 11 December 1945), and the TUDPC remained active until the end of 1947.
5. George Allison, the CP industrial organiser, writing in *World News and Views*, 26 July 1947. See also *Labour Research*, May 1947, p. 84.
6. *Metalworker*, September 1947.
7. H. Humphries, 'Joint Consultative Machinery in the Midlands Region, 20 January 1949, LAB 10/724.
8. G.H. Gallup (ed.), *op. cit.* Only 2% had not heard of 'the crisis and 75% believed it to be serious rather than 'something we shall get over without much trouble. For the increase in public awareness about the need to export between March 1946 and March 1948 see W. Crofts, *Coercion or Persuasion? Propaganda in Britain after 1945*, 1989, pp. 63–4.
9. 'The Second Stage of the Production Campaign, RG 23/123A; W. Crofts, *op. cit.*, p. 39. See also the view of the Chief Information Officer to the Ministry of Supply that the campaign was positively counter productive: 'In fact the only achievement of the Whitehall Productivity Campaign was to produce an ignorance curtain. The workers were gradually put off from reading the bad propaganda with the result that they ultimately did not read, let alone absorb any of the facts about Britain's dire economic position. And the mention of the word productivity was likely to make them feel physically ill!!' R. Williams-Thompson, *Was I Really Necessary?*, 1951, p. 111n.
10. Norah M. Davies, 'Notes on the attitudes of workers in three factories to the production drive', Medical Research Council, Industrial Health Research Board, in FBI 200/p/3/s2/29/36/f.
11. The Second Stage of the Production Campaign, RG 23/123A.
12. *Idem*. The Ministry of Labour's press officer had pointed this out before the campaign was launched, but he was disregarded: Crofts, *op. cit.*, p. 43. The Ministry of Supply's press officer was equally dismayed: R. Williams-Thompson, *op. cit.*, p. 105.
13. Report on meetings of trade union and employers representatives convened by Midlands Regional Controller of MOS, reproduced in R. Williams-Thompson, *op. cit.*, pp. 106–9; Crofts, *op. cit.*, pp 38–47; The Second Stage of the Production Campaign, RG 23/123A; Visit of Paymaster-General to Scotland, *Report*, July 1947, CAB 124/351.
14. Visit of Paymaster-General to Northern Area, *Report*, July 1947, CAB 124/351. 'The worker, another employer pointed out, wanted to be assured of security of work and the fuel crisis and the steel shortage had filled the average worker with alarm and suspicion. Men would not work hard until they saw a good stock pile of coal and steel.' Visit of Paymaster General to Birmingham, *Report*, July 1947, CAB 124/351.
15. AEU National Committee, *Report*, 1947, pp. 62–7.

16. *Idem*, pp. 266, 269; *Labour Research*, October 1947, pp. 169–71; *World News and Views*, 26 July 1947, p. 332.
17. York Conference, *Minutes*, 3 March 1947, p. 5, in EEF 237/1/13/80.
18. Jack Tanner to AEU National Committee, *Report*, 1947, p. 265.
19. AEU National Committee, *Report*, 1948, p. 77.
20. Draft Brief for Minister, November 1946, SUPP 14/137A.
21. *New Propeller*, February, April 1947.
22. AEU National Committee, *Report*, 1947, pp. 278–9.
23. Kipping to Chairmen of Regional Boards, 5 November 1945, BT 168/102; Conference of Chairmen of Regional Boards, 7 December 1945, BT 168/224.
24. Grindley to Harries, 9 November 1945, BT 168/102. Though happy to give their Regional Committees this responsibility, the TUC was reluctant to promote any new district-level organisation in place of the now largely defunct TUDPCs, preferring to wait and see how things developed. (Harries to Grindley, 31 December 1945, BT 168/102; NPACI GC-side, 7 December 1945, TUC 557.1/1; TUC Circular, 2 January 1946, TUC 557.4/1; Harries to White, 4 June 1946, TUC 106.44/1.) There is, however, no reason to doubt that the TUC would have authorised new district machinery had the demand for co-ordination been created by an upsurge of JPC-activity in the factories. (Harries to Walker, 6 June 1946, *loc. cit.*) In December 1946, responding to increasing Trades Council interest in issues of local economic planning, the TUC informed Trades Councils that they could use the Regional Advisory Committees to raise issues with the Regional Boards. (TUC circular, 20 December 1946, TUC 557.4/1; NPACI GC-side, 5 December 1946, TUC 557.1/1.) During the war the TUC had been anxious to keep the Trades Councils at arm's length from production issues.
25. Belson to Pankhurst, 9 January 1946, BT 168/26.
26. NPACI, *Minutes*, 21 June 1946; NPACI, Note by Board of Trade, 2 August 1946; NPACI, note by Sir Clive Baillieu, September 1946; NPACI, Regional Division Report, December 1946; all in TUC 557.1/1 and 557.12/1.
27. 'JPCs and the Production Drive', Whitwell to NPACI, 31 January 1947, TUC 557.12/1. Whitwell had already been persuaded of the need for a JPC revival by trade union arguments in May 1946: Whitwell to Kipping, 11 May 1946, FBI F/3/S2/29/36 (c).
28. Hilary Marquand, Draft Report to Lord President, July 1947, p. 3, CAB 124/351.
29. JWB to Lord President's Committee, 1 April 1946, PREM 8 440. The NPACI held emergency meetings on the coal situation on 31 October and 7 November, 1946.
30. *Board of Trade Journal*, 19 July 1947; A.J. Robertson, *The Bleak Midwinter, 1947*, 1987, has little to say about them – but see pp. 331–33.
31. Joint Consultation in British Industry. A Report of an Inquiry undertaken by the National Institute of Industrial Psychology sponsored by the Human Factors Panel of the Committee on Industrial Reconstruction, 1952, pp. 226–7. The EEF produced other examples of workers agreeing to forgo overtime payments in its unsuccessful attempt to persuade the unions to suspend existing agreements for the duration. (AEU National Committee, *Report*, 1947, p. 62.) The AEU wrote to District Secretaries, worried by press reports that local agreements to suspend these payments were in fact being made. (*Idem*, p. 67.)
32. *New Propeller*, March, April 1947; NPACI, *Minutes*, 3 October 1946, 6 July 1947, TUC 292/557.1/1.
33. Dickson to Kipping, 21 January 1947, Dickson to Canny, 18 January 1944, FBI 200/f/3/s2/29/36/f; *Winget News*, December 1946.
34. *New Propeller*, April 1947; J. Campbell, *Plan for Prosperity*, 1947, p. 112.
35. NPACI GC-side, 11 April 1947, TUC 557.1/1.
36. *Minutes* of Meeting of Regional Board Chairmen, 6 June 1947, p. 5, TUC 292/557.4/1; MRB, *Minutes*, 20 May, 22 July 1947, BT 170/73; Coventry AEU

District Committee, *Minutes*, 11 December 1945; Memorandum from MRB, 11 February 1946 and MRB Circular, 1 May 1947, BT 168/170.

37. Luce to Wood, 26 March 1947, BT 168/170.
38. 'Production under Full Employment', 5 November 1946, TUC 292/225/3.
39. NPACI, *Minutes*, 6 February 1947, TUC 292/557.1/1.
40. BEC draft statement, 26 February 1947, agreed at NJAC, 23 April 1947, BEC 200/B/3/2/C961/1. The allowance for regional, as against workplace, JPCs reflected the experience of the building industry where such regional committees had been established because militants had successfully colonised the site ones. (Summary of Comments on TUC memo on 'Production under Full Employment', 3 January 1947, BEC 200/B/3/2/C961/1.)
41. Minutes of Meeting of Regional Board Chairmen, 6 June 1947, TUC 292/557.4/1; TUC Advisory Committee, Midlands Region 25 June 1947, TUC 292/557.5 (5); Gough to Dibben, 3 July 1947, FBI 200/F/3//S2/29/36/f; Reports of Marquand's visit to Eastern Region and to Birmingham July 1947; H.A. Marquand, Draft Report to Lord President, July 1957, CAB 124/351.
42. *Idem.*
43. TUC Midlands Regional Advisory Committee, Meeting of Trade Union representatives, 25 June 1947, TUC 292/557.5 (5); NPACI, 8 August 1947, TUC 292/557.1/1. The Birmingham District Committee had prepared a long memo on the need for a direct link between RBs and JPCs (Visit of Paymaster-General to Birmingham, 30 June 1947, CAB 124/351).
44. J.R. Campbell, 'State Capitalism and the Fight for Socialism', *Communist Review*, March 1946. 'We must be prepared to adapt our policy to the fact that the labour movement is to some extent in the political and economic leadership of the country. (Campbell, 'Where is that Production Drive?', *Labour Monthly*, June 1946.)
45. H. Pollitt, *Looking Ahead*, August 1947, p. 75; *New Propeller*, July 1946, September 1947.
46. J.R. Campbell, *Engineering Prospects and Wages*, March 1945, quoted in G. Norris, 'Communism and British Politics, 1944–1948', Warwick MA thesis, 1981; G. Allison in *World News and Views*, 5 April and 26 July 1947. In a similar vein, the Association of Scientific Workers, many of whose members were well placed to understand policy-making at company level, declared that 'in the coming months and years it should increasingly be the function of [JPCs] to concern themselves not only with day to day problems but also to mould the policy of the particular establishment concerned to conform with the national interest', *The Scientific Worker*, August 1946, p. 16.
47. *New Propeller*, June, October 1946, January, 1947; *Metalworker*, August, October, November 1947. For pressure from Trades Councils for legislation on JPCs see TUC 292/225/3.
48. Coventry East Divisional Labour Party GMC, *Minutes*, 17 September 1947; Coventry Trades Council EC, *Minutes*, 2 October 1947; R. Williams, 'The Meaning of Industrial Democracy', *AEU Monthly Journal*, September 1948. In April the Coventry Trades Council had called for the establishment of 'compulsory fuel committees ... in each factory, with equal representation of trade unions and management, to be linked up to appropriate regional committees to be controlled nationally. (*Minutes*, 3 April 1947.)
49. AEU National Committee, *Report*, 1946, p. 238; *idem*, 1947, p. 274.
50. *Minutes* of meeting of RB Chairmen, 6 June 1947, TUC 557.4/1.
51. Marquand to Cripps, 8 October 1947, BT 171/14.
52. NJAC, *Minutes*, 23 July, 1947 in BEC 200/B/3/2/C961/2. They also ruled out a proposal from the trade unions to revive the wartime practice of allowing JPCs to refer issues directly to the Board, when both sides could agree to do so, rather than sending them through the appropriate trade union or employers' organisation.

53. NJAC, *Minutes*, 23 July, 1947 in BEC 200/B/3/2/C961/2. But the trade union leaders Bagnall and Deakin also opposed the item on reference to Regional Boards, preferring problems to go to Boards via appropriate trade union or employers' organisations (Report of NPACI meeting by Harries, 2 October 1947, TUC 292/557.4/1), 'I am satisfied there is a genuine fear in the Ministry of Labour, and on the NJAC, that direct contact between the Boards and the JPCs would in the long run be injurious to the recognised local Trade Union machinery. (Patterson memo on JPCs, 18 November 1947, BT 171/206.) While upholding the line in theory, Pankhurst subsequently encouraged his officials to circumvent it if they could. (Pankhurst to Hutchins, 24 February 1948, BT 171/206.)

54. Harries to Tewson, 5 August 1947: 'I think we ought to try compulsion, TUC 292/225/3. This view was endorsed by the GC-side of the NPACI two days later, TUC 292/557.1/1.

55. *The Times*, 13 September 1947. The General Council discussed the possibility of pressing it (GC, *Minutes*, 18 September 1947, TUC 292/225/3). Earlier in the year, however, Cripps had turned down the possibility, pressed by some Labour backbenchers, of opening up a second front on JPCs by building them into his legislation on Development Councils. (Hughes to Brown, 29 May 1947, BT 168/170; *HC Deb*, 3 June 1947, cols 83f, 97f).

56. TUC, *Report*, 1947, pp. 433–7.

57. Correspondence with Middlesborough Trades Council, October–November 1947, TUC 292/225/3.

58. AEU National Committee, *Report*, 1949, p. 255; TUC GC *Minutes*, 23 June 1948, TUC 292/225/3; NPACI, GC-side, 2 December 1948, TUC 292/225/4.

59. MRB, *Minutes*, 15 October 1947, BT 170/73.

60. In June 1947 the MoL had even proposed dropping the word 'production' altogether from the name of the JPCs, but this was rejected by the TUC: Harries to MoL, 18 June 1947, TUC 292/225/3. At the NJAC meeting on 23 July it was agreed to keep the title JPC – without prejudice to right of any industry to choose a different name if they wanted to.

61. Pankhurst to Spicer, 31 October 1947; Brief for Harold Wilson's discussion with Morrison, Isaacs and Ince on 3 November 1947, BT 171/206.

62. Pankhurst, memo on JPCs, 18 November 1947; third draft of circular, pp. 7–8, BT 171/206. In deference to the decision of the NJAC, however, this latter proposal was hedged around with strict conditions that such meetings must 'on no account ... be used to discuss production problems in the factories or to attempt in any way to co-ordinate the normal activities of JPCs'. Hilary Marquand pressed for something less restrictive: 'surely there should be exchange and helpful information at such meetings. Good ideas adopted could be described. Works visits might be arranged'. But Pankhurst appears to have calculated that at this juncture discretion was the better part of valour. (How the meetings he proposed could be prevented from doing the things Marquand wanted he did not explain.) An earlier draft had urged RBs to stimulate local firms to put pressure on employers' associations to reach national agreements on establishing JPCs.

63. Circular RB 1.37, 2 December 1947, TUC 292/225/3. RBs were still allowed to handle shop floor grievances that came up through the correct procedure: and some even cheated and took direct references: Tewson to Halliwell, 5 March 1948, TUC 292/225/3.

64. Pankhurst, 'Joint Production Committees, 18 November 1947, BT 171/206.

65. Briefing for meeting on 5 December 1947, LAB 10/720.

66. E.g. decision to add COI officers to the Regional Boards to circumvent Ministry of Labour objections to the use of the Boards to promote economic information. (*Idem.*) In December 1947 the North Midlands Board was encouraged by Marquand to stimulate demand for JPCs 'without any appearance of interfering BT 171/206.

67. Dickson to Kipping, 21 January 1947, 18 January 1944, FBI 200/f/3/s2/29/36/f.
68. H.A. Marquand, Draft Report to Lord President, July 1947, CAB 124/351. Marquand rejected the demands of some Board members, hankering for a return of executive powers to the Boards, that responsibility for the Boards be transferred from the Board of Trade to the Lord President (Herbert Morrison) whose co-ordinating authority could then be devolved to the Boards themselves.
69. Johnson to Lord President, 24 July 1947, CAB 124/351.
70. Lord President's Committee, *Minutes*, 25 July 1947, CAB 132/6.
71. Meeting of Regional Board Chairmen, *Minutes*, 16 October 1947, BT 171/14.
72. Fuel Committee, *Minutes*, 6 April 1947, CAB 134/272; President's Morning Meeting, *Minutes*, 3 June 1947, BT 13/220; Lord President's Committee, *Minutes*, 25 July 1947, CAB 132/6.
73. Notes of meeting with Harold Wilson, 8 October 1947, TUC 292/556/1.
74. Government Organisation Committee, *Minutes*, 25 October 1947, CAB 134/307.
75. Confederation of Shipbuilding and Engineering Unions, *Report*, 1948, pp. 43, 187; 'Engineering and the Crisis', 8 December 1947, TUC 292/615.2/5.
76. Dickson to Mayhew, 6 October 1946, 1944 Association Correspondence, Labour Party Archive.
77. P. Hennessy, *Whitehall*, 1990, p. 120 and *passim*; K. Middlemass, *Power, Competition and the State*, 1986, pp. 78-9.
78. 'Some Thoughts on the Present Economic Position', 16 February 1947, CAB 124/1079.

10 Going Through the Motions

In the absence of major structural reforms in state/industry relations, the Labour Government's attempts to address what was increasingly recognised as a productivity problem in British industry had to rely mainly on exhortation.[1] Alongside general propaganda campaigns, initiatives on management training and the work of the Anglo-American Productivity Council, Stafford Cripps, while rejecting compulsion, continued to press for the re-establishment of joint consultation in the factories. Under his influence both the Regional Boards and the Ministry of Labour – following their different agendas and continuing to argue about their respective spheres of authority – kept up sustained pressure on the employers. This produced a late flowering of JPCs on a scale comparable with their wartime extent. Quite what these committees achieved is less clear. Most of the initiative came from Whitehall, workers remained generally indifferent, and employers were mainly concerned merely to go through the motions of joint consultation in order to avoid provoking the Government into legislation. As the Government's turn away from wartime physical controls made the engineering unions' ideas about planning appear increasingly unrealistic, those activists who had previously invested great hopes in the JPCs now saw little purpose in them. It was as potential instruments of democratic planning, not merely as a means of ameliorating conflict on the shop floor or of enhancing productivity in an unplanned private sector, that trade union activists had embraced the JPCs.

For two years after the end of the war, the EEF had done nothing about JPCs, hoping that they would quietly fade away.[2] It was only when the National Joint Advisory Committee agreement of April 1947 reassured them that the Government was committed to a voluntarist approach, that the Federation broke its silence to formally reject year-old union demands for the amalgamation of JPCs with shop steward committees. Despite a clause, inserted at the EEF's insistence in 1942, to the effect that the JPC agreement would lapse with the ending of the war, the employers now indicated that they would continue to observe the agreement for the time being.[3]

What finally forced the Federation to abandon this policy of letting sleeping dogs lie was the threat made by Stafford Cripps in September 1947 to enforce JPCs by statutory means unless positive signs of progress were forthcoming. Within three weeks the Federation had circulated its members urging them to resuscitate lapsed JPCs. In a constructive spirit quite foreign to its normal approach, the Federation encouraged members 'to make their JPC a success by taking a personal interest in them, making suggestions as to points to be included in the agenda for meetings and in general to take the initiative in these matters'.[4] Anticipating problems with the membership, members of the Management Board were deputed to explain verbally to local associations what could not safely be put in a circular – that the show of activity was a tactic designed to prevent 'the risk of something much worse ... being forced on employers by the Government'.[5]

Many employers – fed up with wasting time in what they saw as perfectly futile exercises in token consultation[6] – lacked the patience for this kind of political gamesmanship, protesting that they should not be:

> intimidated by statements from Sir Stafford Cripps and other members of the Government that if [they] did not co-operate they would be forced by statute to do so. [They] ... deprecated the idea of the Federation adopting a policy of fear of what the Government might do by statute. They felt that if the Federation took a firm stand and made it known that generally speaking the JPCs were a failure and that their contribution towards increased production was negligible, the Government would not force the Employers by statute to carry on these Joint Committees.[7]

As long as Labour remained in office, however, the EEF leadership continued to hold their militants in check. But employers remained vigilant in resisting any Government activity which threatened, however remotely, to transform JPCs from purely domestic institutions into agencies through which the state could interfere with the day-to-day running of industry.[8]

The result of the EEF policy was a rapid increase in the number of JPCs – at least on paper. Figures collected by the Midlands Regional

Board in November 1948 showed that the number of firms operating
some kind of joint consultation had risen by 74% since the previous
summer. Over half the Birmingham firms employing 500 or more
workers had JPCs. In Coventry the equivalent figure was 71%, and
the total number of JPCs functioning in the city was almost exactly
the same as in 1943.[9] In Manchester engineering employers claimed
in June 1948 that JPCs existed in 72 of the 127 federated firms
employing more than 150 workers; most of the remaining firms
either had other agreed machinery for joint consultation, or were
said to be in the process of setting up committees. Trade union
figures were less optimistic, showing only 30 JPCs in Manchester,
but the unions were satisfied that the Employers' Association was
pressing reluctant firms to act.[10]   Overall, according to an EEF
survey, the proportion of firms operating joint consultative
committees – 69% of those employing 150 or more workers – was
roughly the same in the summer of 1948 as it had been at the
wartime peak in the early months of 1943.[11] Alongside this revival
in engineering, joint consultation arrangements were negotiated in a
wide range of other industries, as the Ministry of Labour prodded
the British Employers' Confederation to deliver on the April 1947
National Joint Advisory Committee agreement.[12]   In some cases
deals were successfully struck along the lines of the 1942
engineering agreement. In others unions were forced to accept
employer insistence that membership of joint production committees
should not be limited to trade unionists.[13] By 1950 joint consultation
was probably more widespread in British industry than ever before
or since.

   Fear of Cripps, the key consideration for the EEF, was no less
influential within Whitehall. In March 1948 the permanent secretary
at the Ministry of Labour, minuted his anxiety about the 'very slow
progress that is being made in the establishment of JPCs.
Responsibility for this has been put definitely on our shoulders and I
am quite sure that if some very substantial progress is not made in
the next two or three months we are likely to be most severely
criticised by the Chancellor of the Exchequer.'[14] Equally worrying,
perhaps, was the fact that the Ministry had been unable to prevent
Cripps from encouraging the Regional Boards to take the initiative in

promoting JPCs; and, where they had done so, local Ministry of Labour officials had little choice but to co-operate in the work.[15]

In an effort to prevent Cripps and Regional Board productionists from setting the tone of the new JPC movement, the Ministry of Labour took two initiatives in the spring of 1948. First, regional controllers were instructed to actively campaign for the establishment of JPCs in individual factories, co-operating with the Regional Boards where they were already active on the issue.[16] Many of the controllers were worried by this apparent departure from 'the Department's normal practice of leaving industry to work out its own salvation within the terms of agreements voluntarily entered into.... We must ... proceed with caution for fear we may lose something of our reputation for non-political impartiality and at the end of it perhaps be told to mind our own business by both sides of industry.'[17] In fact such reminders were hardly necessary. The new departure was hedged around with cautions against taking any action without prior agreement from local employers and unions; trying to force joint consultation on unwilling firms; or jeopardising 'the good will and co-operation of those industrialists who have done so much in this field'.[18] Most importantly, in the present context, controllers were warned not to make direct contact with any federated engineering firms. These were only to be approached via the local Engineering Employers' Association.[19] Far from preparing to force JPCs down the throats of reluctant employers, the Ministry's concern was to reassert its traditional agenda – promoting 'the slow but sure organic processes of industrial negotiation' – while doing just enough to hold Cripps at bay and contain 'injudicious stimulation' by the Regional Boards.[20]

The second initiative was the appointment of Lloyd Roberts, the ex-ICI Labour Director who had played a central role in initiating the JPCs in 1941–2, to co-ordinate the Ministry's work in promoting joint consultation.[21] As a leading exponent of the 'human relations' school of management thinking, Lloyd Roberts wholeheartedly supported the Ministry of Labour objective of switching the emphasis, as he put it on one occasion, from 'exhortation to production' to 'persuasion to consultation'.[22] One reason for resistance, he believed, was that employers saw JPCs as part of a deep-laid stratagem being pursued by Cripps to undermine their power in industry. 'It would,' therefore, 'have a beneficial effect ... if gradually the Minister of Labour came to be recognised as the sponsoring Minister, and if, simultaneously, the emphasis in the campaign were put on the industrial relations value of joint consultation rather than on its contribution to increased productivity as a direct objective.'[23] To this end Lloyd Roberts launched a new attempt to put a stop to Regional Board promotion of JPCs, but this was blocked by the Regional Division and the Treasury's Economic Information Unit which had been co-operating with the Boards to organise conferences in the regions.[24] In February 1949 the Ministry of Labour was forced to accept not only that Boards could continue to host these meetings, but also that the meetings could discuss issues of joint consultation as well as economic questions. The only remaining restriction was that the meetings organised by the Regional Board were supposed to be aimed at firms which had not yet established JPCs. The Ministry of Labour preserved its exclusive right to organise meetings of managers and workers actually involved in joint consultation – so-called 'Know-How' meetings.[25]

In practice, this was a distinction without a difference. Surviving reports from the Midlands show that it was, by and large, only firms already practising joint consultation who responded to invitations to attend conferences; and once there, they could hardly be prevented from exchanging their experiences. The only real difference between meetings called by the Regional Board, and the 'Know-How' meetings was that fewer firms sent worker members of their JPCs to the latter, and this made for a rather more frank discussion. The 'Know-How' meetings consisted largely of personnel managers, many of whom had worked for the Ministry of Labour as wartime Labour Supply officers, and they used the occasions to bemoan the unenlightened attitude of most of top management towards the joint consultation exercises they were charged with running.[26] The division of responsibility between the Boards and the Ministry of Labour, which in 1947 had seemed so important a matter to reformers like Dickson or Stokes, had turned out to be a matter of little consequence. The Regional Boards had, with the assistance of

Cripps' Treasury, effectively won their battle to be allowed to convene meetings of JPCs. But the productionist groundswell to which the reformers had imagined such meetings would give form and direction had failed to materialise.

After four months as the Ministry of Labour's progress chaser on joint consultation, Lloyd Roberts reported that the chief cause of slow progress was the apathy of workers and local trade union officials, 'an apathy of which employers are quite willing to take advantage.'[27] A year later, Isaacs told his Cabinet colleagues that the only hope of further progress with joint consultation lay in mobilising local trade union officials and shop stewards, 'because the fundamental difficulty is the lack of interest on the part of the ordinary rank and file employee.'[28] Such comments applied to industry as a whole: but the Ministry of Labour's conciliation officer in the Midlands remarked on the indifference of both unions and workers in engineering as well as in other industries.[29] Some leading trade unionists were positively hostile to any intervention by the state to promote JPCs. This had long been the position of the trade union chairman of the Scottish Regional Board, and when, in the autumn of 1949, the Ministry of Labour proposed co-operation between their local officials and trade unions to encourage individual firms to form JPCs, this was opposed not only by the British Employers' Confederation but also by the leader of the Transport and General Workers' Union, Arthur Deakin.[30]

A great many JPCs were established in the late 1940s, but contemporary studies of what they actually did suggest that, outside a handful of exceptionally progressive firms, both management and workers were simply going through the motions.[31] Summing up the findings of a study of joint consultation in engineering conducted in 1948–49, Zweig remarked: 'it is generally felt that there is something missing from their life which could bring out their usefulness to full force'.[32] In 1941–42 Government intervention had forced employers to respond constructively to pressure from below: in 1948–49 it had them taking the initiative to meet a demand that hardly existed on the shop floor. With some justice the employers could claim that even when they set up JPCs the workers showed little interest.[33] Moreover those activists who did involve themselves in JPCs were, even more than in wartime, vulnerable to accusations of co-option.[34]   The late 1940s' revival of joint consultation, impressive though the statistics are, was largely a token exercise, carried out by employers to stave off more drastic Government intervention and involving little of the genuine worker participation that had occurred, however patchily, during the war.

If anyone, outside Government, was keen it was the personnel managers striving to implement their doctrines of human relations in industry in the face of scepticism, or worse, from both top management and shop stewards.[35]   One survey of *Industrial Democracy at Work*, published by a Tory MP in 1950, asserted that the trade union insistence on their exclusive right to nominate candidates for JPCs vitiated the whole purpose of joint consultation by perpetuating 'the vicious doctrine of divergent interest'.[36] In this usage, 'industrial democracy' was actually being counterpoised to trade unionism. Not everyone was quite so naive about the place of class conflict in industrial life, but the heavy influence of psychology in the intellectual climate of the late 1940s encouraged the efforts of the 'human relations' school to soften, if not abolish, adversarial bargaining.[37]   Writing in the journal of the Workers' Education Association in 1950, Cripps' Parliamentary Private Secretary deplored the effect of current intellectual trends on the content of WEA classes. Politics and economics were being neglected: 'Study of these topics had ceased to be fashionable. We had, in effect, gone all psychic. Psychology was the thing.'[38] But Cripps himself had fully embraced the psychological approach, setting up a 'Human Factors' panel of Mawdsley psychologists, led by an enlightened businessman, to prize open the secrets of worker resistance to management invitations to more active participation in the productive community of the firm.[39] The possibility that the root of the matter might be located in economic and political, rather than psychological, structures was not on the agenda of the Human Factors team.[40]

One major reason why shop stewards were no longer interested in joint consultation was the complete failure of trade union efforts to integrate the JPCs into the planning process. Peacetime joint consultation was a two-way dialogue between management and worker, systematically fenced off from any contact with the state: 'self-expression,' as the Tory MP quoted earlier put it (approvingly), 'removed from considerations of national or industrial policy.'[41] In the absence of a sense of direct participation in the national effort, there was no basis for shop floor leaders to mobilise productive effort, or even convince themselves that it was worth trying to do so. In an effort to counter the cynical attitude that increasing production would serve only to line the bosses' pockets, reformers had demanded the publication of factory and workshop targets clearly derived from the Government's overall plan for economic reconstruction.[42] As part of its response to the sterling crisis of August 1947, the Government introduced export targets and set up tripartite export committees in the regions to chase them. The targets were conveyed to industry via the trade associations. The contribution of individual firms was determined by the allocation of materials, and they were told how much of their production was to go to home and how much to export markets.[43] These targets were not, however, in the public domain, unless individual employers chose to communicate them to their workers. According to Strauss, the Minister of Supply, many of the JPCs he met in his factory visits 'had been told practically nothing about the firm's contributions to exports both [sic] generally or to specially desirable markets, or to essential home requirements.'[44] Union officials confirmed that most shop stewards 'did not know where their products were being sold.'[45] The unions argued that targets should be broken down to factory level, not through trade associations, but through the tripartite machinery of Regional Boards and their District Advisory Committees.[46] In April 1948, Strauss assured the unions that he was indeed thinking about 'the fundamental problems of how to secure industrial as well as political democracy – how to bring in the representatives of the workers in a system of private enterprise working under specific controls'. But he was not in a position to issue targets for individual firms, both because the Ministry lacked the detailed information and because 'he could not go over the heads of the managements'. Instead he promised to bring pressure to bear on the employers, through the Engineering Advisory Council, to give their own workers more information about their production targets and export markets.[47]

Responding to repeated appeals from Strauss, the engineering employers assured him that, while most of their members were happy to disclose 'the whole of the information that might properly and usefully be given', it was only in the more standardised mass production sections of the industry that it was feasible to present targets in a form that workers would understand. Consequently the matter would have to be left 'to the knowledge and goodwill of individuals'.[48] This was disingenuous. In practice most employers were parsimonious in the extreme about giving information to their workforce. Understanding that knowledge is power, they had no wish to place details of production targets and export markets in the hands of shop stewards, commercial rivals or, indeed, the Regional Boards.[49] In July 1948, Norman Kipping made clear the FBI's opposition to the suggestion that firms should inform the Regional Boards about their targets and the progress they were making towards them. Any such information flow would open the way to intolerable interference by the Boards in the day-to-day running of industry.[50] The information that, in the opinion of most employers, it was 'proper and useful' to give out was not extensive. Against this wall of employer resistance there was little that Strauss could do. Indeed his own Ministry cited the need for commercial confidentiality as the reason for declining to give target figures to Regional Export Committees.[51] As long as the employers continued to hold untrammelled executive power in industry, the balance of forces in the state–business–labour triangle would be bound to yield such results.

The engineering employers were equally insistent on keeping the JPC issue quite separate from the Government's concern with the endemic inefficiency in the management of smaller firms. When, in November 1948, Dickson again tried to revivify his Capacity Clearing Centres to tackle this problem, Norman Kipping remarked: 'I have my doubts as to whether the opinion among employers in general is sufficiently advanced yet to welcome local trade union participation in any local scheme for spreading managerial know-how.'[52] Strauss accepted the logic of this, preferring even at national level to meet separately with the employers' side of the Engineering Advisory Council to discuss issues of managerial efficiency.[53] He was not prepared to jeopardise the pursuit of managerial efficiency by linking it to the less important goal of enhancing industrial democracy. The delicacy of Strauss's position is indicated by his decision not to supply the unions with a copy of the minutes of the meeting of April 1948, presumably fearing that union leaders might let slip to employers his statement about industrial democracy.[54] Despite understanding that taking the workers into full partnership was one key to increasing productivity, neither Strauss nor the Government as a whole were prepared to push the issue of democracy to the point where it might undermine the employer co-operation which, in their view, was even more vital to Britain's economic recovery. Government policy was shaped by the priority given to establishing a *modus vivendi* with the employers – an orientation not compatible with the union agenda of releasing workers' creative energies through a radical democratisation of authority relations in industry.[55]

In 1954, reviewing the disappointing record of joint consultation since the war, Hugh Clegg remarked that the unity of national purpose which underpinned wartime experience was lacking in peacetime. Vague talk of a common interest in economic growth was insufficient to overcome the reality of structural conflict in industry: 'Unfortunately, most decisions are determined by the small issues which divide us, rather than the great issues on which we are united'.[56] In fact, even in wartime, unity on the great issues had been far from carrying all before it. A more pertinent explanation of the persistently disappointing performance of joint consultation since the 1940s would point to the absence, not of a spirit of unity, but of structures of power capable of giving shop floor workers real leverage in negotiating their partnership in productive effort.[57] As G.D.H. Cole pointed out in 1947, joint consultation in private industry made sense as a strategy of worker empowerment only 'to the extent to which [both parties] are acting under the auspices of the State ... and the power vested in the Government can be used to secure employers' conformity with the public interest'.[58] This is what the unions had argued for, and what had been denied. There was little trace of the tripartite negotiation of collaboration in production under the leadership of the state which had been the basis of activist enthusiasm for JPCs in the crisis years of the war. It should not therefore be surprising that the Labour Government's campaign for joint consultation, premised on an imaginary identity of interest between workers and employers, was subject to all the normal resistance of shop floor workers to offers of responsibility without power.

NOTES

1. On the Labour Government's productivity campaigns see N. Tiratsoo and J. Tomlinson, *Industrial efficiency and state intervention: Labour 1939–51*, Routledge, 1993; W. Crofts, *Coercion or Persuasion? Propaganda in Britain after 1945*, 1989.
2. EEF Management Board, *Minutes*, 20 December 1945, 21 November, 19 December 1946; EEF General Council, *Minutes*, 28 February 1946, EEF 237/1/1/43–44.
3. EEF Management Board, *Minutes*, 24 April, 1947, EEF 237/1/1/44.
4. EEF Management Board, *Minutes*, 25 September 1947, EEF 237/1/1/44; EEF Circular, 29 September 1947, LAB 10/213.
5. EEF General Council, *Minutes*, 26 February 1948, EEF 237/1/1/45; EEF Policy Committee, *Minutes*, 3 September 1947, EEF 237/1/9/3.
6. In late 1946 a Yorkshire mill owner told the BEC: 'I have yet to come across an Engineering employer in this Region who had experience of [a JPC], who was not heartily sick of it.' (Summary of Comments on TUC memo on 'Production under Full Employment', 3 January 1947, BEC 200/B/3/2/C961/1.)
7. EEF Management Board, *Minutes*, 25 November 1948, EEF 237/1/1/45.
8. As the secretary of the EEF told the BEC: 'I do not want to encourage Mr Lloyd Roberts [appointed to co-ordinate the promotion of joint consultation by the Ministry of Labour] to intervene in any way with our domestic affairs.' (Low to Honey, 14 March 1949, BEC 200/3/2/C961/3.) See in particular employer resistance to any direct approach by the Ministry of Labour to individual firms; to the promotion of exchange visits between JPCs; or even to the investigations of the 'Human Factors Panel' into joint consultation at factory level: 'Summary of recent history of JPCs', nd (1949), BEC 200/B/3/2/C961/3; EEF Management Board, Minutes, 20 June, 27 October 1949, EEF 237/1/1/46; NJAC GC-side, 24 January, 25 April 1950, TUC 292/225/4.
9. In both cases the giant factories (5,000+ workers) all had JPCs. Belson to Pankhurst, 25 November 1948, BT 171/207.
10. North West Regional Board, *Minutes*, 15 June 1948, BT 171/207. Later that year the Ministry of Labour identified 48 federated firms without JPCs in the North West region and the EEF undertook to bring pressure to bear. (*Idem*, 18 November 1948.) But in Glasgow the EEF met with a lot more resistance from employers: Scottish Regional Controller to Ince, 8 May 1948, LAB 10/722.
11. EEF Management Board, *Minutes*, 14 October 1948, EEF 237/1/1/45.
12. See surveys in BEC 200/B/3/2/C961 and BT 171/206.
13. Thus the TGWU met stiff resistance in its attempts to extend the principle accepted in engineering to the chemical industry, Association of Chemical and Allied Employers to BEC, 16 December 1947, BEC 200/B/3/2/C961/2. In the car industry

the National Union of Vehicle Builders pressed for a much more ambitious series of demands, involving not merely joint consultation but the formal ceding of a measure of executive authority to the unions. Unsurprisingly they got nowhere. As Tewson explained, when the union asked the TUC for help in its campaign: 'I think the practical politics of the difficulties which you have met are that the alternative to JPCs on the lines of the National Engineering Agreement in the present circumstances is – no JPCs at all.' Tewson to Halliwell, 20 February 1948; Halliwell to Tewson, 7 October 1947, 17 February 1948, TUC 292/225/3; leader in NUVB *Journal*, January 1948, NUVB 126/VB/4/1/15.

14. Ince to Myrddin Evans, 6 March 1948, LAB 10/722.
15. Circular RB 1.37, 2 December 1947, TUC 292/225/3. Weston Howard, the pro-Labour businessman who chaired the Eastern Region Board was particularly enthusiastic about the work. 'Summary of Reports by Regional Controllers on the Development of Joint Consultative Machinery up to the end of 1948'; Fraser to Ince, 7 May 1948, PRO LAB 10/722; Kipping to Pankhurst, January 1948, BT 171/206.
16. Ince to Isaacs, 13 May 1948; memo for meeting of Regional Controllers on 12 May 1948, LAB 10/722.
17. Scottish Regional Controller to Ince, 8 May 1948, LAB 10/722. See also letters from London (5 May) and Midlands (7 May) Regional Controllers in *idem*.
18. Circular IR 297/28/1948, 3 June 1948, LAB 10/722.
19. Conference of Regional Controllers, *Minutes*, 12 May 1948, LAB 10/722.
20. Scottish Regional Controller to Ince, 8 May 1948, LAB 10/722.
21. Ince to Myrddin Evans, 6 March 1948; Ince to Isaacs, 13 May 1948, LAB 10/722.
22. Meeting of Ministry of Labour and Treasury officials, *Minutes*, 14 January 1949, LAB 10/722. In line with this Lloyd Roberts wanted to remove the word 'production' and talk simply about joint consultation. Lloyd Roberts, memo, 12 April 1949, in *idem*.
23. Lloyd Roberts, 'Memorandum on Joint Consultation', 17 September 1948, LAB 10/722.
24. Blaker to Pankhurst, 10 January 1949, BT 171/207; Conference of Regional Controllers, *Minutes*, 12 January 1949, LAB 10/722.
25. Meeting of Chairmen of Regional Boards, *Minutes*, 4 February 1949; 'Notes of a Meeting held to discuss the relationship between Joint Consultation and Production…', 24 February 1949; RB Circular 1/59, 15 June 1949, LAB 10/722.
26. LAB 10/724, *passim*.
27. Lloyd Roberts, 'Memorandum on Joint Consultation', 17 September 1948, LAB 10/722.
28. Draft Cabinet Paper, 27 October 1949, LAB 10/722. See also TUC, *Report*, 1949, p. 201.
29. Humphries, 'Joint Consultation in the Midlands', 28 October 1049, LAB 10/724.
30. NJAC, *Minutes*, 23 November 1949; Scottish Regional Controller to Ince, 8 May 1948, LAB 10/722.
31. A notable exception was Glacier Metals – see Chapter 6 above, note 26. For some other 'advanced' experiments see: H. Weston Howard, 'An Approach to Joint Consultation', *Industrial Welfare*, July–August, 1947; *Planning*, 279, 5 March 1948, pp. 271–74; National Institute of Industrial Psychology, *Joint Consultation in British Industry*. (Sponsored by the Human Factors Panel of the Committee on Industrial Productivity), London, 1952, p. 243.
32. F. Zweig, *Productivity and Trade Unions*, Oxford 1951, pp.238–40.
33. National Institute of Industrial Psychology, *op. cit.*, 1952, p. 163.
34. *Ibid*, pp. 77, 80, 85; H.A. Clegg & T.E. Chester, 'Joint Consultation', in A. Flanders & H.A. Clegg (eds), *The System of Industrial Relations in Great Britain*, 1954, pp. 344–6; H.A. Clegg, *The System of Industrial Relations in Great Britain*, 1970, pp. 191–93.

35. Humphries, 'Joint Consultation in the Midlands', 28 October 1949; Humphries, 'Joint Consultation – Know How Conference Survey', 27 July 1950, LAB 10/724.
36. W. Robson Brown and N.A. Howell-Everson, *Industrial Democracy at Work. A Factual Survey*, 1950, p. 79.
37. John Child, British Management Thought. A Critical Analysis, 1969, pp. 114–36.
38. *The Highway*, October 1950. I am grateful to Peter Thompson for drawing my attention to this article.
39. J. Tomlinson, 'Productivity, Joint Consultation and Human Relations: The Attlee Government and the Workplace', paper for Conference on Management, Production and Politics, Glasgow University, 24–25 April 1992, pp. 14–15.
40. But they were well aware that 'the "two sides" conception of workers and management which has its main foundation in the economic relationship casts a threatening shadow over the whole movement.' *National Institute of Industrial Psychology, op. cit.,* p. 227. One of the few non-trade union voices to challenge this approach was James Gillespie, a management consultant with a career as a left-wing shop steward (and many years of unemployment) behind him, who published a brilliant 'social-psychological' study of *Free Expression in Industry* in 1948 in which he set out to chart a route to genuine citizenship for the workers premised on the recognition that the only democracy currently existing in industry was that organised by the trade unions. Gillespie did not undervalue the insights of psychology – he is extremely interesting about them – but he situated those insights within a hard-headed understanding of the realities of divergent class interests. J.J. Gillespie, *Free Expression in Industry*, 1948. For a trade union critique of the psychological emphasis see the article by Lawrence in *AEU Monthly Journal*, October 1948.
41. W. Robson Brown and N.A. Howell-Everson, *op. cit.,* pp. 21–2. For a lonely exception to this generalisation see the case of the Stroud firm forced by its JPC to take up an export order cited by Jack Jones at a conference on Manpower and the Economic Crisis in Coventry: Coventry East DLP, *Minutes*, 19 December 1947.
42. Curiously, in the summer of 1946, it was the employers who took the lead on this issue. 'The workers in the factories' they argued, '... are not going to let themselves be urged to a repetition of their wartime effort on a diet of mere generalisations put over to them by their employers,' 'The White Paper', 2 August 1946, FBI 200/F/3/S2/29/36 (e). Privately, one FBI official suggested that an overriding concern to promote wage restraint – for which only global data about the danger of inflation was required – had crowded out productionist arguments for detailed target-setting in the Government's approach to economic propaganda. Walker to Kipping, 29 July 1946, FBI F/3/S2/29/36 (c).
43. Meeting between CSEU and Minister of Supply, *Minutes*, 5 April 1948, SUPP 14/137.
44. Engineering Advisory Council, *Minutes*, 7 April 1948, BT 171/206.
45. Meeting between CSEU and Minister of Supply, *Minutes*, 5 April 1948, SUPP 14/137.
46. 'Engineering and the Crisis', 8 December 1947, TUC 292/615.2/5; 'Visit of the Paymaster-General to Birmingham', 1 July 1947, p. 4, CAB 124/351; *Labour Research*, September 1947, p. 153.
47. Meeting between CSEU and Minister of Supply, *Minutes*, 5 April 1948, SUPP 14/137.
48. EEF Management Board, *Minutes*, 25 November, 14 October, 24 June 1948, EEF 237/1/1/45; Engineering Advisory Council, *Minutes*, 7 April 1948, BT 171/206.
49. EEF Management Board, *Minutes*, 14 October 1948, EEF 237/1/1/45.
50. Kipping to Chemical Plant Manufacturers' Association, 30 July 1948, FBI 200/F/3/S2/29/36 (g).
51. NPACI, *Minutes*, 4 June 1948, TUC, 292/557.1/2.

52. Kipping to Leggett, 19 November 1948, FBI 200/F/3/S2/29/36 (g). Kipping probably favoured involving trade associations in a measure of joint consultation, as the FBI–BEC report had cautiously recommended in October 1946. But he was well aware that such suggestions were way ahead of general employer opinion: Kipping to Dickson, 27 January 1947, FBI 200/F/3/S2/29/36 (f).

53. Employer Representatives on EAC, *Minutes*, 4 May 1948; Hunnisette to Davidson, 6 May 1948; Hunnisette, 'Production Efficiency', 29 May 1948, FBI 200/F/3/S1/46/2; EEF Management Board, 24 June 1948, pp. 149–50, EEF 237/1/1/45.

54. Meeting between CSEU and Minister of Supply, *Minutes*, 5 April 1948, SUPP 14/137: 'If we are asked we may offer to supply a brief summary but not disclose the existence of the full minutes.'

55. H. Mercer, 'Labour and Private Industry, 1945–51', in N. Tiratsoo (ed.) *The Attlee Years*, 1991, *passim.*

56. H.A. Clegg, *op. cit.*, 1954, p. 364.

57. J. MacInnes, 'Conjuring up Consultation: the role and extent of Joint Consultation in post-war private manufacturing industry', *British Journal of Industrial Relations*, 23 1 1985.

58. G.D.H. Cole, 'Preface', in N. Barou, *British Trade Unions*, London, 1947, p. ix.

11 'The Adventure Has Gone'

In the summer of 1947, Reg Birch, a leading Communist shop steward in London, wrote an angry and nostalgic article about the contrast between wartime productionism and post-war apathy on the shop floor:

> Oh yes, we were aware (and cynically amused by it) that our working harder meant bigger profits for the governor. We gave up many of our hard-won privileges: we supported the introduction of dilutees, and taught our skill and all the tricks of the trade gained by many years of experience to the newcomer, the greenhorn. The urgency of war brought this about – yes, and also the fact that the strategy and tactics of war were applied to industry, not only from on high but, more importantly, on the shop floor, by shop leaders. One could not enter a shop without the knowledge of the link between the product and its use in war. On the walls were propaganda posters, charts of progress, etc. The JPCs were active and busy.... Yes, we were made to feel part, and an important part, of the whole 'managerial functions'. They were no longer sacrosanct and were assailed on every side by circumstances. But today we enter the factory with none of these elements. Gone is the added interest, the extra sense of importance and responsibility. The adventure has gone again.[1]

The Communist Party, of course, had its own reasons for giving up on productionism as the Cold War set in. But Communists were not alone in feeling that the adventure had gone. By the end of 1947 it was impossible to sustain the hope, temporarily revived during the coal crisis six months earlier, that progress towards participatory planning could be achieved by pressure from below.[2] While the engineering unions kept up their demands for planning and industrial democracy throughout the Labour Government's term of office, after 1947 it was clear that no major new initiative could be expected from the state.[3] With the Government declining to establish structures within which workers could participate effectively in industrial decision-making, productionist visions of encroaching control lost their appeal to trade union activists. Already in the summer of 1947 Jack Tanner was backing away from ideas of encroaching control, arguing that JPCs should not seek to expand their brief from production to commercial policy because 'we cannot afford to be associated ... with the less pleasant aspects of management.'[4] It was in December 1947 that the Coventry unions finally abandoned their struggle to revive the wartime JPCs, dissolving the Trade Union District Production Committee which, at its foundation in 1942, had spearheaded the attack on 'managerial functions'.[5]

The subsequent revival of JPCs was, as we have seen, largely a token exercise which did nothing to rehabilitate democratic productionism among industrial militants. At a Fabian Society conference in 1950, Alan Flanders explained that, since workers had no interest in controlling production, the way to promote joint consultation was as an extension of ordinary trade union bargaining, not as a stepping stone to participatory planning. The only dissent came from G.D.H. Cole – 'as much as ever a believer in Guild Socialism' – who protested vigorously against the shrunken notion of industrial democracy represented by Flanders' new orthodoxy. Only genuine worker participation, guaranteed by wider structures of participation at regional and national levels, would 'square industrial conditions with the requirements of a democratic society – democratic not only in politics, but in all its essential aspects.'[6] By 1950, however, wartime hopes for a thoroughgoing democratic transformation of British society had run into the sands.

The Attlee Government had gone a long way to meet the demand, famously formulated in E.H. Carr's July 1940 *Times* leader, that henceforth political democracy would have to be combined with a measure of social equality. The 'social citizenship' described in 1949 by the political theorist of the welfare state, T.H. Marshall, had been embodied in the welfare state. But Marshall's philosophy had no space for participatory democracy;[7] and, in this, it faithfully reflected the limitations of the Attlee Government which extended new social rights to the citizens without attempting any equivalent transformation of the nature of political citizenship in Britain. Michael Young, who as PEP's wartime director and post-war secretary of the Labour Party's research department had been one of the most thoughtful advocates of 'active democracy' throughout the

1940s, identified this democratic deficit as the key to Labour's
malaise. While Labour had hugely extended the reach of the state
into ordinary lives, and done more than any previous administration
to keep the population informed about Government programmes,
progress towards actively involving the masses in their own
governance had been minimal: 'the more difficult problem remains.'
Little had been done to extend democracy in the local community,
for the consumer, in the workplace; to enable 'the small man at the
bottom to make his own contribution to running the whole mighty
and many-sided apparatus.'[8]

At the 1948 Labour Party Conference Herbert Morrison deployed
the language of participatory democracy to urge Party members to
give a personal lead in the campaign for wage restraint and increased
industrial production:

> Ballot-box democracy, where people go and vote ... every few years and do
> nothing much in between, is out of date. We must have an active, living
> democracy in our country and we must whip up our citizens to their
> responsibilities just as we canvass them in elections or just as the air-raid
> wardens did in the war.[9]

In the confusion of the immediate post-war period, argued Morrison,
the ordinary citizen had been content to leave it to the Labour
Government to sort out the problems of getting the country back on
its feet. Well, the Government had done its bit. The legislative
framework existed and 'the ball is now passed back to the citizen. It
is the citizen's task to match the new legislation with a new spirit
and a new effort.'[10] Subsequently Nye Bevan, well briefed by the
Ministry of Labour, explained to the Conference that legislation
would do little to advance joint consultation, since successful JPCs
were those established with the free consent of both parties.[11]
Within this framework of voluntarism, as we have seen, joint
consultation became a token exercise. So long as employer
autocracy remained essentially unimpaired in the factories, no
amount of ministerial exhortation, not even a Labour Party activist
whip in hand, could persuade workers to behave as though industrial
democracy had arrived. As a writer in the *AEU Monthly Journal*
remarked: 'the trade unionist is asked to put his civic responsibilities
first. Yet the state cannot regard the worker as a citizen ... in his

workshop activities, and deny him a civic status in that sphere.'[12] Shop floor citizenship required structural reforms, profound transformations of authority relations. In the absence of such changes, Labour rhetoric about 'Production the Bridge to Socialism' – the policy statement to which Morrison was speaking – was unlikely to light many fires.

In 1950, Harold Wilson, reflecting on his three years at the Board of Trade, circulated to his Cabinet colleagues his own diagnosis of what had gone wrong. In a lengthy paper Wilson argued that the key weakness of the Government in its dealings with private industry was inability to control the behaviour of the 9,400 individual firms which accounted for 75% of industrial output: 'the real decisions which control our economic policy are taken at the board-room level.... Government has little knowledge of them and little influence on them.'[13] As the history of joint consultation had shown, while employer organisations could be cajoled into co-operating with Government, their value as transmission belts to individual firms was limited. However impressive the statistics produced by the EEF, in reality few firms approached joint consultation in the spirit desired by the Government. 'Here again', wrote Wilson, 'national policy ... [is] being frustrated at the board-room level, and we are virtually powerless as a Government to influence decisions at this level'.[14] To tackle this problem, Wilson proposed a series of radical ideas for taking power to direct the key firms including a plan to put Government-appointed directors on their boards to represent the public interest.[15] In discussing the role that joint consultation might play in advancing Government policy, Wilson showed a grasp – unique among Labour ministers – of the arguments that had been put forward by the engineering unions. JPCs, he noted, had been advocated not only as a way of harnessing the productive energies of the shop floor, but also 'as a means of enabling the workers' representatives to put pressure on the management to bring the industrial policy of the firm in question more closely into harmony with national policy, e.g., on the export drive.'[16] This brought Wilson close to the Communist vision of JPCs acting 'not merely as an advisory chorus but as essential levers of the administrative machinery through which alone central decisions as to priority and allocation can be efficiently transmitted, right down to the individual factory and workshop.' To act effectively in such a way, JPCs would have required a statutory basis and guaranteed access to the relevant information about production targets and achievements.[17]

Wilson's paper provides evidence that a differently constituted Labour Government, with different priorities, might have been able to respond positively to the ideas put forward by engineering trade unionists, Communists and others for an alliance between state intervention and shop floor organisation to bring the power of the board-room under democratic control. What is also significant, however, is that, having recognised this possibility, Wilson did not recommend that it be pursued. Instead he remarked: 'one reason why the Government has so far refused to contemplate statutory measures to enforce' the establishment of JPCs was 'the danger that they might be used by extremist elements for furthering other policies.'[18] There was, that is to say, a critical political difficulty. The fault-line between social democracy and communism ran, broadly speaking, between the Labour Government and its potential allies on the shop floor. Any alliance between the shop floor and the state would have to be, at the same time, an alliance between the Labour and Communist Parties.

This had been clearly spelled out by Jack Tanner, proposing Communist affiliation at the Labour Party Conference in 1946:

> It is said that the Communist Party would be an embarrassment to the Government.... As I think most of you are aware, during the war the shop stewards in the engineering industry played a very important part in increasing production through the Joint Production Committees, and it is ... generally known that a very large proportion of the leading shop stewards in the engineering industry are Communists. We urgently need a similar enthusiasm and a similar movement to that which we had during the war.... The efforts to increase production by the Communists ... would be very much more effective if they were also part of the mainstream of our movement.[19]

However, the relationship between communism and social democracy was ultimately determined by international relations. In 1941–42, the Communists had been able to provide the key to unlock shop floor productionism only because Hitler had invaded the Soviet Union. Any attempt by the Labour Government to mobilise similar efforts as a way out of the crisis of 1947 would have demanded similar support from Communist shop stewards – a support which, at the time, they were eagerly offering. The assumption of those who, overwhelmingly, voted down Communist affiliation in 1946 was that the Communists could not be trusted not to somersault again as dramatically as they had done in 1939 or 1941.[20] This assumption was well founded. By the time Wilson was writing, in 1950, the Communists were no longer interested in forging any kind of alliance with the Labour lieutenants of American imperialism. One could speculate as to whether things would have been different if the Labour Government had listened with more sympathy to the ideas of planning and participation expounded by the engineering unions. Those non-Communists who backed affiliation in 1946 argued that it was precisely by admission to the mainstream of Labour politics that the Communist Party could be won from its slavish dependence on Moscow.[21] But it is difficult, in retrospect, not to see this as a hopelessly optimistic judgement.

Those who sought to create an alliance between shop floor militancy and state intervention found themselves up against not merely the split between social democracy and communism but some of the most deeply rooted characteristics of Britain's political culture. In any capitalist society employers were likely to defend their autocratic powers against notions of shop floor citizenship, but their capacity to do so in Britain was enhanced by the appeal of voluntarist codes of behaviour to both trade unions and the state itself. The primacy given to the defence of free collective bargaining by British trade unions tended to inhibit support for that purposive partnership between workers and the state which would be the indispensable condition for any system of participatory planning. Despite the access to Whitehall guaranteed by the wartime and post-war political balance, TUC leaders were well aware that their influence in Whitehall did not match that of the business community, and that their capacity to mediate between the state and their own membership would be compromised by too close an integration of trade unionism into the operations of the wartime state. Consequently it made sense to have a foot in both camps, using the state where they could to strengthen trade unionism, but, in the name of voluntarism, sustaining their freedom of action. For many trade unionists, Bevin's championship of a limited measure of freedom *from* the state, seemed therefore more realistic than radical demands for power in partnership *with* the state. For their part, the managers of the British state allowed the fostering of class harmony within a de-politicised industrial relations system to take precedence over any more dirigist intervention in the industrial life of the country.

The voluntaristic codes of behaviour which governed state/industry relations in Britain were deeply rooted in the peculiarities of Britain's political and economic history: the seventeenth-century defeat of absolutism, the early industrial revolution, the gradualism with which parliamentary government was democratised. All this tended to produce a relationship between state and civil society characterised more by codes of mutual non-interference, than of partnership. Civil society in Britain was characterised by an exceptionally dense and rich articulation of voluntary effort and organisation. Within this free associational culture Britons could pursue their lives without worrying over much that, in constitutional theory, they remained subjects of a medieval monarchy not citizens of a modern state. This combination of civic freedom with relatively undemocratised political arrangements made Britain particularly resistant to the kind of positive state action which may be indispensable to success in twentieth-century industrial life. Democracy, for the British, was to be found more in voluntary organisations operating beyond the reach of the central state – and in relatively autonomous local government – than in the operational modes of the central state itself. The combination of democracy with economic planning was, therefore, a particularly problematic notion in Britain.

Wartime conditions enabled reformers to map out a programme of institutional reform whose realisation would have laid the foundations for a productionist culture of shop floor citizenship. Through the JPCs and the Regional Boards reformers could glimpse possibilities for the democratisation of British industrial life. While the political balance of the wartime coalition ruled out any far-reaching programme of democratisation, reformers hoped that the election of a majority Labour Government in 1945 might have opened the way to more substantial transformations. But the reluctance of the Attlee Government to confront the sensibilities of employers combined with its indifference to institutional reform in Whitehall to marginalise those who challenged established governing codes in the name of the productionist alliance between shop floor workers and the state advocated by Harry Pollitt and glimpsed by Harold Wilson.

It has not been the purpose of this book to suggest that the industrial democrats could have won their battles in the 1940s, or that, had they done so, all the problems of the British economy and polity would have been solved. Rather, I have sought to rescue from obscurity a group of people who subjected some of the most fundamental norms of Britain's political culture to thoughtful and persistent challenge. The point is not that they came close to success, but that they existed at all. I hope that where previous historians have perceived only vacuum and silence, future ones may acknowledge a significant presence. The fact that their defeat was inevitable is not a good reason for consigning them to oblivion. It is precisely by listening to voices drowned out by the clamour of History's winners that we may be able to understand where our society went wrong and how it might yet reform itself.

NOTES

1. Reg Birch, 'From the Engineering Workshop', *Labour Monthly*, July 1947.
2. Thus the insistent calls for a restoration of the wartime links between Regional Boards and JPCs could have little concrete meaning in a situation where JPCs were moribund. J. Campbell, *Britain's Plan for Prosperity*, 1947, p. 110.
3. AEU National Committee, *Report*, 1948, pp. 58, 76–7, 219, 270; idem, 1949, p. 255; CSEU, *Plan for Engineering*, 1951; TUC 292/615.2/5, *passim*.
4. *AEU Monthly Journal*, August 1947, p. 236.
5. AEU Coventry District Committee, *Minutes*, 23 December 1947.
6. 'If he did not get a few points in before the session ended he felt he would burst. He was as much as ever a believer in Guild Socialism and industrial democracy.' Problems Ahead Conference, March 1950, *Minutes*, p. 24, Fabian Society Papers, G 50/3.
7. Bryan S. Turner, Outline of a Theory of Citizenship, *Sociology*, 24, 2, 1990, pp. 200–201.
8. 'A Plea for Restatement of Socialism', RD 353, April 1950 in Labour Party Archive; M. Francis, 'Old realisms: Policy reviews of the past', *Labour History Review*, 56, 1, 1991, pp. 21–2.
9. Labour Party Conference, *Report*, 1948, p. 132.

10. *Ibid.*, pp. 129–30.
11. *Ibid.*, p. 139.
12. R.M. Fox, 'Freedom of the Workshop', *AEU Monthly Journal*, January 1950.
13. H. Wilson, 'The State and Private Industry', 4 May 1950, pp. 10, 13, CAB 124/1200.
14. *Ibid.*, p. 5.
15. *Ibid.*, pp. 14, 18. For further discussion of Wilson's proposals see K. Middlemass, *Power Competition and the State Vol. 1: Britain in Search of Balance 1940–61*, 1988, pp. 181–4; J.Cronin, *The Politics of State Expansion, War, State and Society in Twentieth Century Britain*, 1991, pp. 180–81.
16. H. Wilson, *op. cit.* p. 5.
17. *Labour Research*, September 1947.
18. H. Wilson, *op. cit.*, p. 5.
19. Labour Party Conference, *Report*, 1946, p. 224.
20. 'The Labour Party and the Communist Party', 27 February 1946, Labour Party Archive, GS/1/4.
21. Labour Party Conference, *Report*, 1943, pp. 162, 165.

Bibliography

A. Manuscript Collections

1. Public Record Office, Kew

Ministry of Aircraft Production

AVIA 9
AVIA 15

Board of Trade
BT 13
BT 28
BT 168
BT 169
BT 170
BT 171

Cabinet
CAB 66
CAB 92
CAB 102
CAB 124
CAB 127
CAB 129
CAB 132
CAB 134

Ministry of Labour
LAB 8
LAB 10

Prime Minister's Office
PREM 4
PREM 8

Wartime Social Survey
RG 23

Ministry of Supply
SUPP 14

War Office
WO 185

2. Modern Records Centre, University of Warwick

AEU, Amalgamated Engineering Union, Mss 259
CEEA, Coventry and District Engineering Employers' Association, Mss 66
CLP, Coventry East Divisional Labour Party, Mss 85
CTC, Coventry Trades Council, Mss 5
EEF, Engineering Employers' Federation, Mss 237
Etheridge Papers, Mss 202
FBI, Federation of British Industries, Mss 200
Michaelson Papers, Mss 233
Powell Papers, Mss 79
Steele Papers, Mss 344
Stokes Papers, Mss 180 and Mss 289
TGWU, Transport and General Workers' Union, Mss 126
TUC, Trade Union Congress, Mss 292
Young Papers, Mss 242

3. Working-Class Movement Library, Manchester

AEU Manchester District Committee, *Minutes*
Fairey Aviation Combine Committee, *Correspondence*

4. Labour Party Archive, Manchester

1944 Association Papers
Morgan Phillips Papers
Research Department Papers

5. Communist Party Archive, Manchester

Executive Committee Papers
Political Letters
Weekly Letters

6. Tom Harrison Mass Observation Archive, University of Sussex

File Reports
Industry Topic Collection
Town Boxes

7. British Library of Economic and Political Science (LSE)

Chevins Papers
Citrine Papers
PEP Papers

8. ESRC Data Archive, University of Essex

BIPO, British Institute of Public Opinion (Gallup), raw data of polls, 1939–1946. Except where otherwise stated in the footnotes, BIPO poll results have been computed from this data.

9. Other Papers

Beaverbrook Papers, House of Lords Library
Cole Papers, Nuffield College, Oxford
Darling Papers, Hoover Institution, Stanford University
Dutt Papers, British Library
Fabian Society Papers, Nuffield College, Oxford
Kapp Papers, in possession of Yvonne Kapp
People's Convention Papers, Marx Memorial Library

B. Official Publications

Committee on Regional Boards (Citrine Committee), *Report*, Cmd. 6360, 1942
House of Commons Debates
D. Mcquail, *Analysis of Newspaper Content*, Royal Commission on the Press, Research Series 4, Cmnd. 6810, 1977
Report of the Committee of Inquiry on Industrial Democracy (Bullock Report), January 1977, Cmnd. 6706
White Paper on Employment Policy After the War, Cmd. 6404, 1944

C. Newspapers, Periodicals and Reports

1. Newspapers

a) National
Daily Express
Daily Herald
Daily Mail
Daily Mirror
Daily Sketch
Daily Telegraph

Daily Worker
Financial News
News Chronicle
The Times

b) Local and Regional
Chatham Observer
Chatham, Rochester and Gillingham News
Coventry Evening Telegraph
Express and Star (Wolverhampton)
Lancashire Daily Post
Manchester Evening News
Midland Daily Telegraph
Rochester, Chatham and Gillingham Journal

2. Periodicals

AEU Monthly Journal
Communist Review
Copartnership
The Draughtsman
Economist
Factory News (Vickers Armstrong, Openshaw)
Industrial Welfare
Labour Monthly
Labour Research Metalworker
New Propeller
New Statesman
Picture Post
Planning
The Scientific Worker
Socialist Commentary
Tribune
Winget Life
World News and Views

3. Reports

AEU, Proceedings of National Committee, *Reports*, 1941–1951
AEU, *Third Report on Production*, 1942
Communist Party, *Congress Reports*, 1942–1949
Confederation of Shipbuilding and Engineering Unions, *Annual Reports*, 1946–1951.
Labour Party, *Conference Reports*, 1941–1951
TUC, *Reports*, 1941-1951

D. Contemporary Published Works

Place of publication is London unless otherwise stated

1. Books

A. Albu, *Management in Transition*, Fabian Society Research Series, 68, 1942

Argonaut, *Give Us the Tools*, Secter and Warburg, 1942

N. Barou, *British Trade Unions*, Gollancz, 1947

Mark Benney, *Over to Bombers*, Allen and Unwin, 1943

W. Robson Brown and N.A. Howell-Everson, *Industrial Democracy at Work. A Factual Survey*, Pitman,1950

R.P. Dutt, *Britain in the World Front*, Hardy, Bournemouth, 1942

M. Edleman, *Production for Victory, not Profit!*, Left Book Club, 1941

Fabian Society, *Plan for Britain*, Routledge, 1943

A. Flanders, *The Battle for Production*, International Publishing Co., 1941

J.J. Gillespie, *Free Expression in Industry. A Social-Psychological Study of Work and Leisure*, Pilot Press, 1948

W. Hannington, *The Rights of Engineers*, Gollancz, 1944

E. Jacques, *The Changing Culture of a Factory*, Tavistock, 1951

Mass Observation, *People in Production. An Enquiry into British War Production*, Penguin Special, 1942

Mass Observation, *An Enquiry into People's Homes*, John Marrag, 1943,

Mass Observation, *Puzzled people. A study in popular attitudes to religion, ethics, progress and politics in a London borough*, Gollancz, 1947

Mass Observation, *The Journey Home*, John Murray, 1944

J.T. Murphy, *Victory Production*, John Lane, 1942

National Institute of Industrial Psychology, *Joint Consultation in British Industry*, (sponsored by the Human Factors Panel of the Committee on Industrial Productivity), 1952

Jack Owen, *War in the Workshops*, Lawrence and Wishart, 1942

H. Pollitt, *Answers to Questions*, Communist Party, 1945

H. Pollitt, *How to Win the Peace*, Communist Party, 1945

C. Reaveley and J. Winnington, *Democracy and Industry*, Chatto and Windus, 1947

C. Riegelman, *British Joint Production Machinery*, International Labour Office, Montreal, 1944

G.S. Walpole, *Management and Men. A Study of the Theory and Practice of Joint Consultation at all Levels*, Jonathan Cape, 1944

S. and B. Webb, *Soviet Communism: a New Civilisation*, Left Book Club, 1937

G. Williams, *Women and Work*, Nicholson and Watson, 1945

F. Zweig, *Productivity and Trade Unions*, Blackwell, Oxford, 1951

2. Chapters and Articles

T.W. Agar, 'Towards Industrial Democracy', in Fabian Society, *Can Planning be Democratic?*, 1944

G. Dickson, 'Evolution in Management', in J.R.M. Bramwell (ed.), *This Changing World*, 1944

T. Harrison, 'What is Public Opinion?', *Political Quarterly*, August 1940

B. Wootton, *Freedom Under Planning*, in H. Morrison *et al.*, *Can Planning be Democratic?* 1944

3. Pamphlets

Anon, *Party Organisation for Victory*, Communist Party, March 1943

Anon, *Shock Brigades – A Guide. How to start them. How they work.*, Y.C.L. n.d. (1942?)

Anon, *We Pledge the Lads*, Communist Party group at Napiers (Sabre Engines), Liverpool, n.d. (1944)

Sam Blackwell, *Birmingham Against Hitler*, Communist Party, n.d. (1943?)

E. Burns, *Labour's Way Forward*, Communist Party, July 1942

G.D.H. Cole, *Guide to the Elements of Socialism*, Labour Party Research Department, 1947

Confederation of Shipbuilding and Engineering Unions, *Plan for Engineering*, 1951

CP, *Britain's Plan for Prosperity*, 1947

CP, *Britain for the People*, 1944

CP, *Party Organisation for Victory*, 1943

CP, *For Britain Free and Independent*, 1948

CP, *The Communist Party and the National Front*, n.d. (late 1941?)

G. Dickson, *Industrial Democracy*, Talk given to British Institute of Industrial Administration, Waldorf Hotel, 20 November 1946

M. Dobb, *Economics of Capitalism. An Introductory Outline*, Marx House Syllabus, n.d. (1942?)

Engineering and Allied Trades Shop Stewards' National Council, *Arms and the Men*, Report of Conference, 19 October 1941

Engineering and Allied Trades Shop Stewards' National Council, *Millions Like Us*, Report of Conference, 12 March 1944

Engineering and Allied Trades Shop Stewards' National Council, *JPCs – How to Get the Best Results*, 1942

Engineering and Allied Trades Shop Stewards' National Council, *Shop Stewards and the Future.* n.d. (1945?)

Engineering and Shipbuilding Shop Stewards' Committee for Scotland, *Shop Stewards' Next Step*, n.d. (1944?)

J.B. Jefferys, *Trade Unions in a Labour Britain*, Fabian Society Pamphlet, 1947

Labour Party, *Let Us Face the Future*, 1945

C. Madge and T. Harrison, *Mass Observation*, 1937

National Engineering Joint Trades Movement, *Memorandum on Post-war Reconstruction in the Engineering Industry*, 1945

TUC, *Quiz on Joint Production Committees*, February 1943

M. Young, *Small Man: Big World. A Discussion of Socialist Democracy*, Labour
Party, 1949

E. Memoirs

Place of publication is London unless otherwise stated

D. Hyde, *I Believed. The Autobiography of a Former British Communist*,
Reprint Society, 1952

J. Jones, *Union Man*, Collins, 1986

N. Kipping, *Summing Up*, Hutchinson, 1972

J. McCulloch, *Medway Adventure*, Joseph, 1946

R. Williams-Thompson, *Was I Really Necessary?*, Worlds Press News, 1951

F. Secondary Sources

Place of publication is London unless otherwise stated

1. Books

Paul Addison, *The Road to 1945. British Politics and the Second World War*,
Quartet, 1982

P. Addison, *Now the War is Over*, Jonathan Cape, 1985

C. Barnett, *The Audit of War*, MacMillan, 1987

S. Beer, *Britain Against Itself. The Political Contradictions of Collectivism*,
Faber, 1982

S. Blank, *Industry and Government in Britain. The FBI in Politics, 1945-65*,
Saxon House, Farnborough, 1973

S. Brooke, *Labour's War. The Labour Party during the Second World War*,
Oxford, Clarendon, 1992

W. Brown, *Exploration in Management*, Heineman, 1960

Alan Bullock, *The Life and Times of Ernest Bevin, Vol. 2, Minister of Labour*,
Heineman, 1967

J. Bulpitt, *Territory and Power in the United Kingdom: An Interpretation*,
Manchester University Press, Manchester, 1983

Angus Calder, *The People's War. Britain 1939-45*, Cape, 1971

H. Chapman, *State Capitalism and Working-class Radicalism in the French
Aircraft Industry*, University of California Press, Oxford, 1991

John Child, *British Management Thought. A Critical Analysis*, Allen and Unwin,
1969

A. Chisholm and M. Davie, *Beaverbrook. A Life*, Hutchinson, 1992

W. Crofts, *Coercion or Persuasion? Propaganda in Britain after 1945*,
Routledge, 1989

J. Cronin, *Labour and Society in Britain 1918-1979*, Batsford, 1984

J. Cronin, *The Politics of State Expansion, War, State and Society in Twentieth Century Britain*, Routledge, 1991

R. Croucher, *Engineers at War, 1939–1945*, Merlin, 1982

J. Curran and J. Seaton, *Power Without Responsibility. The Press and Broadcasting in Britain*, Routledge, 1988

E. Durbin, *New Jerusalems: The Labour Party and the Economics of Democratic Socialism*, Routledge, 1985

A. Flanders and H.A. Clegg, *The System of Industrial Relations in Great Britain*, Blackwell, Oxford, 1954

E. and R. Frow, *Engineering Struggles. Episodes in the story of the shop stewards' movement*, Manchester Free Press, Manchester, 1982

G.H. Gallup (ed.), *The Gallup International Public Opinon Polls, Great Britain, 1937–1975*, Vol. 1 (1937–1964), New York, 1977

Nigel Harris, *Competition and the Corporate Society*, Methuen, 1972

P. Hennessy, *Whitehall*, Penguin, 1990

P. Inman, *Labour in the Munitions Industries*, HMSO, 1957

E. Jacques, *Employee Participation and Managerial Authority*, 1968

T. Jeffery, *Mass Observation – A Short History*, CCCS, Birmingham, 1978

Kevin Jefferys, *The Churchill Coalition and Wartime Politics, 1940–45*, Manchester University Press, Manchester, 1991

J. Kelly, *Is Scientific Management Possible?*, Faber, 1968

S. Koss, *The Rise and Fall of the Political Press in Britain, Vol. 2*, Hamilton, 1984

Tony Lane, *The Merchant Seamen's War*, Manchester University Press, Manchester, 1990

J.M. Lee, *The Churchill Coalition, 1940–1945*, Batsford, 1980

J. Leruez, *Economic Planning and Politics in Britain*, Robertson, London, 1975

Rodney Lowe, *Adjusting to Democracy. The Role of the Ministry of Labour in British Politics, 1916–39*, Clarendon, Oxford, 1986

D. Marquand, *The Unprincipled Society. New Demands and Old Politics*, Fontana, 1988

K. Middlemass, *Politics in Industrial Society*, Deutsch, 1979

K. Middlemass, *Power, Competition and the State Vol. 1: Britain in Search of Balance 1940–61*, Macmillan, 1986

L. Minkin, *The Labour Party Conference. A Study in the Politics of Intra-Party Democracy*, Allen Lane, 1978

K.O. Morgan, *Labour in Power, 1945–1951*, Clarendon, Oxford, 1984

K. Morgan, *Against Fascism and War*, Manchester University Press, Manchester, 1989

K. Morgan, *Harry Pollitt*, Manchester University Press, Manchester, 1993

J.E. Mortimer, *A History of the Association of Engineering and Shipbuilding Draughtsmen*, AESD, 1960

T. Nichols, *The British Worker Question: A New Look at Workers and Productivity in Manufacturing*, Routledge, 1986

H. Perkin, *The Rise of Professional Society. England since 1880*, Routledge, 1989

B. Pimlott, *Hugh Dalton*, Cape, 1985

J. Pinder (ed.), *Fifty Years of Political and Economic Planning*, Heinemann, 1981

J.M. Preston, *Industrial Medway: an Historical Survey*, Berry Wiggins, 1977

R. Price, *Labour in British Society*, Croom Helm, 1986

W.J. Reader, *Imperial Chemical Industries, A History, Vol. II*, Oxford University Press, 1975

A.A. Rogow and P. Shore, *The Labour Government and British Industry*, Blackwell, Oxford, 1955

A.J. Robertson, *The Bleak Midwinter, 1947*, Manchester University Press, Manchester, 1987

J.D. Scott and R. Hughes, *The Administration of British War Production*, HMSO, 1955

Jonathan Schneer, *Labour's Conscience: The Labour Left 1945-1951*, Unwin Hyman, 1988

T. Smith, *The Politics of the Corporate Economy*, 1979

P. Summerfield, *Women Workers in the Second World War*, Croom Helm, 1984

A.J.P. Taylor, *Beaverbrook*, Hamilton, 1972

N. Tiratsoo and J. Tomlinson, *Industrial efficiency and state intervention: Labour 1939-51*, Routledge, 1993

S. Tolliday and J. Zeitlin, (eds), *Shop Floor Bargaining and the State. Historical and Comparative Perspectives*, Cambridge University Press, Cambridge, 1985

J. Turnstall, *The Problem of Industrial Relations News in the Press*, Royal Commission on the Press, Working Paper 3,

A.W. Wright, *G.D.H. Cole and Socialist Democracy*, Clarendon, Oxford, 1979

2. Chapters

Paul Addison, 'By-Elections of the Second World War', in C. Cook and J. Ramsden (eds), *By-Elections in British Politics*, 1973

A. Calder, 'Mass Observation', in M. Bulmer (ed.), *Essays on the History of British Sociological Research*, Cambridge University Press, Cambridge, 1985

S. Fielding, 'Don't Know Don't Care', in N. Tiratsoo, (ed.), *The Attlee Years*, Pinter, 1991

A. Mason and P. Thompson, 'Reflections on a revolution? The political mood in wartime Britain', in N. Tiratsoo, (ed), *The Attlee Years*, Pinter, 1991

H. Mercer, 'Labour and Private Industry, 1945-51', in N. Tiratsoo, (ed.), *The Attlee Years*, Pinter, 1991

A.J. Robertson, 'Lord Beaverbrook and the Supply of Aircraft, 1940-41', in A. Slaven and D.H. Aldcroft (eds), *Business, Banking and Urban History*, Donald, Edinburgh, 1982.

R. Roberts, 'The Administrative Origins of Industrial Diplomacy: an Aspect of Government–Industry Relations, 1929-1935', in J.Turner, (ed), *Businessmen and Politics*, Heinemman, 1984

W. Streek, 'Co-determination: the fourth decade', in B. Wilpert and A. Sorge (eds), *International Perspectives on Organisational Democracy*, Wiley, Chichester, 1984

3. Articles

A. Booth, 'Economic Advice at the Centre of British Government', *Historical Journal*, 29, 1986

A. Exell, 'Morris Motors in the 1940s', *History Workshop*, 9, 1980

S. Fielding, 'What did the people Want. The meaning of the 1945 General Election', *Historical Journal*, 35, 1992

G. Finlayson, 'A Moving Frontier: Voluntarism and the State in British Social Welfare, 1941–49', *Twentieth-century British History*, 1, 2, 1990

J. Hinton, review of Chapman, *Social History*, 17, 3, 1992

J. MacInnes, 'Conjuring up Consultation: the role and extent of Joint Consultation in post-war private manufacturing industry', *British Journal of Industrial Relations*, 23, 1, 1985

D. Ritschel, 'A Corporatist Economy in Britain? Capitalist planning for industrial self-government in the 1930s', *English Historical Review*, 1, 1991

Richard Sibley, 'The swing to Labour during the Second World War: when and why', *Labour History Review*, 55, 1, 1990

P. Summerfield, 'Mass Observation: Social Research or Social Movement?', *Journal of Contemporary History*, 20, 3, 1985

P. Thompson, 'Playing at being skilled men; factory culture and pride in work skills among Coventry car workers', *Social History*, 13, 1, 1988

J. Tomlinson, 'Mr Attlee's supply side socialism', *Economic History Review*, 46, 1993

J. Tomlinson, 'Labour's management of the national economy, 1945–51', *Economy and Society*, 18, 1, 1989

Bryan S. Turner, 'Outline of a Theory of Citizenship', *Sociology*, 24, 2, 1990

4. Unpublished Manuscripts

R. Croucher, 'Communist Politics and Shop Stewards in Engineering, 1935–46', Warwick PhD, 1977

G. Dickson, *Already Our Children Sneer*, 1941

S. Fielding, 'The movement away from party: wartime popular politics reconsidered', unpublished paper, 1992

N. Fishman, 'The British Communist Party and the Trade Unions, 1933–1945: the dilemmas of revolutionary pragmatism', London PhD, 1991

K. Morgan, 'Against Fascism and War. Ruptures and Continuities in British Communist Politics, 1935–1941', Manchester PhD, 1987

G. Norris, 'Communism and British Politics, 1944–1948', Warwick MA thesis, 1981

H. Rees, 'The Medway Towns – their settlement, growth and economic development', London PhD, 1954

J. Tomlinson, 'Productivity, Joint Consultation and Human Relations: The Attlee Government and the Workplace', paper for Conference on Management, Production and Politics, Glasgow University, 24–25 April 1992

Index